The Royal Navy in Battle

The Royal Navy in Battle
An Analysis of Sea-Power and Actions
During the First World War, 1914-18

ILLUSTRATED

Arthur H. Pollen

The Royal Navy in Battle
An Analysis of Sea-Power and Actions During the First World War, 1914-18
by Arthur H. Pollen

ILLUSTRATED

First published under the title
The British Navy in Battle

Leonaur is an imprint of Oakpast Ltd
Copyright in this form © 2022 Oakpast Ltd

ISBN: 978-1-915234-18-6 (hardcover)
ISBN: 978-1-915234-19-3 (softcover)

http://www.leonaur.com

Publisher's Notes

The views expressed in this book are not necessarily those of the publisher.

Contents

A Greeting by Way of Dedication	7
A Retrospect	13
Sea Fallacies: A Plea for First Principles	29
Some Root Doctrines	40
Elements of Sea Force	49
The Actions	62
1. Naval Gunnery, Weapons, and Technique	72
The Action That Never Was Fought	83
The Destruction of "Koenigsberg"	91
Capture of H.I.G.M.S. "Emden"	115
The Career of Von Spee	126
Battle of the Falkland Islands (1)	138
Battle of the Falkland Islands (2)	147
Battle of the Falkland Islands (3)	156
Battle of the Falkland Islands (4)	165
The Heligoland Affair	179
The Action off the Dogger Bank	190
The Dogger Bank 2	195
The Battle of Jutland	207

The Battle of Jutland (Continued)	219
The Battle of Jutland (Continued)	229
The Battle of Jutland (Continued)	242
The Battle of Jutland (Continued)	251
The Battle of Jutland (Continued)	264
Zeebrügge and Ostend	274
Third Phase Sketches	287

CHAPTER 1

A Greeting by Way of Dedication

Xmas, 1915.

To the Admirals, Captains, Officers and Men of the Royal Navy and of the Royal Naval Reserve:

To the men of the merchant service and the landsmen who have volunteered for work afloat:

To all who are serving or fighting for their country at sea:

To all naval officers who are serving—much against their will—on land:

Greetings, good wishes and gratitude from all landsmen.

We do not wish you a Merry Christmas, for to none of us, neither to you at sea nor to us on land, can Christmas be a merry season now. Nor, amid so much misery and sorrow, does it seem, at first sight, reasonable to carry the conventional phrase further and wish you a Happy New Year. But happiness is a different thing from merriment. In the strictest sense of the word you are happy in your great task, and we doubly and trebly happy in the security that your great duties, so finely discharged, confer. So, after all it is a Happy New Year that we wish you.

If you could have your wish, you of the Grand Fleet—well, we can guess what it would be. It is that the war would so shape itself as to force the enemy fleet out, and make it put its past work and its once high hopes to the test against the power which you command and use with all the skill your long vigil and faithful service have made so singly yours today. And in one sense—and for your sakes, because your glory would be somehow lessened if it did not happen—we too could wish that this could happen. But we wish it only because you do. Although you do not grumble, though we hear no fretful word, we realise how wearing and how wearying your ceaseless watch must be.

It is a watchfulness that could not be what it is, unless you hoped, and indeed more than hoped, *expected* that the enemy must early or late prove your readiness to meet him, either seeking you, or letting you find him, in a High Seas fight of ship to ship and man to man. We, like you, look forward to such a time with no misgiving as to the result, though, unlike you, we dread the price in noble lives and gallant ships that even an overwhelming victory may cost.

Your hopes and expectation for this dreadful, but glorious, end to all your work do not date from August, eighteen months ago. When as little boys you went to the *Britannia*, you went drawn there by the magic of the sea. It was not the sea that carries the argosies of fabled wealth; it was not the sea of yachts and pleasure boats. It was the sea that had been ruled so proudly by your fathers that drew you. And you, as the youngest of the race, went to it as the heirs to a stern and noble heritage. So, almost from the nursery have you been vowed to a life of hardship and of self-denial, of peril and of poverty—a fitting apprenticeship for those who were destined to bear themselves so nobly in the day of strain and battle. To the mission confided to you in boyhood you have been true in youth and true in manhood. So that when war came it was not war that surprised you, but you that surprised war.

When the war came, you from the beginning did your work as simply, as skilfully, and as easily as you had always done it. Not one of you ever met the enemy, however inferior the force you might be in, but you fought him resolutely and to the end. Twice and only twice was he engaged to no purpose. *Pegasus*, disabled and outraged, fell nobly, and the valiant Cradock faced overwhelming odds because duty pointed to fighting. Should the certainty of death stand between him and that which England expects of every seaman? There could only be one answer. In no other case has an enemy ship sought action with a British ship. In every other case the enemy has been forced to fight, and made to fly. It was so from the first.

When two small cruisers penetrated the waters of Heligoland with a flotilla of destroyers, the enemy kept his High Seas Fleet, his fast cruisers, and his well-gunned armoured ships in the ignoble safety of his harbours and his canal. He left, to his shame, his small cruisers to fight their battle alone. Tyrwhitt and Blount might, and should, have been the objects of overwhelming attack. But the Germans were not to be drawn into battle. The ascendancy that you gained in the first three weeks of war you have maintained ever since. Three times under the cover of darkness or of fog, the greater, faster units of the German force have—in a frenzy of fearful daring—ventured to cross or enter the sea that once was known as the German Ocean. Three times they have known no alternative but precipitate flight to the place from which they came.

Not once has a single merchant ship bound for England been stopped or taken by an enemy ship in home waters. But fifty-six out of eight thousand were overtaken in distant seas. It has been yours to shepherd and protect the vast armies we have sent out from England, and so completely have you done it that not a single transport or supply ship has been impeded between this country and France. From the first there has not been, nor can there now ever be, the slightest threat or the remotest danger of these islands being invaded. Indeed, so utter and complete has been your work that the phrase "Command of the Sea" has a new meaning. The sea holds no danger for us. Allied to other great land powers, we find ourselves able and compelled to become a great land power also. The army of four millions is thus not the least of your creations.

So thorough is your work that Britain stands today on a pinnacle of power unsurpassed by any nation at any time.

Has the completeness of your work been impaired by the ravages of the submarine? Its gift of invisibility has seemed to some so mystic a thing that its powers become magnified. Because it clearly sometimes might strike a deadly blow, it was thought that it always could so strike, till madness was piled upon madness, and it seemed as if the very laws of force had been upset, and ships and guns things obsolete and of no use. But you have always known—and we at last are learning—that this is idle talk, and that as things were and as they are, so must they always be; and that sea-power rests as it always has, and as it always will, with the largest fleet of the strongest ships, and with big guns well directed and truly aimed.

It did not take you long to learn the trick of the submarine in war, and had things been ordered differently, you might have learned much of what you know in the years of peace. But you learned its tricks so well that it has failed completely to hurt the navy or the army which the navy carries over the sea, and has found its only success in attacking unarmed merchant ships. These are only unarmed because the people of Christendom had never realised that any of its component nations could turn to barbarism, piracy, and even murder in war. It would have been so easy, had this utter lapse into devilry been expected, to have armed every merchant ship—and then where would the submarine have been? But even with the merchantmen unarmed, the submarine success has been greatly thwarted by your splendid ingenuity and resource, your sleepless guard, your ceaseless activity, and the buccaneers of a new brutality have been made to pay a bloody toll.

Take it for all in all, never in the history of war has organised force accomplished its purpose at so small a cost in unpreventable loss, or with such utter thoroughness, or in face of such unanticipated difficulties.

It was inevitable that there should be some failures. Not every opportunity has been seized, nor every chance of victory pushed to the utmost. Who can doubt that there are a hundred points of detail in which your material, the methods open to you, the plans which tied you, might have been more ample, better adapted to their purpose, more closely and wisely considered? For when so much had changed, the details of naval war had to differ greatly from the anticipation. In the long years of peace—that seem so infinitely far behind us now—you had for a generation and a half been administered by a department almost entirely civilian in its spirit and authority. It was a control that had to make some errors in policy, in provision, in selection. But your skill counter-balanced bad policy when it could; your resources supplied the defects of material; too few of you were of anything but the highest merit for many errors of selection to be possible.

And the nation understood you very little. Your countrymen, it is true, paid you the lip service of admitting that you alone stood between the nation and defeat if war should come. But war seemed so unreal and remote to them, that it was only a few that took the trouble to ask what more you needed for war than you already had.

And you were so absorbed in the grinding toil of your daily work to be articulate in criticism; too occupied in trying to get the right result with indifferent means—because the right means cost too much and could not be given to you—to strive for better treatment; too wholly wedded to your task to be angry that your task was not made more easy for you. Hence you took civilian domination, civilian ignorance, and civilian indifference to the things that matter, all for granted, and submitted to them dumbly and humbly, as you submitted silent and unprotesting to your other hardships; you were resigned to this being so; and were resigned without resentment. If, then, the plans were sometimes wrong, if you and your force were at other times cruelly misused, if the methods available to you were often inadequate, it was not your fault—unless, indeed, it be a fault to be too loyal and too proud to make complaint.

If we took little trouble to understand you, we took still less to pay and praise you. There is surely no other profession in the world which combines so hard a life, such great responsibilities, such pitiful remuneration. But small as the pay is, we seize eagerly every chance to lessen it. If we waste our money, we do not waste it on you. But we fully expect you to spend your money in our service. The naval officer's pay is calculated to meet his expenses in time of peace. Now a very large proportion of the pay of cadets, midshipmen, sub-lieutenants, and lieutenants necessarily goes in uniform and clothes. The life of a uniform can be measured by the sea work done by the wearer. Sea work in war is—what shall we say?—three to six times what it is in peace. But we do nothing to help young officers to meet these very ugly attacks on their very exiguous pay. We do not even distribute the prize money that the fleet has earned.

Someday, when this war is won, it may be realised that it has been won because there is a great deal more water than land upon the world, and because the British Fleet commands the use of all the water, and the enemy the use of only a tiny fraction of all the land. If France can endure, and if Russia can "come again"; if Great Britain has the time to raise the armies that will turn the scale; if the Allies can draw upon the world for the metal and food that make victory—and waiting for victory—possible; if the effort to shatter European civilization and to rob the Western world of its Christian tradition fails, it is because our enemies counted upon a war in which England would not fight. Someday, then, we shall see what we and all the world owe to you.

We may then be tempted to be generous and pay you perhaps a living wage for your work, and not cut it down to a half or a third if there is no ship in which to employ you. And if you lose your health and strength in the nation's service, we may pay you a pension proportionate to the value of your work, and the dangers and responsibilities that you have shouldered, and to the strenuous, self-sacrificing lives that you have led, for our sakes. We may do more. We may see to it that honours are given to you in something like the same proportion that they are given, say, to civilians and to the army. We may do more still. We may realise that to get the best work out of you, you must be ordered and governed and organised by yourselves.

But then again, we may do nothing of the kind. We may continue to treat you as we have always treated you; and if we do, there is at any rate this bright side to it. You will continue to serve us as you have always served us, working for nothing, content so you are allowed to remain the pattern and mirror of chivalry and knightly service, and to wear "the iron fetters" of duty as your noblest decoration.

Chapter 2

A Retrospect

August, 1918.

In looking back over the last four years, the sharpest outlines in the retrospect are the ups and downs of hopes and fears. Indeed, so acutely must everyone bear these alternations in mind, that to remark on them is almost to incur the guilt of commonplace. For they illustrate the tritest of all the axioms of war. It is human to err—and every error has to be paid for. If the greatest general is he who makes the fewest mistakes, then the making of some mistakes must be common to all generals. The rises and reversals of fortune on all the fronts are of necessity the indices of right or wrong strategy. These transformations have been far more numerous on land than at sea, and locally have in many instances been seemingly final.

Thus, to take a few of many examples, Serbia, Montenegro, and Russia are almost completely eliminated as factors; our effort in the Dardanelles had to be acknowledged as a complete failure. But at no stage was any victory or defeat of so overwhelming and wholesale a nature as to promise an immediate decision. The retreat from Mons, Gallipoli, Neuve Chapelle, Hulloch, Kut—the British Army could stand all of these, and much more. France never seemed to be beaten, whatever the strain. Even after the defection of Russia, a German victory seemed impossible on land. Never once did either side see defeat, immediate and final, threatened. A right calculation of all the forces engaged may have shown a discerning few where the final preponderance lay. The point is that, despite extraordinary and numerous vicissitudes, there never was a moment when the land war seemed settled once and for all.

This has not been the case at sea. The transformations here have been fewer; but they have been extreme. For two and a half years the sea-power of the Allies appeared both so overwhelmingly established and so abjectly accepted by the enemy, that it seemed incredible that this condition could ever alter materially. Yet between the months of February and May, 1917, the change was so abrupt and so terrific that for a period it seemed as if the enemy had established a form of superiority which must, at a date that was not doubtful, be absolutely fatal to the alliance. And again, in six months' time, the situation was transformed, so that sea-power, on which the only hope of Allied victory has ever rested was once more assured.

Thus, after the most anxious year in our history, we came back to where we started. This nation, France, Italy, and America no less, we have all returned to that absolute and unwavering confidence in the navy as the chief anchor of all Allied hopes. Not that the navy had ever failed to justify that confidence in the past. There was no task to which any ship was ever set that had not been tackled in that heroic spirit of self-sacrifice which we have been taught to expect from our officers and men; there had never been a recorded case of a single ship declining action with the enemy. There were scores of cases in which a smaller and weaker British force had attacked a larger and stronger German. Ships had been mined, torpedoed, sunk in battle, and the men on board had gone to their death smiling, calm, and unperturbed.

If heroism, goodwill, a blind passion for duty could have won the war, if devotion and zeal in training, patient submission to discipline, a fiery spirit of enterprise could have won—then we never should have had a single disappointment at sea. The traditions of the past, the noble character of the seamen of today—we hoped for a great deal, nor ever was our hope disappointed. And when the time of danger came, when our tonnage was slipping away at more than six million tons a year, so that it was literally possible to calculate how long the country could endure before surrender, it never occurred to the most panic-stricken to blame the navy for our danger. The nation saw quite clearly where the fault lay, and the government, sensitive to the popular feeling, at last took the right course.

But it was a course that should have been taken long before. For, though the purposes for which sea-power exists seemed perfectly secure and never in danger at all till little more than a year ago, yet there had been a series of unaccountable miscarriages of sea-power. Battles were fought in which the finest ships in the world, armed with the best and heaviest guns, commanded by officers of unrivalled skill and resolution, and manned by officers and crews perfectly trained, and acting in battle with just the same swift, calm exactitude that they had shown in drill—and yet the enemy was not sunk and victory was not won. Though, seemingly, we possessed overwhelming numbers, the enemy seemed to be able to flout us, first in one place and then in another, and we seemed powerless to strike back. Almost since the war began, we kept running into disappointments which our belief in and knowledge of the navy convinced us were gratuitous disappointments A rapid survey of the chief events since August, 1914, will illustrate what I mean.

The First Crisis

The opening of the war at sea was in every respect auspicious for the Allies. By what looked like a happy accident, the British Navy had just been mobilised on an unprecedented scale. It was actually in process of returning to its normal establishment when the international crisis became acute, and, by a dramatic stroke, it was kept at war strength and the main fleet sent to its war stations before the British ultimatum was despatched to Berlin. The effect was instantaneous. Within a week transports were carrying British troops into France and trade was continuing its normal course, exactly as if there were no German Navy in existence. The German sea service actually went out of existence.

Before a month was over a small squadron of battle-cruisers raided the Bight between Heligoland and the German harbours, sank there small cruisers and half-a-dozen destroyers, challenged the High Seas Fleet to battle, and came away without the enemy having attempted to use his capital ships to defend his small craft or to pick up the glove so audaciously thrown down. The mere mobilisation of the British Fleet seemed to have paralyzed the enemy, and it looked as if our ability to control sea communications was not only surprisingly complete, but promised to be enduring. The nation's confidence in the navy had been absolute from the beginning, and it seemed as if that confidence could not be shaken.

Before another two months had passed, we had run into one of those crises which were to recur not once, but again and again. During September an accumulation of errors came to light. The enormity of the political and naval blunder which had allowed *Goeben* and *Breslau* to slip through our fingers in the Mediterranean, and so bring Turkey into the war against us, at last become patent. (*Vide The*

Goeben & the Breslau: the Imperial German Navy in the Mediterranean, 1914—The Flight of the Goeben and Breslau A. Berkeley Milne, Julian S. Corbett, W. L. Wyllie and Others; Leonaur 2020.)

There was no blockade. There were the raids which *Emden* and *Karlsruhe* were making on our trade in the Indian Ocean and between the Atlantic and the Caribbean. The enemy's submarines had sunk some of our cruisers—three in succession on a single day and in the same area. Then rumours gained ground that the Grand Fleet, driven from its anchorages by submarines, was fugitive, hiding now in one remote loch, now in another, and losing one of its greatest units in its flight. For a moment it looked as if the old warnings, that surface craft were impotent against under-water craft, had suddenly been proved true. Von Spee, with a powerful pair of armoured cruisers, was known to be at large. As a final insult, German battle-cruisers crossed the North Sea, and battered and ravaged the defenceless inhabitants of a small seaport town on the east coast. Something was evidently wrong. But nobody seemed to know quite what it was.

The crisis was met by a typical expedient. We are a nation of hero-worshippers and proverbially loyal to our favourites long after they have lost any title to our favour. In the concert-room, in the cricket-field, on the stage, in Parliament—in every phase of life—it is the old and tried friend in whom we confide, even if we have conveniently to overlook the fact that he has not only been tried, but convicted. This blind loyalty is, perhaps, amiable as a weakness, and almost peculiar to this nation. But we have another which is neither amiable nor peculiar.

We hate having our complacency disturbed by being proved to be wrong and, rather than acknowledge our fault, are easily persuaded that the cause of our misfortune is some hidden and malign influence. And so, in October, 1914, the explanation of things being wrong at sea was suddenly found to be quite simple. It was that the First Sea Lord of the Admiralty was of German birth. With the evil eye gone the spell would be removed. And so a most accomplished officer retired, and Lord Fisher, now almost a mythological hero, took his place.

Within very few weeks the scene suffered—

. . . a sea change.
Into something rich and strange.

Von Spee was left but a month in which to enjoy his triumph over Cradock; *Emden* was defeated and captured by *Sydney*; *Karlsruhe* vanished as by enchantment from the sea; and Von Hipper's battle-cruisers, going once too often near the British coast, had been driven in ignominious flight across the North Sea and paid for their temerity by the loss of *Blücher*. Three months of the Fisher-Churchill *régime* had seemingly put the navy on a pinnacle that even the most sanguine—and the most ignorant—had hardly dared to hope for in the early days. The spectacle, in August, of the transports plying between France and England, as securely as the motor-buses between Fleet Street and the Fulham Road, had been a tremendous proof of confidence in sea-power. The unaccepted challenge at Heligoland had told a tale. The British fleet had indeed seemed unchallengeable. But the justification of our confidence was, after all, based only on the fact that the enemy had not disputed it. It was a negative triumph.

But the capture of *Emden*, the obliteration of Von Spee, the un-camouflaged flight of Von Hipper, here were things positive, proofs of power in action, the meaning of which was patent to the simplest. No man in his senses could pretend that our troubles in October had not been attributed to their right origin, nor that the right remedy for them had been found and applied.

There was but one cloud on the horizon. The submarine—despite the loss of *Hogue, Cressy, Aboukir, Hawk, Hermes,* and *Niger,* and the disturbing rumours that the fleet's bases were insecure—had been a failure as an agent for the attrition of our main sea forces. The loss of *Formidable*, that clouded the opening of the year, had not restored its prestige. But Von Tirpitz had made an ominous threat. The submarine might have failed against naval ships. It certainly would not fail, he said, against trading ships. He gave the world fair warning that at the right moment an under-water blockade of the British Isles would be proclaimed; then woe to all belligerents or neutrals that ventured into those death-doomed waters. The naval writers were not very greatly alarmed. For four months, after all, trading ships—turned into transports—had used the narrow waters of the Channel as if the submarines were no threat at all.

Yet, on pre-war reasoning, it was precisely in narrow waters crowded with traffic that under-water war should have been of greatest effect. These transports and these narrow waters were the ideal victims and the ideal field, and coast and harbour defence and the prevention of invasion, by common consent, the obvious and indeed the supreme functions the submarine would be called upon to discharge. From a military point of view the landing of British troops in France was but the first stage towards an invasion of Germany and, from a naval point of view, it looked as if to defend the French ports from being entered by British ships was just as clearly the first objective of the German submarine as the defence of any German port. Now six months of war had shown that, if they had tried to stop the transports, the submarines had been thwarted.

Means and methods had evidently been found of preventing their attack or parrying it when made. Was it not obvious that it could be no more than a question of extending these methods to merchant shipping at large to turn the greater threat to futility? It was this reasoning that, in January and February, made it easy for the writers to stem any tendency of the public to panic, and when, towards the end of February, the First Lord addressed Parliament on the subject, and dealt with the conscienceless threat of piracy with a placid and defiant confidence, all were justified in thinking that the naval critics had been right.

And so, the beginning of the submarine campaign, though somewhat disconcerting, caused no wide alarm. An initial success was expected. It would take time to build the destroyers and the convoying craft on the scale that was called for, and so to organise the trade that the attack must be narrowed to protected focal points. And as absolute secrecy was maintained, both as to our actual defensive methods and as to our preparations for the future, there was neither the occasion nor the material for questioning whether the serene contentment of Whitehall was rightly founded.

Meantime, as we have seen, success had justified the solution of the October crisis. The attempt to probe deeper and to get at the cause of things was a thankless task. Those who could see beneath the surface could not fail to note in December and January that, while an exuberant optimism had become the mark of the British attitude towards the war at sea, a movement curiously parallel to it was going forward in Germany. The shifts to which the Grand Fleet had been put by the defenceless state of its harbours, though rigidly excluded from the British Press, has been triumphantly exploited in the German. Hence, when the enemy's only oversea squadron was annihilated by Sir Doveton Sturdee, his Press responded with an outcry on the cowardice of the British Fleet that, while glad to overwhelm an inferior force abroad, dared not show itself in the North Sea.

And, as if to prove the charge, Whitby and the Hartlepools were forthwith bombarded by a force we were unable to bring to action while returning from this exploit. The enemy naval writers surpassed themselves after this. And it looked so certain that the German Higher

Command might itself become hypnotized by such talk that, before the New Year, it seemed prudent to note these phenomena and warn the public that we might be challenged to action after all, of the kind of action the enemy would dare us to, and what the problems were that such an action would present. And in particular it seemed advisable to state explicitly that much less must be expected from naval guns in battle than those had hoped, whose notions were founded upon battle practice.

A battle-cruiser manoeuvring at twenty-eight knots—instead of a canvas screen towed at six—mines scattered by a squadron in retreat, a line of retreat that would draw the pursuers into minefields set to trap them; the attacks on the pursuing squadrons by flotillas of destroyers, firing long-range torpedoes—these new elements would upset, it was said, all experiences of peace gunnery, because in peace practices it is impossible to provide a target of the speed which enemy ships would have in action, and because there had been no practice while executing the manoeuvres which torpedo attack would make compulsory in battle.

Within a fortnight the action of the Dogger Bank was fought and Von Hipper's battle-cruisers were subjected to the fire of Sir David Beatty's Fleet from nine o'clock until twelve, without one being sunk or so damaged as to lose speed. The enemy's tactics included attacks by submarine and destroyer which had imposed the manoeuvres as anticipated—and the best of gunnery had failed. But *Blücher* had been sunk; the enemy had run away; so, the warning fell on deaf ears; the lesson of the battle was misread. Optimism reigned supreme.

THE SECOND CRISIS

Within a month a naval adventure of a new kind was embarked upon, based on the theory that if only you had naval guns enough, any fort against which they were directed must be pulverized as were the forts of Liège, Namur, Maubeuge, and Antwerp. The simplest comprehension of the principles of naval gunnery would have shown the theory to be fallacious. It originated in the fertile brain of the lay Chief of the Admiralty, and though it would seem as if his naval advisers felt the theory to be wrong, none of them, in the absence of a competent and independent gunnery staff, could say why. And so, the essentially military operation of forcing the passage of the Dardanelles was undertaken as if it were a purely naval operation, with the result that, just as naval success had never been conceivable, so now the failure of the ships made military success impossible also.

It was thus we came to our second naval crisis. The first we had solved by putting Lord Fisher into Prince Louis's place. The lesson of the second seemed to be that there was only one mistake that could be made with the navy and that was for the government to ask it to do anything. Mr. Churchill, as King Stork, had taken the initiative. Lord Fisher, the naval superman, had not been able to save us. It was clear that lay interference with the navy was wrong—equally clear that it would be wiser to leave the initiative to the enemy. And so, a new *régime* began.

But, in reality, the lessons of the first crisis and the second crisis were the same. To suppose that a civilian First Lord is bound to be mischievous if he is energetic, and certain to be harmless if, in administering the navy as an instrument of war, he is a cipher, were errors just as great as to suppose that a seaman with a long, loyal, and brilliant record in the public service had put an evil enchantment over the whole British Navy because, fifty years before, he had been born a subject of a Power with which till now we had never been at war. Things went wrong in October, 1914, for precisely the same reasons that they went wrong in February, March, and April, 1915.

The German battle-cruisers escaped at Heligoland for exactly the same reasons that the attempt to take the Dardanelles forts by naval artillery was futile. We had prepared for war and gone into war with no clear doctrine as to what war meant, because we lacked the organism that could have produced the doctrine in peace time, prepared and trained the navy to a common understanding of it, and supplied it with plans and equipped it with means for their execution. What was needed in October, 1914, was not a new First Sea Lord, but a Higher Command charged only with the study of the principles and the direction of fighting.

But in May, 1915, this truth was not recognised. And in the next year which passed, all efforts to make this truth understood were without effect. And so, the submarine campaign went on till it spent itself in October and revived again in the following March, when it was stopped by the threat of American intervention. The enemy, thwarted in the only form of sea activity that promised him great results, found himself suddenly threatened on land and humiliated at sea, and to restore his waning prestige, ventured out with his forces, was brought to battle—and escaped practically unhurt.

The controversies to which the Battle of Jutland gave rise will be in everyone's recollection. Another of the many indecisive battles with which history is full had been fought, and the critics established themselves in two camps. One side was for facing risks and sinking the enemy at any cost. The other would have it that so long as the British Fleet was unconquered it was invincible, and that the distinction between "invincible" and "victorious" could be neglected. After all, as Mr. Churchill told us, while our fleet was crushing the life breath out of Germany, the German Navy could carry on no corresponding attack on us; and when the other camp denounced this doctrine of tame defence, he retorted that victory was not unnecessary but that the torpedo had made it impossible.

The Third Crisis

Yet, within two months of the Battle of Jutland, the submarine campaign had begun again, and, at the time of Mr. Churchill's rejoinder, the world was losing shipping at the rate of three million tons a year! As there never had been the least dispute that to mine the submarine into German harbours was the best, if not the only, antidote, never the least doubt that it was only the German Fleet that prevented this operation from being carried out it seemed strange that an ex-First Lord of the Admiralty should be telling the world first, that the German Fleet in its home bases delivered no attack on us and therefore need not be defeated! And, secondly, as if to clinch the matter and silence any doubts as to the cogency of his argument, we were to make the best of it because victory was impossible.

This utter confusion of mind was typical of the public attitude. If a man who had been First Lord at the most critical period of our history had understood events so little, could the man in the street know any better?

Once more the root principles of war were urged on public notice. But it was already too late. Jutland, whether a victory, or something far less than a victory, had at any rate left the public in the comfortable assurance that the ability of the British Fleet was virtually unimpaired to preserve the flow of provisions, raw material, and manufactures into Allied harbours and to maintain our military communications. But soon after the third year of the war began, a change came over the scene. The highest level that the submarine campaign had reached in the past was regained, and then surpassed month by month. Gradually it came to be seen that the thing might become critical—and this though the campaign was not ruthless. Yet it was carried out on a larger scale and with bolder methods which the possession of a larger fleet of submarines made possible.

The element of surprise in the thing was not that the Germans had renewed the attempt—for it was clear from the terms of surrender to America that they would renew it at their own time. The surprise was in its success. The public, still trusting to the attitude of mind induced by the critics and by the authorities in 1915, had taken it for granted that the two previous campaigns had stopped in December, 1915, and in March, 1916, because of the efficiency of our counter-measures. The revelation of the autumn of 1916, was that these counter-measures had failed.

It was this that brought about the third naval crisis of the war. Once more the old wrong remedy was tried. The government and the public had learned nothing from the revelation that we had gone to war on the doctrine that the fleet *need* not, and *ought* not, to fight the enemy, and were apparently unconcerned at discovering that it *could* not fight with success. And so, still not realising the root cause of all our trouble, once more a remedy was sought by changing the chief naval adviser to the government.

But on this occasion, it was not only the chief that was replaced, as had happened when Lord Fisher succeeded Prince Louis of Battenberg, and when Sir Henry Jackson succeeded Lord Fisher. When Admiral Jellicoe came to Whitehall several colleagues accompanied him from the Grand Fleet. There was nothing approaching to a complete change of personnel, but the infusion of new blood was considerable. But this notwithstanding, the menace from the submarine grew, when ruthlessness was adopted as a method, until the rate of loss by April had doubled, trebled, and quadrupled that of the previous year. All the world then saw that, with shipping vanishing at the rate of more than a million tons a month, the period during which the Allies could maintain the fight against the Central Powers must be strictly limited.

Thus, without having lost a battle at sea—but because we had failed to win one—a complete reverse in the naval situation was brought about. Instead of enjoying the complete command Mr. Churchill had spoken of, we were counting the months before surrender might be inevitable. During the ten weeks leading up to the culminating losses of April, a final effort was made to make the public and the government realise that failure of the Admiralty to protect the sea-borne commerce of a seagirt people was due less to the government's reliance on advisers ill-equipped for their task, than that the task itself was beyond human performance, so long as the Higher Command of the navy was wrongly constituted for its task. It was, of course, an old warning vainly urged on successive governments year after year in peace time, and month after month during the war. Evidences of inadequate preparation of imperfect plans, of a wrong theory of command, of action founded on wrong doctrine but endorsed by authority, had all been numerous during the previous two and a half years.

THE FOURTH CRISIS

But where reason and argument had been powerless to prevail, the logic of facts gained the victory. At last, in the fourth naval crisis of the war, it was realised that changes in personnel at Whitehall were not sufficient, that changes of system were necessary. Before the end of May the machinery of administration was reorganised and a new Higher Command developed, largely on the long-resisted staff principle.

Thus, after repeated failures—not of the Fleet but of its directing minds in London—a complete revolution was effected in the command of the most important of all the fighting forces in the war, *viz.*, the British Navy. It was actually brought about because criticism had shown that the old *régime* had first failed to anticipate and then to thwart a new kind of attack on sea communications—just as it had failed to anticipate the conditions of surface war. It was at last realised that two kinds of naval war could go on together, one almost independent of the other.

A power might command the surface of the sea against the surface force of an enemy, and do so more absolutely than had ever happened before, and yet see that command brought, for its main purposes, almost to nothing by a new naval force, from which, though naval ships could defend themselves, they seemingly could not defend the carrying and travelling ships, upon which the life of the nation and the continuance of its military effort on land depended. The revolution of May saved the situation. At last the principle of convoy, vainly urged on the old *régime*, was adopted, and within six months the rate at which ships were being lost was practically halved. In twelve months, it had been reduced by sixty *per cent*.

But the departure made in the summer of 1917, though radical as to principle, was less than half-hearted as to persons. Many of the men identified with all our previous failures and responsible for the methods and plans that have led to them, were retained in full authority. The mere adoption of the staff principle did indeed bring about an effect so singular and striking as completely to transform all Allied prospects. In April, defeat seemed to be a matter of a few months only.

By October it had become clear that the submarine could not by itself assure a German victory. If such extraordinary consequences could follow—exactly as it was predicted they must—from a change in system which all experience of war had proved to be essential, why, it may be asked, was the adoption of the staff principle so bitterly opposed? Partly, no doubt, because of the natural conservatism of men who have grown old and attained to high rank in a service to which they have given their lives in all devotion and sincerity. The singularity of the sailor's training and experience tends to make the naval profession both isolated and exclusive.

And that its daily life is based upon the strictest discipline, that gives absolute power to the captain of a ship because it is necessary to hold him absolutely responsible, inevitably grafts upon this exclusiveness a respect for seniority which gives to its action in every field the indisputable finality bred of the quarter-deck habit. Thus, there was no place in Admiralty organisation for the independent and expert work of junior men, because no authority could attach to their counsel. It is of the essence of the staff principle that special knowledge, sound, impartial, trained judgment, grasp of principle and proved powers of constructive imagination, are higher titles to dictatorship in policy than the character and experience called for in the discharge of executive command.

But to a service not bred to seeing all questions of policy first investigated, analysed, and, finally, defined by a staff which necessarily will consist more of younger than of older men, the suggestion that the higher ranks should accept the guiding co-operation of their juniors seemed altogether anarchical. The long resistance to the establishment of a Higher Command based on rational principles may be set down to these two elements of human psychology.

That successive governments failed to break down this conservatism must, I think, be explained by their fear of the hold which men of great professional reputation had upon the public mind and public affections. It was notable, for example, that when our original troubles came to us at the first crisis, the government, instead of seeking the help of the youngest and most accomplished of our admirals and captains, chose as chief advisers the oldest and least in touch with our modern conditions. It was, perhaps, the same fear of public opinion that delayed the completion of the 1917, reforms until the beginning of the next year. But, with all its defects and its limitations, the solution sought of the fourth sea crisis had made the history of the past twelve months the most hopeful of any since the war began.

The New Era

The period divides itself into two unequal portions. Between June and January, 1918, was seen the slowly growing mastery of the submarine. The rate of loss was halved and the methods by which this result was achieved were applied as widely as possible. But in the next six or eight months no improvement in the position corresponding to that which followed in the first period was obtained. The explanation is simple enough. The old autocratic *régime* had not understood the nature of the new war any better than the nature of the old. It had from the first, under successive chief naval advisers, repudiated convoy as though it were a pestilent heresy.

In June, 1917, the very men who, as absolutist advisers, had taken this attitude, were compelled to sanction the hated thing itself. It yielded exactly the results claimed for it, but no more. It was in its nature so simple and so obvious that it did not take long to get it into working order. It was the best form of defence. But defence is the weakest form of war. The stronger form, the offensive, needed planning and long preparations. In the nature of things these could not take effect either in six months or in twelve.

Nor is it likely that, while the old personnel was suffered to remain at Whitehall, those engaged on the plans and charged with the preparations for this were able to work with the expedition which the situation called for. For the first six months after the revolution, then, little occurred to prove its efficiency, except the fruits of the policy which instructed opinion had forced on Whitehall. But these, so far as the final issue of the war was concerned, were surely sufficient. For the losses by submarines were brought below the danger point.

It was not until the revolution made its next step forward by the changes in personnel announced in January that marked progress was shown in the other fields of naval war. The late autumn had been marked, as it was fully expected, once the submarine was thwarted, by various efforts on the part of the enemy to assert himself by other means at sea. A Lerwick convoy, very inadequately protected, was raided by fast and powerful enemy cruisers, and many ships sunk in circumstances of extraordinary barbarity. The destroyers protecting them sacrificed themselves with fruitless gallantry. There were ravages on the coast as well. Both things pointed to salient weaknesses in the naval position.

At the time of the third naval crisis at the end of 1916, it had been pointed out that the repeated evidences of our inability to hold the enemy in the Narrow Seas ought not to be allowed to pass uncensured or unremedied. But the fatal habit of refusing to recognise that an old favourite had failed prevented any reform for a year. It was not until Sir Roger Keyes was appointed to the Dover Command and a new atmosphere was created that remarkable departures in new policy were inaugurated.

This policy took two forms. First, there was the establishment of a mine barrage from coast to coast across the Channel, and simultaneously with this, North Sea minefields stretching, one from Norwegian territorial waters almost to the Scottish foreshore, and another in the Kattegat, to intercept such German U-boats as base their activities upon the enemy's Baltic force. Two great minefields on such a scale as this are works of time. Nor can their effect upon the submarine campaign be expected to be seen until they are very near completion; but then the effect may possibly be immediate and overwhelming.

Principally to facilitate the creation and maintenance of the barrages, a second new departure in policy was the organisation of attacks on the German bases in Flanders. Of these Zeebrügge was infinitely the more important, because it is from here that the deep water canal runs to the docks and wharves of Bruges some miles inland. The value of Zeebrügge, robbed of the facilities for equipment and reparation which the Bruges docks afford, is little indeed. It is little more than an anchorage and a refuge. To close Zeebrügge to the enemy called for an operation as daring and as intricate as was ever attempted. Success depended upon so many factors, of which the right weather was the least certain, that it was no wonder that the expedition started again and again without attempting the blow it set out to strike. Its final complete success at Zeebrügge was a veritable triumph of perfect planning and organisation and command.

It came at a critical moment in the campaign. A month before the enemy, by his great attack at St. Quentin, had achieved by far the greatest land victory of the war. He had followed this up by further attacks, and seemed to add to endless resources in men a ruthless determination to employ them for victory. The British and French were driven to the defensive. Not to be beaten, not to yield too much ground, to exact the highest price for what was yielded, this was not a very glorious *rôle* when the triumphs on the Somme and in Flanders of 1916, and 1917, were remembered. It cannot be questioned that the originality, the audacity, and the success of Vice-Admiral Keyes' attacks on Zeebrügge and Ostend, gave to all the Allies just that encouragement which a dashing initiative alone can give. It broke the monotony of being always passive.

But the new minefields, the barrages, the sealing of Zeebrügge, these were far from being the only fruits of the changes at Whitehall. A sortie by *Breslau* and *Goeben* from the Dardanelles, which ended in the sinking of a couple of German monitors and the loss of a light German cruiser on a minefield, directed attention sharply to the situation in the Middle Sea. There was a manifest peril that the Russian Fleet might fall into German hands and make a junction with the Austrian Fleet at Pola. Further, the losses of the Allies by submarines in this sea had for long been unduly heavy. A visit of the First Lord to the Mediterranean did much to put these things right. First steps were taken in reorganising the command and, before the changes had advanced very far, an astounding exploit by two officers of the Italian Navy resulted in the destruction of two Austrian Dreadnoughts, and relieved the Allies of any grave danger in this quarter.

Meantime, it had become known that a powerful American squadron had joined the Grand Fleet, that our gallant and accomplished Allies had adopted British signals and British ways, and had become in every respect perfectly amalgamated with the force they had so greatly strengthened. And though little was said about it in the Press, it was evident enough that the moral of the Lerwick convoy had been learned, nor was there the least doubt that the Grand Fleet, under the command of Sir David Beatty, had become an instrument of war infinitely more flexible and efficient than it had ever been. His plans and battle orders took every contingency into council so far as human foresight made possible.

At Jutland, at the Dogger Bank, and in the Heligoland Bight, Admiral Beatty had shown his power to animate a fleet by his own fighting spirit and to combine a unity of action with the independent initiative of his admirals, simply because he had inspired all of them with a common doctrine of fighting. Under such auspices there could be little doubt that our main forces in northern waters were ready for battle with a completeness and an elasticity that left nothing to chance.

But if we are to look for the chief fruit of last year's revolution, we shall not find it in the reorganised Grand Fleet, nor in the new initiative and aggression in the Narrow Seas, for the ultimate results of which we still have to wait. If the enemy despairs both of victory on land or of such success as will give him a compromise peace, if he is faced by disintegration at home and, driven to a desperate stroke, sends out his Fleet to fight, we shall then see, but perhaps not till then, what the changes of last year have brought about in our fighting forces. Meantime, the success of the great reforms can be measured quite definitely. In the months of May and June over half a million American soldiers were landed in France, sixty *per cent.* of whom were carried in British ships. No one in his senses in May or June last year would have thought this possible.

Looked at largely, then, last year's revolution at Whitehall is in all ways the most astonishing and the most satisfactory naval event of the last four years. It is the most satisfactory event, because its results have been so nearly what was foretold and because it only needs for the work to be completed for all the lessons of the war to be rightly applied.

CHAPTER 3

Sea Fallacies: A Plea for First Principles

What do we mean by "sea-power" and "command of the sea"? What really is a navy and how does it gain these things? How come navies into existence? Of what constituents, human and material, are they composed? How are the human elements taught, trained, commanded, and led? How are the ships grouped and distributed, and the weapons fought in war?

To the countrymen of Nelson, and to those of his great interpreter, Mahan, these might at first sight seem very superfluous questions, for they, almost of natural instinct, should understand that strange but overwhelming force that has made them. To the Kingdom of Great Britain and Ireland, to the Empires that owe allegiance to the British Crown, to the United States of America, sea-power is at once their origin and the fundamental essential of their continued free and independent existence. And it is their predominant races that have produced the world's greatest sea fighters and sea writers. It is to the British Fleet that the world owes its promise of safety from German diabolism bred of autocracy. It is to sea-power that America must look if she is to finish the work the Allies have begun. With so great a stake in the sea, Great Britain and America should have fathomed its mysteries.

But, despite the fighters and the writers, the sea in a great measure has kept its secret hidden. In every age the truth has been the possession of but a few. Countries for a time have followed the light, and have then, as it were, been suddenly struck blind, and the fall of empires has followed the loss of vision. The world explains the British Empire of today, (1919), and the great American nation which has sprung from it, by a happy congenital talent for colonising waste places, for self-government, for assimilating and making friends with the unprogressive peoples, by giving them a better government than they had before. And certainly, without such gifts the British races could not have overspread so large a portion of the earth. But the world is apt to forget that there were other empires sprung from other European peoples—Portuguese, French, Spanish, and Dutch—each at some time larger in wealth, area, or population, than that which owed allegiance to the British Crown. In each case it was the power of their navies that gave each country these great possessions.

Of some of these empires only insignificant traces remain today. They have been merged in the British Empire or have become independent. And the merging or the freeing has always followed from war at sea. It is the British sailors, and not the British colonists, that have made the British Empire. It is not because the settlers in New England were better fighters or had more talent for self-government, but because Holland had the weaker navy, that the city which must shortly be the greatest in the world is named after the ancient capital of Northern England, and not after Amsterdam. It was not England's half-hearted fight on land, but her failure to preserve an unquestionable command of the sea that secured the extraordinary success of Washington and Hamilton's military plans.

To all these truths we have long paid lip service. Years ago, it passed into a commonplace that should ever national existence be threatened by an outside force, it would be on the sea that we should have to rely for defence. With so tremendous an issue at stake, why was our knowledge so vague, why has our curiosity to know the truth been so feeble? Perhaps it is that communities that are very rich and very comfortable are slow to believe that danger can hang over them. In the catechism used to teach Catholic children the elements of their religion, the death that awaits every mortal, the instant judgment before the throne of God, the awful alternatives, Heaven or Hell, that depend on the issue, are spoken of as the "Four Last Things." Their title has been flippantly explained by the admitted fact that they are the very last things that most people ever think of. So, has it been with America and England in the matter of war. The threat seemed too far off to be a common and universal concern.

It could be left to the governments. So long as we voted all the money that was asked for officially, we had done our share. And, if statesmen told us that our naval force was large enough, and that it was in a state of high efficiency, and ready for war, we felt no obligation to ask what war meant, in what efficiency consisted, or how its existence could be either presumed or proved. We had no incentive to master the thing for ourselves. We were not challenged to inquire whether in fact the semblance of sea-power corresponded with its reality. The fact that it was on sea-power that we relied for defence against invasion should, of course, have quickened our vigilance. It, in fact, deadened it. For we had never refused a pound the Admiralty had asked for. We took the sufficiency of the navy for granted and, with the buffer of the fleet between ourselves and ruin, the threat of ruin seemed all the more remote.

A minority, no doubt, was uneasy and did inquire. But they found their path crossed by difficulties almost insuperable. The literature of sea-power was based entirely upon the history of the great sea wars of a dim past. Mahan, it is true, had so elucidated the broad doctrines of sea strategy that it seemed as if he who ran might read. But lucid and convincing as is his analysis, urbane and judicial as is his style, Mahan's work could not make the bulk of his readers adepts in naval doctrine. The fact seems to be that the fabled mysteries of the sea make every truth concerning it elusive, difficult for anyone but a sailor to grasp. The difficulties were hardly lessened by Mahan's chief work having dealt completely with the past. The most important of the world's sea wars may be said to begin with the Armada and to end in 1815. In these two and one quarter centuries the implements of naval warfare changed hardly at all. Broadly speaking, from the days of Howard of Effingham to those of Fulton and Watt, man used three-masted ships and muzzle-loading cannon. Hence the history of the Great Age deals very little with the technique of war.

To the lay reader, therefore, the study of sea-power, based upon these ancient campaigns, seemed not only the pursuit of a subject vague and elusive in itself, but one that becomes doubly unreal through the successive revolutions of modern times. It was like studying the politics of an extinct community told in records of a dead language. The incendiary shell, armour to keep the shell out, steam that made ships completely dirigible in the sense that they could with great rapidity be turned to any chosen course, these alone had, by the middle of the last century, completely revolutionized the tactical employment of sea force.

Steam, which made a ship easier to aim than a gun, gave birth to ramming; and naval thought was hypnotized by this fallacy for nearly two generations. By the end of the century the whole art had again been changed, first by the development of the monster cannon, and next, a far more important invention, the mountings that made first light, and then heavy, guns so flexible in use that they could be aimed in a moderate sea way. These and the invention of the fish torpedo and the high-speed boat for carrying it—that in the twilight of dawn and eve would make it practically invisible—brought about fresh changes that altered not only the tactics of battle, but those of blockade and of many other naval operations.

But great and surprising as were the changes and developments in naval weapons and the material in the last half of the nineteenth century, they were completely eclipsed by the number and nature of the advances made in the first decade and a half of the twentieth. If, to the ordinary reader, the lessons of the past seemed of doubtful value in the light of what steam, the explosive shell, the torpedo, and the heavy gun had effected, what was to be said in the light of the kaleidoscope of novelties sprung upon the world *after* the latest of all the naval wars? For between 1906, and 1914, there came a succession of naval sensations so startling as to make clear and connected thinking appear a visionary hope.

First, we heard that naval guns, that until 1904, had nowhere been fired at a greater range than two miles, were actually being used in practice—and used with success—at distances of ten, twelve, and fourteen thousand yards. It was not only that guns were increasing their range, they were growing monstrously in size and still more monstrously in the numbers put into each individual ship, so that the ships grew faster than the guns themselves, until the capital ship of today is more than double the displacement of that of ten years ago. And with size came speed, not only the speed that would follow naturally from the increase in length, but the further speed that was got by a more compact and lighter form of prime mover.

Ten years ago, (as at 1919), the highest action pace a fleet of capital ships would have been, perhaps, seventeen knots. Now whole squadrons can do twenty-five *per cent.* better. And with the battle-cruiser we have now a capital ship carrying the biggest guns there are, that can take them into action literally twice as fast as a twelve-inch gun could be carried into battle twelve years ago. Thus, with range increased out of all imagination, and vastly greater speed, the tactics of battle were obviously in the melting pot.

But these were far from being the only revolutionary elements. There followed in quick succession a new torpedo that ran with almost perfect accuracy for five or six miles and carried an explosive charge three or four times larger than anything previously known. It had seemed but yesterday that a mile was the torpedo's almost outside range. Then, at the beginning of the decade of which I speak, the submarine had a low speed on the surface, and half of that below it, with a very limited area of manoeuvre in which it could work. It seemed little more, many thought, than an ingenious toy capable, perhaps, of an occasional deadly surprise if an enemy's fleet should come too near a harbour, but seemingly not destined to influence the grand tactics of war.

But in an incredibly short time the submarine became a submersible ocean cruiser, with three times the radius of a pre-Dreadnought battleship, with a far higher surface speed, and able to carry guns of such power that they could sink a merchant ship with half-a-dozen rounds at four miles. In this, even the dullest could see something more than a change in naval tactics. Might not the whole nature of naval war be changed? For the long range torpedo that could be used in action, at a range equal to that at which the greatest guns could be expected to hit; the submarine that, completely hidden, could bring the torpedo to such short range that hits would be a certainty, the invisible boat that could evade the closest surface cordon and, almost undisturbed, hunt and destroy merchantmen on the trade routes—that, but for the submarine, would have been completely protected by the command won by the predominant fleet—wonderful as these new things were, they were far from exhausting the new developments of under-water war.

Great ingenuity had been shown not only in developing very powerful mines, but in devising means of laying them by the fastest ships, so that not only could these deadly traps be set by merchantmen disguised as neutrals, but by fast cruisers whose speed could at any time enable them to evade the patrols. And, finally, it was equally obvious that the submarine could become a mine layer also. There was, then, literally no spot in the ocean that might not at any moment be mined.

Add to all this, that while wireless introduced an almost instant means of sending orders to or getting news from such distant spots that space was annihilated, airships and aeroplanes—with some, as many thought, with a decisive capacity for attacking fleets in harbour—seemed to make scouting possible over unthought of areas. Can we blame the landsman who set himself patiently to learn the rudiments of the naval art if, after a painful study of the past, he found himself so bemused by the changes of the present as to wonder if a single accepted dogma could survive the high-explosive bombardment of today's (1919) inventions? It almost looked as if nothing could be learned from the past and less, if possible, be foretold about the future. If the understanding of sea-power in the days of old had been the possession of but a few, it seemed that today it must be denied to all.

It is, therefore, not surprising that extraordinary misunderstandings were—and are—prevalent. Only one truth seemed to survive—the supremacy of the capital ship. But this, too, became an error, because it excluded other truths. To the vast bulk of laymen, the word "navy" suggested no more than a panorama of great super-Dreadnought battleships. From time to time naval reviews had been held, and the illustrated papers had shown these great vessels, long vistas of them, anchored in perfectly kept lines, with light cruisers and destroyers fading away into the distance. Both in the pictures and in the descriptions all emphasis was laid upon the ships. And in this the current official naval thought of the day was reflected.

If anyone wished to compare the British Fleet with the German or the German with the American, he confined himself to enumerating their respective totals in Dreadnoughts, and let it go at that. His mental picture of a fleet was thus a perspective of vast mastodons armed with guns of fabulous reach and still more fabulous power, gifted, some of them, with speed that could outstrip the fastest liner, and encased, at least in part, in almost impenetrable armour.

He would know generally, of course, that such things as cruisers, destroyers, and submarines not only existed, but were indeed necessary. He would know vaguely that cruisers were useful for cruising, and destroyers for their eponymous duties—though he would have been sorely puzzled if he had been asked to say exactly what the cruising was for, or what the destroyers were intended to destroy. He would have heard of the mystic properties of torpedoes, and of mines, and of certain weird possibilities that lay before the combination of the torpedo with the submarine. Similarly, if one challenged him, he would admit, of course, that guns could only be formidable if they hit, and that fleets could only succeed in battle if their officers and crews were properly trained and skilfully led.

But these were things that could not be tabulated or scheduled. They did not figure in Naval Annuals, nor in Admiralty statements. They were stumbling blocks to the layman's desire to be satisfied—and he took it for granted that they were all right, and was content to measure naval strength by the number of the biggest ships, and so rate the navies of the world by what they possessed in these colossal units only. Thus, he would always put Great Britain first, and recently

Germany second, with the United States, Japan, and France taking the third place in succession, as their annual programmes of construction were announced. And just as he thought of navies in terms of battleships, so he thought of naval war in terms of great sea battles. A reaction was inevitable.

Four years have now passed since Germany struck her felon blow at the Christian tradition the nations have been struggling to maintain—and so far, there has been no Trafalgar. The German Fleet, hidden behind its defences, is still integral and afloat, and though the British Fleet has again and again come out, its battleships have got into action but once, and then for a few minutes only. For four years, therefore, the two greatest battle fleets in the world seem to have been doing nothing; and to be doing nothing now! And so, if you ask the average layman for a broad opinion on sea-power today, (1919), he will tell you that battle fleets are useless. For a year or more he has heard little of any work at sea except of the work of the submarine. To him, therefore, it seemed manifest that the torpedo has superseded the gun and the submarine the battleship. His opinions, in other words, have swung full cycle. Was he right before and is he wrong now, or was his first view an error and has he at last, under the stern teachings of war, attained the truth?

He was wrong then and he is wrong now. It was an error to think of sea-power *only* in terms of battleships. It is a still greater error to suppose that sea-power can exist in any useful form *unless* based on battleships in overwhelming strength. It is true that the German submarines did for a period so threaten the world's shipping as to make it possible that the overwhelming military resources of the Allies might never be brought to bear against the full strength of the German line in France. It is also true that they have added years to the duration of the war, millions and millions to its cost, and have brought us to straits that are hard to bear. They were truly Germany's most powerful defence, the only useful form of sea force for her. But it is, nevertheless, quite impossible that the submarine can give to Germany any of the direct advantages which the command of the sea confers.

These simple truths will come home convincingly to us if we suppose for a minute that, at the only encounter in which the battle fleets met, it had been the German Fleet that was victorious. Had Scheer and Von Hipper met Beatty and Jellicoe in a fair, well-fought-out action, and sunk or captured the greater part of the British Fleet so that but a crippled remnant could struggle back to harbour—as little left of the mighty British Armada as survived of Villeneuve's and Gravina's forces after Trafalgar—would it ever have been necessary for Germany to have challenged the forbearance of the world by reckless and piratical attacks on peaceful shipping?

Quite obviously not. For with her battle-cruisers patrolling unchallenged in the Channel, the North Sea, and the Atlantic, with all her destroyers and light cruisers working under their protection, no British merchantman could have cleared or entered any British port, no neutral could have passed the blockading lines.

British submarines might, indeed, have held up German shipping—but we should have lost the use of merchant shipping ourselves. Our armies would have been cut off from their overseas base, our fighting Allies would have been robbed of the food and material now reaching them from North and South America and the British Dominions, and the civil population of England, Scotland, Ireland, and Wales, would have been threatened by immediate invasion or by not very far distant famine. And this is so because command of the sea is conditioned by a superior battleship strength, and can only be exercised by surface craft which cannot be driven off the sea.

Let us look at this question again from another angle. It is probable that Germany possessed, during the summer of 1917, some two hundred submarines at least. She may have possessed more. These submarines were, for many months, sinking on an average of from twenty to twenty-four British ships a week, and perhaps rather more than half as many Allied and neutral ships as well. It was, of course, a very formidable loss. But of every seventeen ships that went into the danger zone, sixteen did actually escape. How many would have escaped if Germany could have maintained a fleet of fifty surface ships—light cruisers, armed merchantmen, swift destroyers—in these waters? Supposing trade ships were to put to sea and try to get past such a cordon just as they risk passing the submarines, how many could possibly escape? What would be the toll each surface ship would take—one a fortnight? One a week? One a day?

These are all ridiculous questions, because, could such a cordon be maintained, no ship bound for Great Britain would put to sea at all. It would not be sixteen escaping to one captured; the whole seventeen would so certainly be doomed that they all would stay in port. So much the war has certainly taught us. When, on August 4, 1914, the British Government declared war on Germany, the sailing of every German ship the world over was then and there stopped. A hundred that were at sea could not be warned and were captured. Those that escaped capture made German or neutral ports. But the order not to sail did not wait upon results. The stoppage of the German merchant service was automatic and instantaneous. It would have been raving insanity to have risked encounter with a navy that held the surface command.

Three months later the situation was locally reversed in South American waters. Von Spee, with two very powerful armoured cruisers and three light fast vessels, encountered a very inferior British force under Admiral Cradock off Coronel, and defeated it decisively. Von Spee's victory meant that in the Southern Atlantic there was no force capable of opposing him. Instantly every South American port was closed. No one knew where Von Spee might turn up next. Not a captain dared clear for England. Even in South Africa General Botha's hands were tied. A section of the Transvaal and Orange Colony Dutch had risen in rebellion, and had made common cause with the Germans in South West Africa. With Von Spee at large there was no saying what help he would bring to the enemy, and the risk that communications with the mother country might be cut, was a real one. For four weeks the South African Government was paralyzed.

Then followed the most brilliant piece of sea strategy in the war. Two battle-cruisers were sent secretly and at top speed to the Falkland Islands. They reached Port Stanley on December 7, and on the next morning at eight o'clock, Von Spee, in obedience to some inexplicable instinct, brought the whole of his forces to attack the islands. It was the most extraordinary coincidence in the history of war. It was as if a man had been told that a sixty-pound salmon had been seen in a certain river, had thrown a fly at random, and had got a bite and landed him with his first cast.

The verdict of Coronel was reversed. Four out of five German ships were sunk. The *Dresden* escaped, but only to hide herself in the *fjords* of Patagonia. Germany's brief spell of sea command in the South Atlantic had ended as dramatically as it began. And within twenty-four hours the laden ships of Chile and the Argentine had put to sea, the underwriters had dropped their premiums to the pre-war rate, and the arrangements for the invasion of South West Africa had begun.

Once more it had been proved that the course of sea traffic is governed by sea command, and sea command means the general power to use the ocean for what it truly is, the highway that connects all the ports of the world together. To use, that is to say, exclusively; to limit its use to the power possessing that command, and to those other powers that might be friendly to them, or to neutrals unconcerned with the war altogether. Never in history has this command been complete. From Trafalgar to 1815, the British, if ever, commanded the sea adversely against their enemies. But they lost anything from six hundred to one thousand ships a year, and it was never possible to stop the whole of the enemy's trade.

Before submarines were ever heard of, then, command could not be made absolute. Strangely enough, steam changed all this. Today (1919) the surface command against surface force is virtually absolute. In August, 1914, Germany had in all a dozen armed vessels on the high seas prepared to attack British shipping. They took and destroyed fifty-six vessels only. All but three were destroyed or driven to intern in very few months. Save for a raider or two—exceptions that prove the rule—no surface attack has been made on the Allies' ocean trade since then. And there has been no ocean trade in German bottoms at all. In a sense, then, the submarine has only restored to the weaker belligerent a part—and only a small part—of the powers he possessed in the days of sailing fleets. It gives him a limited power of attack on his enemy's supply.

But, two cruises of the *Deutschland* notwithstanding, it has returned him none of his old trading power. And, as the course of the submarine war has shown, so long as he limits the attack on trade to proportions which the neutral world can put up with, the power of attack is so restricted as to be without military value. The attempt, then, to get a kind of command of the sea by submarine alone could only be made at the cost of turning the whole neutral world into an enemy world. And from the German point of view, the tragedy of the thing is this. The attempt was made, the whole world has become hostile, and the thing has failed.

In these two popular fallacies—the pre-war error that battleships were everything, and the present error that they are absolutely useless, and that it is the submarine that reigns at sea—we see, as it appears to me, convincing proofs that an exposition of the A B C of sea fighting would not be a work of supererogation. I have spoken of these fallacies as popular fallacies, but they are not limited to the unlettered, nor are they foreign to men of affairs. They have, on the contrary, flourished most in ministries, and been strongly held by those whose business it should have been not only to follow or express, but to mould, public opinion. A British statesman, afterwards Prime Minister, said once in

Parliament:

> I believe that since the Declaration of Paris, the fleet, valuable as it is for preventing an invasion of these shores, is almost valueless for any other purpose.

Most strange of all, the strongest exponents of these heresies have been certain naval officers themselves. It would be interesting to essay to account for this, as it seems to me the strangest curiosity of our times. Let it suffice for the moment to state that what up to a year ago was a dominating faith, is recognised universally today (1919) as a devastating tissue of errors.

Had the root principles of sea-power been properly understood, these errors never could have prevailed. For it is popular opinion that is ultimately responsible for the kind of government each nation has. On it depends the kind of navy that each government creates, and hence the measure of safety at sea that each nation enjoys. The tragic history of the last four years shows how this opinion can be misguided into an almost fatal tolerance of what is false.

When will a new Mahan arise to set things right? The world needs a naval teacher.

Chapter 4

Some Root Doctrines

War is a condition which arises when the appeal to reason, justice, or fear has failed and a nation wishes, or in self-defence is compelled, to bring another to its will by force.

Force is exerted by armies on land and naval fleets at sea. It is the primary business of the armed force in each element to defeat that of the enemy in battle, and so disintegrate and destroy it. The beaten nation's power to fight is thus brought to naught. Its resolution to renew the attack or to continue resistance is broken down. If defeat throws it open to invasion without power of stopping the invader, its national life, internal and external, is paralyzed and it is compelled to bow to the will of the conqueror. In its simplest conception, then, war is a struggle between nations in which the opposing sides pit their armed forces against each other and have to abide by the issue of that combat.

It is rarely, however, that a single battle between armies has decided the issue of a war. The campaigns of Jena and Sadowa are indeed instances in point. But they are in their way as exceptional as is the Boer War—decided without a pitched battle being fought at all. These may be regarded as the extremes. Normally, war may end victoriously for one side without the other having been deprived of the means of continuing even effective resistance. In such cases it is some moderation in the victor's terms, some change in the ambition of the partially defeated side, or, at least, a sense that no adequate results can be expected from further fighting, that has brought about the cessation of hostilities.

But, again, there are wars in which the issues can admit of no compromise at all. The invasions of Tamerlane, Attila, and the Mohammedan conquerors were not wars but campaigns of extermination. It is in such a war that we are engaged today, (1919). The stake for every country is of a vital character, so that compromise is indistinguishable from defeat, and defeat must carry with it the negation of everything which makes national life tolerable. The Germans have convinced themselves that there is no alternative to world dominion but downfall, and the civilized world is determined that there shall be no German world dominion. Such a struggle by its nature permits of no end by arrangement or negotiation. It must go forward until either one side or the other is either militarily defeated or until the economic strain disintegrates the state. In such conditions a secondary form of military pressure may be of paramount importance.

Now if we go back to our first definition of war, as a struggle in which the opposing sides pit their armed forces against each other and abide by the issue of the combat, we must remember that, just as it is rare for a war to be decided by a single combat, so is it rare for a single combat to dissipate and destroy an army. Ordinary prudence dictates that there shall be protected lines or some strong place into which it can retreat in the event of defeat. And when it is thus compelled to abandon open fighting and seek a position of natural or artificial strength, it becomes the business of the stronger to complete the business by destroying and penetrating the defences. But if this is too costly a proceeding, the stronger tries to contain the force so protected and passes on, if possible, to investment and siege. The simplest case of this is the complete encirclement and siege of the great city or camp, of which the war of 1870, gave two such striking examples in Metz and Paris.

When war calls out the whole manhood of many nations and turns them into fighting forces, it is obvious that there cannot be equality of force in all the theatres. Where either side is weaker, it is compelled locally to adopt the same tactics that a defeated force adopts. It must, that is to say, go upon the defensive. It entrenches and fortifies itself. Thus, as military operations, the attack and defence of fortifications may become general, and this without either side being necessarily able to inflict the pressure of siege upon its opponent, siege being understood to mean severing of communications with the outside world. But, clearly, where siege is possible, as was the case with Metz and Paris, the attacking force becomes also the investing force. It can rely upon the straits to which it can reduce the besieged to bring about that surrender which, *ex hypothesi*, would have been the result of the battle had the weaker not declined it.

Battle and siege are thus in essence complementary modes of war and all military action may roughly be defined as fighting, or some method of postponing fighting, or steps or preparations towards fighting.

Sea War

War at sea is carried on, as we have seen, by naval fleets. The immediate object of a fleet is to find, defeat, and destroy the enemy's fleet. The ultimate or further objective which is gained by such destruction is to monopolise the use of the sea, as the master highway, by retaining freedom for the passage of the victor's ships while denying such passage to those of the defeated. The power to insist on this exclusive control of sea communications is called "command of the sea."

If the war is a purely naval war, that is, limited to the use of naval forces and hence directed solely to naval ends—as was the war between England and France, in the course of which the United States gained their independence—the command of the sea can theoretically be won by a single victorious battle. For if the main force of one side is destroyed, that belligerent becomes incapable of questioning the supremacy of the enemy, and hence must limit his sea action to sporadic attempts on communications. These can never be maintained to a degree that can be decisive, simply because a power greater than can be brought to the attack can be employed for their defence.

Success in such a war, then, can simply be measured in terms of trade or of sea supply; defeat by the economic loss that its cessation must cause. There have been purely naval wars in the past and, could a combination be formed of countries whose aggregate sea-power was greater than that of Great Britain, a purely naval war might occur again. But it could only be brought about by such a conjuncture for the reason that Great Britain is the only country to which a purely naval defeat would mean such utter and immediate ruin, that her surrender to her sea conqueror would follow inevitably and promptly. This is so because, whereas almost every country is to some extent dependent upon sea supplies, Great Britain exists only in virtue of them.

To us, therefore, the advantages that derive from possession of command of the sea are overwhelming; and our possession of it adversely to any other country must be disadvantageous, exactly in proportion as that country is dependent upon sea supplies.

In a war which is both naval and continental, as in the present war, command of the sea means much more than the power to deny the gain and comfort of sea supplies. The side that is defeated at sea, or avoids fighting for fear of defeat, may lose not only everything which can come to it directly or indirectly from the use of ships, but will suffer from the added disadvantage that a military use can be made of sea communications in the enemy's possession. The side that commands the sea can carry on its ocean traffic, and supply not only its civil population but its armies and its fleets from abroad.

It can ally itself with continental nations and send its military forces away in ships and land them in friendly ports. It can prevent the sea invasion of its own, of its allies' territory, and of its colonial possessions. It can stop not only the enemy's own sea trade, but all neutral sea trade that directly or indirectly can benefit him, so that he is cut off from all supplies, whether raw material, food, or manufacture, not produced in his own territories or in those with which he has land communications. If the sea force of the side possessing command includes means of engaging stationary defences with success, and removing passive sea defences from the approaches to the enemy's coast and harbours, then it can even beat down the enemy's coast protection and invade him directly. The nation with sea command, then, threatens its opponents with attack by land at every point and, pending its development, can to the extent to which the enemy is dependent on overseas traffic for the necessaries of life, or for the maintenance of his armies at full fighting strength, subject him to all the rigour of siege.

The command of the sea which makes the exercise of these menaces possible, is, as we have seen, the fruit of victory over the enemy's armed forces. But if that enemy is weaker and follows at sea the course which, as we have seen, an army inferior on land must adopt, *viz.*, declines battle and withdraws his fleet behind defences to postpone it, he thereby to a great extent surrenders the sea command to the stronger. And if the stronger knows his business, he at once uses this command to subject his opponent to the economic disadvantages set out above. Siege by sea, then, like siege on land, may be the consequence of, but is always the alternative to, victorious battle in bringing about a decision. For while victorious battle robs the defeated nation of any possibility of warding off further attack by force, siege undermines the will and resolution of the civil population to endure, and thus calls forces into existence which will compel the enemy's government to surrender.

The command of the ocean ways are, then, of tremendous consequences in war—so great, indeed, that the control of sea communications has often been put forth as the primary object to be aimed at by sea-power. That it is the object of sea-power victoriously used we have already seen. But so long as the enemy possesses forces that actually disturb the tranquil enjoyment of sea communications, command is certainly *qualified*, and if he have in reserve unused and unimpaired forces for attacking and defeating the fleet which secures command, the command of the sea cannot be said to be unconditionally possessed. Consequently, if destruction of the enemy's armed forces is a necessary condition to real—because indisputable—sea command, it is for victorious battle and for nothing else that fleets exist.

These propositions are not only obviously true; they seem to be truly obvious. But in recent history we have witnessed the curious spectacle that an inversion of the order of these two statements did actually create two different and opposed schools of naval thought. The first school saw in victory the first and constant preoccupation of the fleet. It concerned itself, therefore, chiefly with the essentials to victory, and as victory can only come from fighting, it was at the elements of fighting that it worked.

It sought to find the most perfect methods of using weapons, because it realised that it was only from the evolution of these that right tactics could be deduced. It studied the campaigns of the past to discover the two great groups of doctrine that our fighting ancestors have bequeathed to us, the first dealing with the science of strategy, the second with the principles of command. They realised that weapons and the ships that carry them do not fight themselves, but must be fought by men; and they wished those men rightly educated and trained in the subtle and complex science of their high calling. To them, in short, sea war was an affair of knowledge applied by men trained both in the wisdom and in the lofty spirit of those that had excelled in naval war before. And, faithful to the traditions of the past, no less than eager for research into all the undeveloped potentialities of the products of modern progress, they pinned their faith on ability to force the enemy to battle, and to beat him there when battle came.

The other school went for a short cut to naval triumph. If only they could get a fleet of ships so big, so fabulously armed, so numerous as to make it seem to the enemy that his fleet was too feeble to attack, why then battle would be made altogether superfluous, and no further worry over so unlikely a contingency was necessary. They did not, therefore, trouble to inquire either into the processes needed for bringing battle about, or into what was necessary for success when battle came. They passed on to the contemplation of what can only be the fruit of victory—as if victory were not a condition precedent!

It was, unfortunately, this group, hypnotised by a theory it did not understand, which controlled naval policy in Great Britain for the ten years preceding the war, and for the first three and a half years of it. Their error lay, of course, in supposing that a fleet, so materially strong and numerous that its defeat was unimaginable because no attack on it could be conceived, must—so long as any serious lowering of its force by attrition was avoided—be the military equivalent to one which had already defeated the enemy; that "invincible" and "victorious" were, in short, interchangeable terms.

So masterful was this obsession that their apologists—shutting their eyes to the obvious and appalling consequences of this creed in action—two years after the event, still regarded the only encounter between the main fleets in this war as a great victory, because the larger, by avoiding the risk of close contact with the lesser, came out of the conflict with forces as substantially superior to the enemy's as they were before the opportunity of a decisive battle had been offered.

The group in question had, indeed, become possessed of one truth. It was simply that preponderant force is a vital element. But by holding it to the exclusion of all other truths they were blinded not only to the crucial business of studying the intellectual and technical essentials to fighting, but even to the orthodox meaning of the communication theory of sea war, on which they had so eagerly, but ignorantly, seized. For the true doctrine is, as we have already seen, just this, that when an enemy refuses battle, the stronger navy's sole remaining offensive is to cut him off from communication with the sea.

It must do this, as we have seen, to restrict his supplies, to weaken his armed forces, to strike at his prosperity and the comfort of his civil population, and thus obtain that partial paralysis of his national life, the completion of which can only be got by a victory that disarms him. And these things, which are the results of blockade, are also the intended results. But they are not intended for their own sake only, nor, primarily, to make the enemy surrender to avoid them. They are inflicted to force the enemy to the battle which he has refused, because it is only by battle that he can relieve himself from them. A stringent blockade, then, is the primary means of inducing a fleet action, and hence we see that siege, while truly the only alternative to battle, is something much more.

Indeed, it is no exaggeration to say that, viewed in its right relation to the true theory of war—a state of things in which a conflict of wills between nations is settled by a conflict of their armed forces—it is almost the primary object of siege to bring this conflict about and so to hasten the issue. From the definition the aim of war is the enemy's defeat and not merely his surrender. And battle is necessary to defeat.

The failure to realise this elementary truth was the cause of much more than an omission to fathom the technique of fighting, the fruits of which we shall find, when we come to the consideration of the naval actions of the last three years and note the curious result of the Jutland deployment and the inconclusive character of so many of the artillery encounters which have occurred, and the extraordinary prolongation of those which were not inconclusive. It brought about what is, at first sight, something even more astonishing, *viz.*, an actual indisposition by those in control of the British Navy, to adopt, when the enemy refused battle, the only course that could compel him to it, though it was actually the first article of their creed to gain the power to do this very thing.

Great Britain went to war at midnight August 4, 1914. The Grand Fleet went to its war stations. The High Seas Fleet withdrew to the security of the Kiel Canal. Within a day no enemy trading ships dared put to sea. Within a week, transports were carrying a British Army to France. Our merchantmen continued their sea trading almost as if nothing had happened. But, though the German flag vanished from the seas, neutral vessels were free to use the German ports until the following March, and for another six months the enemy was free to import, in almost any quantities that he liked, certain forms of food, cotton, fats, and many of the ores and chemicals which were the indispensable raw material of the propellants and explosives vitally necessary to him in a prolonged war.

By permitting this, we showed that our policy, in other words, was not to attack but to wait attack, and then not to do anything to compel the enemy to attack. Our sea statesmen had not indoctrinated the civil government with a clearly defined policy that it was prepared to enforce at the opening of hostilities. Yet in a matter of this kind it was exactly at the opening of hostilities that a stringent blockade, accompanied by a generous rationing of sea supplies to the neutrals bordering on Germany, could have been proclaimed and enforced with the least friction.

For, in the first place, Germany's declaration of war was so entirely unprovoked and sudden, and her first measure of war, the invasion of Belgium—when her soldiery became at once outrageous—combined the world over to create a neutral opinion strongly in favour of the Allies. Next, the fact that Great Britain's participation in the war was both professedly and actually in loyalty to the identical obligation to Belgium which Germany had violated, predisposed America, for the first time since the colonies proclaimed their independence, to an active sympathy with the British ideal, perhaps because for the first time that ideal appeared to them to be one that was purely chivalrous.

It was then everything that the psychological moment should have been seized. Nor could it have been difficult to see that, if the opportunity was allowed to slip by, the mere fact that a half measure—to wit, the suspense of German shipping—had been enforced, must lead to a new condition, namely, a hugely magnified trade through the neutral ports. This trade, it is true, was nominally confined to goods that were not contraband of war. But contraband is an elastic term, and, to make things worse, the British Government proclaimed its intention—so little had war-trained thought prepared its policy—of accepting the provisions of the unexecuted Declaration of London as defining what contraband was to be.

This gave the enemy the liberty to import materials indispensable to his manufacture of munitions and of armament, was one of which full advantage was taken. It was bad enough that cotton, indispensable ores, the raw materials of glycerine as well as the finished product, were poured into the laboratories, the factories, and the arsenals of Germany without stint or limit. It was, if possible, worse that this traffic created gigantic exporting interests in America which, once vested, made the restriction of them wear the appearance of an intolerable hardship when, many months too late, more stringent measures were taken. So powerful indeed had these interests become, that the real and rigid blockade which, under the doctrines of the "continuous voyage" and the "ultimate destination" would from the first have been fully consonant with international law, was actually never attempted at all until the United States themselves became belligerents.

For fourteen months, then, we witnessed a state of things so paradoxical as to be without parallel in history. It was our professed creed that the fleet existed to seize and control sea communications. The enemy conceded us this control and, so far from using it to straiten him so relentlessly that he would have no choice but to fight for relief from it, we actually permitted him to draw, through sources absolutely under our control, for essentials in the form of overseas supplies that he needed in a war which all the world realised must now be a prolonged one. The traditional naval policy of the country was thus not reflected in the action of the country's government, because that policy had no representation in the navy's counsels. There is, perhaps, no single heresy for which so high and disastrous a price has been paid.

It would appear, then, that our pre-war naval policy did not contemplate that immediate and stringent sea pressure that would compel the enemy to action, nor yet the closest and most vigilant kind of watch that would have brought him to action in the promptest and most fatal manner when circumstances compelled him to come out. Nor is it difficult to see why this was so. To profess the communication theory of sea war without realising that the control of communications is the result of victory, that is, setting up a consequence as an aim while ignoring its cause, inevitably led to the inverted error, an unwillingness so to employ the control of communications, when the enemy ceded them without victory, as to force the enemy into battle as the only hope of escaping an intolerable condition.

Not having contemplated and prepared for battle as the first aim of naval policy, they left an instinctive disinclination to force on an affair which they suddenly realised would be as critical as it was certainly unanticipated. It is this which explains possibly the greatest paradox in history, *viz.*, that Germany proclaimed a strict blockade of Great Britain before Great Britain proclaimed such a blockade of Germany.

CHAPTER 5

Elements of Sea Force

Having established the truth that the primary purpose of a navy is to fight and its immediate object victory, we must next pass on to ask of what it is that naval force consists and by what processes it fights and wins. All fighting is done by men using weapons. At sea the men and weapons have to be carried in ships. The ships and weapons have to be designed and selected, and the men have to be converted from ignorance into accomplished fighting units. Finally, the ships and the weapons must be employed in accordance with certain methods and in obedience to certain dynamic laws—the technique, the tactics, and the strategy of war. It may simplify the subject to summarize the elements of naval force as follows. It may be said to consist:

1. Of the main weapon-bearing ships built for fighting fleet actions.

2. Of smaller armed ships of many kinds necessary for the right use of the main fighting ships and for the subsidiary operations leading up to, or following from, fleet actions.

3. Of means other than ships—aircraft, mines, and the like—for entrapping and injuring the main fleets and cruisers of the enemy, for defending and attacking bases, and for making certain sea areas dangerous or impassable to the enemy's forces.

4. Of the personnel to man, fight, and command the ships and to direct the operations of the separate squadrons and fleets at sea; and

5. Of that higher central command on shore that, by designing and selecting the material, by training the officers and men, creates sea force; that discovers the right method of using weapons; that elucidates the tactics that follow from such use; that develops the strategy which the strength and situation of rival forces makes best; that as a

preparation for war, keeps the whole force ready in all particulars; that in war, directs it to the greatest advantage.

To get the best naval force it is clear, then, that you want:

(*a*) Ships whose tactical properties are superior to those which the enemy possesses, and you want more of them.

(*b*) Weapons delivering a more devastating blow, that can reach to longer ranges, and can be employed with higher rapidity.

(*c*) Methods of employing both the ships and the weapons that will assure to them the utmost scope of efficiency so as to strike at the enemy—if possible—before the enemy can strike, and will keep them in use when conditions of movement, light, and weather have become too difficult for the enemy to overcome.

(*d*) A personnel of higher *morale*, better discipline, and greater skill.

(*e*) A staff of officers to train and command this personnel, adept in all the craft of fighting, instinct with the loftiest patriotism, and masters of the art of leadership.

(*f*) A supreme command, not only equally conversant both with the doctrine that can be gathered from a study of the past and with the resources that modern scientific and industrial development place at the disposal of the fighting men, but consciously cultivating what may be called a prophetic imagination, by which alone future developments can be anticipated, and guided throughout, and always, by regard to the public interest only.

The factors that enter are first, material; secondly, men; and, thirdly, the intellectual, spiritual, and moral activities necessary for shaping and turning the first two to their purpose.

Looked at largely, the elements have been enumerated above in the inverse order of their importance. For, clearly, the qualities of the ship are much less important than the qualities of the weapons that she carries. A slow, unarmoured battleship, carrying accurate, quick-firing, long-range guns, is a better fleet unit than a fast, perfectly protected ship with weapons unlikely to hit, because ill-made, poorly mounted, or badly ammunitioned. And the power and range of the weapons are less important than the science and methods with which they are employed.

An old 12-inch gun that can be used with constant effect at 12,000 yards when the change of range is high, the target often obscured by smoke, and the firing ship constantly under helm, is an infinitely more effective weapon than a new 15-inch that, in spite of a legend range of 20,000 yards, cannot be made to hit in action conditions. And it is from right method that are derived right tactics by which, in turn, the decisive massing of ships in action is obtained. Again, the best of ships' weapons and methods must be absolutely useless unless the discipline, *morale*, and skill of those who use them are equal to the strain of fighting. Again, it is highly improbable that you will have good discipline and skill unless you have good leaders, for the excellent reason that it is the officers who make the men; certainly, if they exist in spite of there not being good leaders, weak or heartless leadership can throw them altogether away.

The Revolution robbed the French Navy of nearly all its trained officers—and, though possessed of better ships and courageous crews, that navy never fought with real effect in the Great War of from 1792 to 1815. Again, however excellent your ships, weapons, and methods, your *morale* and your courage, unskilful command at sea and ignorance of the true principles of tactics may rob you of victory. And, lastly, unless those who are responsible for the creation of the material and the training of human force, and for the chief command and general strategy before and during war, are equal to their task unless they keep in close and real touch with the active service, not only is it almost impossible that a force of very high efficiency can exist, but quite impossible that a right direction can be given to it in war.

The reader will very likely detect in the foregoing category of precedence a trite maxim of Napoleon's elaborated into a series of sonorous, if illustrative, commonplaces. But this is a matter in which, even at the cost of being hackneyed, it is absolutely necessary that certain points should be clearly established. First, looking at the whole subject of sea force as a problem in dynamics, it should be constantly before our eyes that a navy is so highly complex an affair that it can only act rightly when *all* the elements of which it is composed are employed in accord with the principles peculiar to each, and are combined so that each takes its due place in relation to the rest.

It is, for example, quite conceivable that you might have a fleet or a flotilla equipped with the best material, its personnel instructed and expert in the best methods, commanded in detail and directed by the chief command according to the soundest principles of tactics and strategy, and yet that such a unit might fail in winning its legitimate purpose, simply because of some failure to base its operations on correct data. The omission to provide all the means for obtaining intelligence that science and experience suggest, or, having employed them and got the raw material, an inability to interpret and transmit it rightly and promptly to the officer in command, might send a fleet upon its mission either to the wrong place or at the wrong time, or with the wrong dispositions.

In considering naval science, then, it is, so to speak, axiomatic to recognise that, as its extent and variety are almost infinite, the task of elucidating and teaching its principles and their application, so that every person making up the organism which is to set the science into action shall act in the light of true doctrine, requires an intellectual effort of incalculable magnitude, just because the dynamic laws governing each element are extraordinarily obscure, and because the number of elements is so extraordinarily great. To be part perfect, then, may vitiate the whole effort.

But if a whole science must be explored and its principles universally inculcated, it would seem as if a wholly untenable ideal was being put forward. But there is no escape from this ideal. For the laws of science are ruthless. Just as "the wages of sin is death," so is failure the fruit of false doctrine. And the cruelty of the things lies in this, that what seems an almost infinitesimal infidelity may bring a large and noble effort, greatly conceived and gallantly executed, to disaster.

The scale of the task prescribes the scale of the instruments for its discharge. It was clearly beyond the scope of a single individual as chief professional adviser to the Admiralty, I will not say to solve, but even to keep account of, all the intricate problems which require investigation. Indeed, for many years before the war it was fully realised that only a properly organised war staff could even make a beginning from which a right understanding of naval war in modern conditions could derive. The necessity for this had constantly been urged upon successive governments. The matter came to a head when, in 1909, the Cabinet appointed a committee from its own members to consider Lord Charles Beresford's very grave statements as to the condition of the navy.

This committee never published the evidence by which Lord Charles and his associates tried to establish their case. But in the course of a brief report which was published they said that they had been impressed "with the difference of opinion amongst officers of high rank and professional attainments regarding important principles of naval strategy and tactics, and they look forward with much confidence to the further development of a naval war staff, from which naval members of the Board and flag officers and their staffs at sea may be expected to derive common benefit." Observe, that the most experienced officers of the day differed with regard to important principles of tactics!

The technical officers of the navy knew that this absence of doctrine "among officers of high rank and professional attainments" arose very largely out of a total want of exact data as to the precise effect our weapons could be expected to have upon the enemy, and the effect the enemy's weapons could be expected to have upon us. If there was no agreement as to how to use weapons there could be no agreement as to their value and, without such agreement, any common doctrine of tactics must be impossible. And with tactics in the melting-pot, strategy must be pure guesswork.

The 1909, committee had hoped that an extended war staff would bring order out of chaos. But by 1911, there had still been nothing done to realise its pious aspirations. When Mr. Churchill took office, then, in the autumn of that year, he had the conclusions of the Beresford Committee to guide him as to the state of strategy and tactics and a state of things in the matter of guns, torpedoes, and mines, no less than the manifest trend of active naval thought, to show where the beginnings of reform must be made.

Mr. Churchill became First Lord in circumstances which were very unexpected, and his first public announcement raised hope to the highest point. For, over the date of New Year's Day, 1912, there was published by the First Lord a Memorandum which contained a passage on which every optimist fastened. This document defined the root need of naval force with masterly precision. Coming so soon, expressed with such clarity and conviction, it seemed to be not so much a collection of eloquent and thoughtful sentences logically compacted, but a profession of intentions that must definitely turn the current of naval life into the only channel that could assure right progress. Mr. Churchill, in short, had quite evidently grasped the fundamental truth that the whole structure of naval war was based upon the mastery of weapons and, as evidently, intended the pursuit of this mastery to be the watchword of his administration. His actual words were as follows:

> Unit efficiency—that is to say, the individual fighting power of each vessel—is in the sea service for considerable periods entirely independent of all external arrangements and unit efficiency at sea, far more so than on land, is the prime and final factor *without which the combinations of strategy and tactics* are only

the *preliminaries of defeat*, but with which even faulty dispositions can be swiftly and decisively retrieved.

At last, then, the man and the moment had come together. To the new First Lord had been given the vision that the moment called for. At last, the consistent, concerted, co-ordinated effort would be made which, proceeding by investigation, analysis, reason, and experiment, would lead us to the root truths of one weapon after another. When the conditions of action were analysed and the problems they propounded isolated, a measure of our capacity to deal with them would be afforded, and not only would the points of our incapacity be made clear, but the reasons for that incapacity and the character of the measures needed for the remedy would be automatically shown by the analysis.

For the first condition for solving any problem is its accurate, scientific, and exhaustive statement. And, if the statement is sufficiently full, it almost carries the solution with it. Let the problems of the gun, torpedo, mine, and submarine once be set out in full, and the principles on which we should proceed to get the utmost out of them in attack, and the utmost against similar efforts by the enemy in defence, would become very clear indeed. In short, when all available knowledge was put before those capable of appreciating it, weighing it, and drawing from it right deductions, progress in a right direction would be assured because, for the first time, it would be established on a scientific foundation.

Nor, indeed, was this all. For no such inquisition could be made in fundamentals without the work being reflected in every other department of naval activity. In place of uninstructed conjecture, we should have, as a basis of naval thought and plan, the reasoned conclusions of expert knowledge.

There was the more reason for this optimistic view because Mr. Churchill's Memorandum went on to indicate the machinery by which alone right methods can invariably, because together impartially and impersonally, be discovered. For the particular occasion of the Memorandum was the establishment of a new and extended war staff for which, since 1904, we had all been waiting. This, the First Lord explained, must have four carefully differentiated but very important tasks.

It was first, the Memorandum said, "to be the means of preparing and training officers for dealing with the extended problems that await them in stations of high responsibility." Its second function was to sift, develop, and apply the results of history and experience, and to preserve them "as a general stock of reasoned opinion available as an aid and as a guide for all who are called upon to determine in peace or war the naval policy of the country." Its third function was the exhibition of the vast superiority which a well-selected committee of experts possesses over even the most brilliant expert working by himself. The staff was to be:

> A brain far more comprehensive than of any single man, however gifted, and tireless and unceasing in its action, applied continuously to the scientific study of naval strategy and preparation.

Finally, this staff, carefully selected from the most promising officers, whose work would train them for the highest command, making all history and experience the province from which to draw the raw material of its doctrines, engaged tirelessly and unceasingly in applying this doctrine to the guidance of the civilian authorities by defining the requirements of our war preparation and war strategy, was also to be the executive department through which the higher command would issue its authoritative orders. "It is to be an instrument capable of formulating any decision which has been taken, or may be taken, by the executive, in terms of precise and exhaustive detail."

To those hopefully disposed this departure, then, seemed beyond words momentous. For thirty years, whatever disagreement there may have been in the navy, there was absolute unanimity as to the need of a staff for the study of war and the formulation of campaign plans. So long as weapons in use could be mastered by the personnel of the ships without dependence on methods of fire control and so forth extraneously supplied, this was indeed the navy's chief and overmastering need.

Had such a staff existed even sixteen years ago, it is quite inconceivable that we could imperceptibly have drifted into dependence on extraneous methods for the right use of weapons, without the staff responsible for preparation for war, bringing the fact of this dependence to the notice of its chief. And, the principle once recognised that staff organisation is the only road to infallibility, the institution of an additional staff for the study of so vital a matter must inevitably have followed. The existence of one competent, impartial, and impersonal expert body would automatically have resulted in the creation of another.

But actually, when this new staff was so resoundingly established at the beginning of 1912, some amongst the optimists began to wonder whether there might not be a fly in the ointment of their content. It was pointed out that to create a staff for dealing "with the combinations of strategy and tactics" *before* any machinery existed for elucidating the essentials of "unit efficiency" did most certainly have the air of putting the cart before the horse. But to doubt that this machinery would follow seemed too absurd in face of the tremendous emphasis that Mr. Churchill had laid upon its necessity. If, without unit efficiency, "the combinations of strategy and tactics were only the preliminaries of defeat," whereas if it existed a position in which tactics had failed, "could be retrieved with swiftness and decision," it was manifestly unthinkable that such efficiency could be left to chance, or assumed to exist on the *ipse dixit* of any official. Obviously the First Lord, having put his hand to the minor and secondary matter, would not delay action at least as drastic in the major primary.

The institution of the War Staff, then, was watched with sympathetic interest in the full expectation, not only that it must lead to great results, but that it must be followed—as, of course, it should have been preceded—by one for fathoming all the potentialities of the means employed in the attack and defence of fleets.

But the War Staff was never put into the position to discharge the functions which the 1909, committee had designated as its main purpose. So far from being an authority equipped for the exhaustive study of war and how to prepare for it, the whole apparatus of fighting was carefully excluded from its purview. It had no connection with the departments administering gunnery, torpedoes, submarines, aircraft, or mines. As to some of these activities, there were as a fact no departments solely charged with their control before the War Staff was instituted. They were not entrusted to the War Staff. And no new staffs were created! If the strategical vagueness, to which the Beresford Committee had borne witness in 1909, arose largely, as many supposed, from the uncertain state of naval technique, then, so far as the War Staff was concerned, this vagueness had to continue—for technique was not their concern.

The consequences were demonstrated in many striking ways as the war progressed. But not the least curious result was the confusion that arose as to the offensive and defensive aspects of naval strategy and preparation. In the debate on the Naval Estimates of 1916, a violent attack on Admiralty policy by Mr. Churchill left Mr. Balfour with no alternative but to break the brutal truth to us that, at the outbreak of war, we had not a single submarine-proof harbour on the East Coast. Reflect for a minute what this means. In the years which have elapsed since Lord Fisher came to the Admiralty as First Sea Lord, two altogether revolutionary changes have been made in naval war.

1. Until 1904, the 12-inch guns of our battleships were weapons that no one would have thought of using beyond the range of 4,000 yards. The identical guns have been used in this war at 11,000, 12,000, and 13,000 yards. The advance in range owes nothing to improvements in the gun. It has been brought about by improvements in sights, in range-finders, and in the organisation called fire control.

2. Again, in 1904, the submarine, or submersible torpedo-carrying boat, had indeed been proved to be a practical instrument for war, but was still in its infancy. By 1907, when Captain Murray Sueter wrote his well-known work on the subject, it had become obvious that the tactics of battle, no less than the defence of fleets, stood to be completely changed by its actual and probable developments.

Now every new engine of war—and as a long-range weapon the modern gun is such—creates a double problem. There is the art of using it in attack; there is the art of countering it when it is in the enemy's hands. With every new development, then, the navy has to learn a new offensive and a new defensive. In the matter of guns, there is but one defensive that can be perfectly successful. It is to develop a method of using them so rapid, so insistent, and so accurate that the enemy's guns will be out of action before they can be employed against us. Failing this there is a secondary defensive, *viz.*, to protect ships by armour.

Finally, you may keep out of range of the enemy's guns by turning or running away. The adoption of armour calls for no perfection either of tactical organisation or technical practice. It is a matter which can be left to the metallurgists, engineers, and constructors. The purely naval policy, then, would have been either to develop the use of guns offensively, which, as we have seen, must also be the best defence, or with a purely defensive idea, solely to enjoin the tactic that will avoid the risks inseparable from coming under the enemy's fire. To the country that was completing nearly two battleships to any other country's one, that aspired to command the sea, that hoped to be able to blow any enemy fleet out of the water if it got the chance, it would seem obvious that there could be only one gunnery policy; to wit, push the offensive to the highest possible extent.

Again, the distinguishing feature of submarines is their capacity to approach the strongest of vessels unseen and then, in waters superficially under hostile command, to strike with the most deadly of all weapons. As they gained in speed and radius of action, it became obvious that wherever a fleet might be—whether at sea or in harbour—it must, unless it were protected by effective passive defences while in harbour, and by numerous mobile guards when at sea, be exposed to this insidious and, if successful, deadly form of attack.

The basic supposition of British naval policy has been to maintain a fleet sufficiently powerful to drive all enemy's craft within his harbours and defences. The proposition has only to be stated for it to be clear that the navy could not have expected, except in rare circumstances, to have any targets for its submarines, whereas it was as certain as any future thing could be, that every British ship would be a constant target for the enemy's submarines. British policy in regard to submarine war should, then, have been mainly, if, indeed, not wholly, defensive.

Thus, if there was one form of *offensive* imperatively imposed on us, it was that of naval artillery; and if there was one form of *defensive* not less imperatively incumbent, it was the provision of adequate protection against submarines.

It is now, of course, common knowledge that it was exactly in these two particulars that Admiralty policy from 1904–1914, was either discontinuous, vacillating, and self-contradictory, or simply non-existent. So far as it cultivated anything, it was a defensive tactic for the gun and offensive tactics for the submarine! On the latter point let the non-provision of a safe anchorage on the Northeast coast stand for the whole. If you pick up a Navy List for any month in any year prior to August, 1914, you will look in vain for any department of Whitehall, any establishment at a principal port, any appointment of flag officer or captain, to prove that there was at any time an individual or a committee charged with the vital problem of protecting the British Fleet against enemy submarines when war broke out. The necessity had indeed been realised. It was set out by Captain Sueter in 1907. It had been urged on the Board of Admiralty. But no action was taken.

This, of course, was bad enough. The case of gunnery was worse, for if you compare the Navy List of August, 1914, with that of the corresponding month of the year that Mr. Churchill took office, you will find that it was to his administration that we owe the abolition of the only officer and department in the navy competent to advise or direct methods of gunnery adequate for war. From 1908, to 1913, the Inspectorship of Target Practice had been effective in giving shape, and to some extent, a voice, to the alarm, anxiety, and indignation of the navy at the manner in which gunnery administration boxed the compass of conflicting policies. With the suppression of the office there came administrative peace—and technical chaos.

Why were not these problems, each and all of them, thoroughly investigated and their solutions discovered before war began?

Mr. Churchill supplies us with the answer. He closes his article in the *London Magazine* of September, 1916, with a protest against naval operations being more critically and even captiously judged than military operations. They are so judged, he tells us, because of the apparent simplicity of a naval battle, and the obvious character of any disaster that happens to any unit of a fleet. Regiments may be thrown away upon land and no one be any the wiser, but to lose a ship is an event about which there can be no dispute. It is regarded as a disaster, and at once somebody, it is assumed, must be to blame. This is hard measure on the seaman. Surely, an admiral, he tells us, has a greater claim upon the generosity of his countrymen than a general.

> His warfare is almost entirely novel. Scarcely one had ever had any experience of sea fighting. All had to learn the *strange new, unmeasured, and,* in times of peace, *largely immeasurable conditions.*

Now this is really a very striking admission. Whence arose this theory that naval warfare consisted of unfathomable mysteries? Perhaps the explanation is as follows: Popular interest in the navy was first thoroughly aroused by Mr. Stead's *Pall Mall* articles in the middle eighties. It is from the controversies that he aroused that Brassey's and the other annual naval publications emerged. For twenty years newspaper interest in shipbuilding programmes, design, and so forth, advanced in a crescendo of intensity. The many and startling departures in naval policy that characterized Lord Fisher's tenure of the first professional place on the Board of Admiralty, brought this interest to a climax. There was a controversial demand for more costly programmes involving political and journalistic opposition, which in turn provoked greater vigour in those that advocated them.

Thus, the whole of naval policy had to be commended to popular—and civilian—judgment. And it followed that the advocates of expansion had to employ arguments that civilians could understand. They very soon perceived that success lay along the line of sensationalism. Larger and faster ships, heavier and longer range guns carrying bigger and more devastating shells, faster and more terrifying torpedoes, those new craft of weird mystery, the submarines—all these things in turn and for considerable periods were urged upon the public and the statesmen in terms of awe and wonder. But the Augurs, instead of winking behind the veil, came finally to be hypnotised by their own wonder talk.

Who cannot remember that ever-recurring phrase, "the untold possibilities" of the new engines of war? They got to be so convinced on this subject that they made no effort to find out precisely what the possibilities were, and Mr. Churchill's phrase that I have just quoted, "the strange new, unmeasured, and largely immeasurable conditions," exactly summed up the frame of mind of those who were responsible for naval policy up to and including Mr. Churchill's time. If all these problems were insoluble, if the conditions were immeasurable, if the possibilities of new weapons were really untold and untellable, what was the use of worrying about experiment and knowledge, judgment and *expertise*? It was this frame of mind that led a humourist to suggest that the materialists ought really to be called the spiritualists.

It was all very unfortunate, because any rightly organised system of inquiry, investigation, and experiment, would have dissipated this atmosphere of mystery once and for all. When new inventions are made that affect the processes of industry, it is not the men who go about talking of their "untold possibilities," their "incalculable" effects, and their "immeasurable" results, that get the commercial advantage of their development. It is those who take immediate steps to investigate the limits of their action and the precise scope of their operations who turn new discoveries to account. To talk as if the performance of guns, torpedoes, submarines, and aircraft were beyond human calculation, was really a confession of incompetence.

The application to these things of the principles of inquiry universally employed in other fields was always perfectly simple, and had it been employed we should not have begun the war with wondering what we could do, but knowing precisely what we ought to do. It was want of preparation in these matters that was undoubtedly one of the deciding factors in tying us down both to defensive strategy and to defensive tactics.

Once grasp what are the possibilities open to the enemy's armed forces; once realise the scope the mine and torpedo possess; once analyse their influence both on strategy and on tactics, with the new problems that they create both for cruising force and for naval artillery in action, and it becomes exceedingly clear what it is that your own fleet must be prepared to do.

Had these things been realised at any time between 1911, and 1914, should we have had our own naval bases unprotected against submarine attack? Should we have been without any organisation for using mines offensively against the enemy? Still more, should we have been practically without any means whatever of preventing the enemy using mines against us? We should have had a fleet composed of different units, organised, trained, and equipped in a very different way.

CHAPTER 6

The Actions

The naval operations suggested and described in the following chapters are the surprise attack that Germany did *not* deliver, the destruction of *Koenigsberg*, the capture of *Emden*, Cradock's heroic self-sacrifice off Coronel, the destruction of Von Spee's squadron off the Falkland Islands, the affair of the Heligoland Bight, the pursuit of Von Hipper across the Dogger Bank, the battle of Jutland, and finally, the operations carried out against Zeebrügge and Ostend in the fourth year of the war. I have not in these chapters followed strict chronological order, but have arranged them so as to present the problems of sea fighting as they arise in a crescendo of interest and complexity.

Modern war is fought in conditions to which history offers no parallel. Both the British and German Governments have maintained the strictest reserve in regard to every operation. When one reads the despatches, it is quite obvious to the least instructed student of war, that their publication has been guided by the consciousness that within two or three days of issue the text would be in the enemy's hands. Every atom of information, then, that could be of the slightest value to the Germans has been ruthlessly excised, with results to a great extent ruinous to lay comprehension of the events described.

This being so, I wish it clearly to be understood that every opinion or judgment expressed in these chapters must obviously be subject to modification and revision when further information becomes available. Generally speaking, too, the plans I have included with the text have no pretence whatever to be authentic, but are presented simply as diagrammatic ways of making the text intelligible. No more can be claimed for them than that they should not be inconsistent with the information officially given. The plans of the Falkland Islands engagements are the only exceptions. These I believe to be substantially correct.

In the destruction of *Koenigsberg* the main interest is the solution of a gunnery problem in itself not very intricate, if once the means of carrying it out exist and the right method of procedure is recognised. But in the actual operations the men on the spot had to do an immense number of things before the problem could be tackled at all, and in the solution of the gunnery problem they had to learn from the beginning and so discover, from their failure at the first attempt, the method which was so brilliantly successful on the second. In this respect the story isolates a single and, as I have said, a simple problem in gunnery and illustrates what is meant by right technique. Apart from this, the story is full of human interest and exhibits the exceptional advantages which naval training gives to those who have to extemporize methods of dealing with circumstances and difficulties without the guidance of experience.

In the *Sydney-Emden* engagement we have a very good example of the modern single ship action. Not the least of its points of interest is that *Sydney* seems to have lost her rangefinder a very few minutes after the action began. At first sight it would seem to be an absolutely disabling loss. In some quarters more emphasis has been laid on the value of a good rangefinder to fire control than to any other element of that highly debated branch of naval science. But in this engagement, as in that of *Koenigsberg*, the enemy was destroyed by a ship that did not use a rangefinder at all. The action thus not only shows the place which the observation of fire takes in the art of sea fighting, but illustrates in the highest degree the value of long practice in gunnery. Since 1905 every commissioned ship in the fleet has worked assiduously on this problem, and, whether the methods in use have been good, bad, or indifferent, this practice produced a race of officers extraordinarily well equipped for dealing with fire control as a practical problem.

It is highly probable, if the methods and instruments they have been given have not always been of the best, that this fact, by throwing them on their own resources, did much to stimulate that singular capacity for extemporization which we shall see illustrated in the *Koenigsberg* business. Moreover, this is a faculty in which our officers seem to excel the Germans greatly. In this fight, as in so many others, it was the enemy who first opened fire, and it was his opening salvoes that were the most accurate. But the enemy has seldom kept this initial advantage, whereas we shall generally find the British personnel improving as the action proceeds. It would appear, then, that as the material suffers the Germans, who are most dependent on it, have on the whole shown less resource than our own officers.

In the action off Coronel the heroic self-sacrifice of the British force overlays the technical interest. In one respect it is altogether unique, for it is the only action in this war in which the weaker and faster squadron sought action with one of incalculably greater fighting power but of inferior speed. Neither side seems to have manoeuvred in a way that would have added to the difficulties of fire control, but as, apart from manoeuvring, the shooting conditions were extraordinarily difficult, one is forced to the conclusion that the deciding factor was less the great superiority of the enemy's force, as measured by the weight of his broadsides, than the still more marked superiority that arose from his having a more modern and more homogeneous armament.

At the Falkland Islands the all-big-gun ship appeared for the first time in a sea action and, although opposed by vessels whose armament was no match for such heavy metal, it was actually employed according to the tactics officially set out as the basis of the Dreadnought idea in design; the tactics, that is to say, of keeping away from an enemy, so as to maintain a range favourable to the more powerfully gunned ship. The battle resolved itself into three separate actions, and it was on this principle that Sir Doveton Sturdee fought the Graf von Spee and his two battle-cruisers, and that the Captain of the *Cornwall* engaged *Leipzig*. But, curiously enough, in the engagement between *Kent* and *Nürnberg* a different principle is seen at work. Captain Allen pursued at full speed until he had crippled the enemy's engines, and then, as his speed fell off, continued to close till he was able to silence him altogether at a range of 3,000 yards. Thus, on a single day two diametrically opposed tactical doctrines were exemplified by officers under a single command.

In each of these four actions the tactics of the gun escaped complication by the distractions and difficulties which torpedo attack imposes on long-range gunnery. In our next action, the affair off Heligoland, the torpedo figures largely, because visibility was limited to about 6,000 yards. The affair off Heligoland cannot be described as an engagement. It was primarily a reconnaissance in force developed into a series of skirmishes and single ship actions, which began at seven in the morning and ended at mid-day. Submarines, destroyers, cruisers of several types and, finally, battle-cruisers, were employed on the British side. There were sharp artillery engagements between destroyers, there were torpedo attacks made by destroyers on light cruisers and by submarines on battle-cruisers.

But they were not massed attacks on ships in formation, but isolated efforts at marksmanship, and they were all of them unsuccessful. This failure of the torpedo as a weapon of precision is of considerable technical interest. The light thrown on gunnery problems by the events of the day is less easy to define. The chief interest of this raid into the Bight lies in the strategical idea which prompted it and in its moral effects on the British and German naval forces. That Sir David Beatty, in command of four battle-cruisers, should coolly have challenged the German Fleet to fight and that this challenge was not accepted, was extremely significant. It was of special value to our side, for it showed the British Navy to possess a naval leader who knew how to combine dash and caution and marked by a talent for leadership as conspicuous as the personal bravery which had won him his early promotions.

These qualities were still better displayed in the engagement off the Dogger Bank. This action is remarkable in several respects. For the first time destroyers were here employed to make massed torpedo attacks on a squadron of capital ships. The particular defensive functions of such torpedo attacks will be discussed in the proper place. Suffice it to say here that no torpedo hit, but that the British were robbed of victory by a chance shot which disabled Sir David Beatty's flagship, and deprived the squadron of its leader when bold leadership was most needed. Why the action was broken off by Rear-Admiral Moore, who succeeded to the command, has never been explained, and the unfortunate wording of an Admiralty *communiqué* gave the world for some time an impression that Sir David Beatty—of all people—had retreated from the threat of German submarines.

The Battle of Jutland eclipses in technical interest all the other engagements put together. It presents, of course on a far larger scale, all the problems hitherto met separately. We are still far too imperfectly informed as to many of the incidents of this battle for it to be possible to attempt any complete analysis of its tactics, or to indicate the line on which judgment will ultimately declare itself. We are, for example, entirely without information either about the method of deployment prescribed by the Commander-in-Chief of the Grand Fleet at six o'clock, or of the theory on which the night attack by the destroyer on the retreating German Fleet was ordered. We do not know how it was that a misunderstanding arose between the battle-cruiser fleet and the battle fleet as to the time and place of junction, nor the arrangements which resulted in contact with the German Fleet being lost after the action was over.

★★★★★★

The positions of the two fleets at six o'clock had been estimated by dead reckoning, both in *Lion* and in *Iron Duke*. The two reckonings did not agree, and the Commander-in-Chief said in the despatch that such a discrepancy was inevitable. The word "misunderstanding" in the text must not be taken to mean that the calculation in either fleet was avoidable, still less reprehensibly, wrong.

★★★★★★

It is, therefore, only possible to discuss those points on which light has been thrown by the despatch, and the principles of action which the commander-in-chief has set out in various speeches delivered after he had ceased to command at sea.

In the engagement off the Falkland Islands, it will be remembered that there was a marked contrast between the tactical methods followed in the pursuit of Von Spee and those adopted by Captain Allen in his pursuit of *Nürnberg*. In the Battle of Jutland, we shall find a still more marked contrast between the strategic conceptions of the two leaders of the British forces.

Admiral Beatty seems to have acted throughout as if the enemy should be brought to battle and destroyed, almost regardless of risk. The Commander-in-Chief of the Grand Fleet seems to have been willing to engage only if he could do so without jeopardising the forces under his command. The one was bent on victory, the other seemed satisfied—so long as the enemy were thwarted in any ulterior purpose—if only the British Fleet were saved from losses.

It followed from such very opposite views, that their tactical methods differed also. At each stage of the action Sir David Beatty's tactic was to get his forces into action at the first possible moment and to keep them in action as long as possible. Thus, when the news first reaches him that the enemy is to the northeast, he leads his whole fleet at top speed straight for the Horn Reef to get between him and his base. And this he does without waiting for any information about the composition of the enemy's force. Whether it is the battle-cruiser and light forces only, or the whole German Fleet, his first idea is to make sure that *he* is in a position to engage if he wishes to.

As it was at 3:0 p.m., so it was at each stage after he got into action. The reduction of his squadron by one third does not seem to have upset the coolness of his judgment or the firmness of his determination in the least degree. When he found himself opposed, no longer by five battle-cruisers, but by sixteen Dreadnought battleships as well, he reversed the course of the fleet, made Evan-Thomas fall in behind him, and, during a holding action for the next hour, kept the Germans under his guns, risking their fire, threatening the head of their line, and half-cajoling, half-forcing Scheer northward to where the British fleets would be united. The moment contact becomes imminent—knowing that the light might at any moment fail—he forces the pace and discounts risks incalculably greater than at any time during the day, if only the enormous striking power of the Grand Fleet can be brought for once into action as a whole.

And so, regardless of the punishment his fleet had received earlier in the day, he shortens the range from 14,000 yards to 12,000 and then from 12,000 to 8,000, in a last effort to hold the enemy, while the Grand Fleet deploys and comes into action. There is no foolhardiness in his tactics, for the speed that enables him to head the German line is not only the best defence of his own squadron against torpedo attack. He has made it almost impossible for the German destroyers to enfilade the Grand Fleet, if only it deploys at full speed on him. He knows, of course, that at 8,000 yards the side armour of his ships will not keep out the enemy's shells. But he has demoralised the German gunfire by his own once before and, confident in the superior coolness and nerve of his officers and crews, he relies on this element again as the best defence of his squadron.

It is not till 6:50, when he realises that his whole effort has miscarried, that he makes the entry in his despatch which seems to me one of the most tragic phrases ever used by a great master of fighting. He had been baulked of victory at the Dogger Bank by a chance injury to his ship, when his squadron came under the command of an admiral trained in the tenets of Whitehall. Now on May 31 he had executed a master stroke of tactics. The armoured cruiser, designed to be a swift bully over the weak, he had used to confound and paralyze the strong. There had been many a discussion as to the tactical value of speed when the Dreadnought type was first designed, but no thinker had had the daring to forecast any such stroke as Sir David Beatty planned and executed off the Jutland Reefs. But it was a stroke struck in vain.

> By 6:50 the battle-cruisers were clear of our leading Battle Squadron, then bearing about north northwest three miles and I . . . reduced to 18 knots.

There was no more to try for that day. When, a quarter of an hour afterwards, the Grand Fleet starts south, he hunts for and heads the German line again. But it is all to no purpose. Yet he does not give up hope. At half-past nine darkness makes further pursuit impossible, but at any rate:

> Our strategical position was such as to make it appear certain that we should locate the enemy at daylight under most favourable circumstances."

It is plain, then, that he had a plan for next day's battle, just as he had had one for the hard and costly day just passed. To the last the thought still preoccupies him that has been his guide throughout. The enemy must be found and destroyed.

The commander-in-chief, however, whatever his anxiety for victory, is plainly concerned throughout by the enormous responsibility that weighs upon him as the guardian of the fleet under his command. Only one of the ships was hit by gunfire and only one was struck by torpedo! In summing up the story of the day, he says:

> The hardest fighting, fell to the lot of the Battle Cruiser Fleet ... the Fifth Battle Squadron, the First Cruiser Squadron, the Fourth Light Cruiser Squadron, and the flotillas.

But he must add a note, that the units of the Battle Cruiser Fleet were *less heavily armoured* than their opponents! The obsession of the defensive idea is obvious.

> The enemy constantly turned away and opened the range under cover of destroyer attacks and smoke screens.
> The German Fleet appeared to rely very much on torpedo attacks, which were favoured by low visibility, and by the fact that we had arrived in the position of a 'following' or 'chasing' fleet. A large number of torpedoes were apparently fired, but only one took effect (on *Marlborough*), and even in this case the ship was able to remain in the line and to continue the action. The enemy opened the range under cover of destroyer attacks ... which were favoured by the fact ... that we had arrived in the position of a 'following' ... fleet.

Had Admiral Jerram's squadron followed full speed straight into the wake of the battle-cruisers, had the whole Grand Fleet deployed on Sir David Beatty's track, the enemy's business should have been finished, for Scheer never could have turned under such a concentration of fire. But the form of the deployment created the situation that Scheer needed. It exposed the fleet to the torpedoes. And the risk was not faced. Speaking eight months afterwards at the Fishmongers' Hall, Admiral Jellicoe explained why.

> The torpedo, as fired from surface vessels, is effective certainly up to 10,000 yards range, and *this requires* that a ship shall keep beyond this distance to fight her guns. As conditions of visibility, in the North Sea particularly, are frequently such as to make fighting difficult beyond a range of 10,000 yards, and as modern fleets are invariably accompanied by very large numbers of destroyers, whose main duty is to attack with torpedoes the heavy ships of the enemy, it will be recognised how great becomes the responsibility of the admiral in command of a fleet, particularly under the conditions of low visibility to which I have referred. As soon as destroyers tumble upon a fleet within torpedo range the *situation becomes critical for the heavy ships.*

At Jutland three British and one German battle-cruiser were sunk by gunfire. At Dogger Bank *Lion* was disabled by a chance shot. Ten German battleships and one British were struck by torpedoes on May 31. One of these, one only, and she in all probability hit simultaneously by several, blew up. The other nine German ships and *Marlborough* all reached port in safety. Surely, if the situation of heavy ships is "critical" when within torpedo range, their situation when within reach of heavy guns must be more critical still. Is it possible to distinguish and say that one form of risk is *always*, and the other *never*, to be run? Is not the issue identical with that raised by the abandonment of the Dogger Bank pursuit—if it is true that pursuit was abandoned, as the Admiralty told us, on account of the presence of submarines?

At any rate, we see in this attitude one that stands in sharp contrast to Sir David Beatty's. He had faced torpedo attack in the Bight of Heligoland, and submarine attack in the Dogger Bank affair, and seemingly in the early fighting of May 31, without allowing the menace to influence him to avoid action. He took the right precautions against it. He had his cruisers and flotillas out as a screen, but having done all that was humanly possible to parry the attack he then, with a clear conscience, went for victory.

The same contrast is seen in the events of June 1. Sir John Jellicoe was perfectly willing to fight if the Germans would come out and fight on his conditions. At 4:0 a.m. an enemy Zeppelin flew over the fleet, so that its position was known to Scheer. Yet says the commander-in-chief, "the enemy made no sign." His own pre-occupation is not to find the enemy, but his own light forces. He thinks it worth recording that he hung about the scene of the yesterday's battle, "in spite of the ... danger incurred in waters adjacent to enemy coasts from submarine and torpedo craft." Napoleon speaks bitterly of his admirals, who acted as though they could win victory without taking risks.

A strong case can, of course, be made for the doctrine on which Sir John Jellicoe acted on these two days, a doctrine endorsed by the Admiralty, so far at least as it was shown in action on the first and only opportunity the British Fleet was given of utterly destroying the enemy. The defence can hardly be put better than it was by Mr. Churchill in his *London Magazine* article. Nor am I concerned here to argue the pros and cons on a point on which there can be little doubt as to the judgment of posterity. I direct attention to the singular fact that the British Fleet on May 31 fought as two separate units until six o'clock, and that the leaders of the two sections were animated by conflicting theories of war. One admiral represents the fighting fervour of the fleet: the other the caution—perhaps the wise caution—of the Higher Command.

There is no getting out of this dilemma. If Admiral Jellicoe was right in refusing to face the risks inseparable from a resolute effort to make the battle decisive, then Sir David Beatty must have been wrong to have fought in a way which cannot be intelligently explained except on the basis that from first to last he had decisive victory as his object. If the tender care that brought the Grand Fleet through the action with hardly a man killed and only two ships touched, was right and wise, then the clear vision, all the more luminous for seeing and counting the cost, which exposed *Indefatigable*, *Queen Mary*, and *Invincible* to destruction, was woefully wrong. Now it seems extraordinary, if the strategy of waiting to fight till the Germans attacked was right—if this was the Admiralty doctrine—that it was not communicated to Sir David Beatty as well as to Sir John Jellicoe.

If it was axiomatic to avoid the risk of ships being destroyed, so that Admiral Moore was right to break off the action at the Dogger Bank and Admiral Jellicoe right in letting the enemy "open the range under the cover of torpedo attacks," why was not Admiral Beatty forbidden to jeopardise his ships, and Admiral Arbuthnot warned against any pursuit of the enemy's cruisers or destroyers, that might possibly bring him within range of the German gunfire? How are we to explain

Bingham's attack on the head of the German line or Goodenough's reconnaissance which brought him under the salvoes of the German guns at 12,000 yards? Is the doctrine of caution and ship conservation to apply only to battleships and not to battle-cruisers, armoured cruisers, light cruisers, and destroyers? Is it only the battle fleet that is not to fight except when it risks practically nothing by doing so? All these questions are forced to the student's attention when he reviews the events here recorded.

Many defects in our preparations for war have been attributed to our lack of staff machinery in the years preceding the war. The defenceless state of the fleet's bases, the absence of any policy for using mines, or the means for carrying one out, the contrast between our pre-war confidence in our gunnery methods and what they have achieved in action, these and a score of other deficiencies have been attributed, and probably rightly, to our failure to appreciate the fact that modern war is so various and complicated a thing, and employs instruments and weapons and methods, the full possibilities of which are so obscure that only a long concerted effort could analyse and unravel them, that no organ except a General Staff could possibly have laid down the right doctrine of war or ensured the means of its application.

But of all the evidence of what we had lost by its absence, I know of none more striking than that from the outbreak of war until Sir David Beatty took command of the whole main forces of the navy, those forces should have been divided, and the two divisions commanded by men whose views as to the main purpose for which the force existed were utterly incompatible. It is amazing that Whitehall either never knew that this divergency of doctrine existed, or, knowing it, should not have secured that one or the other doctrine should predominate.

No official despatches descriptive of the attacks on Zeebrügge and Ostend have been published. For these extraordinary events, then, we have to rely upon the stories officially given out by the Admiralty's descriptive writer and the interviews which the officers concerned were allowed to give to different journalists.

Chapter 7

1. Naval Gunnery, Weapons, and Technique

Before passing to the actions, it is important to have a clear idea of two things which these actions illustrate. The first is the nature of the advantage which heavy guns have over lighter pieces. In each of these actions the side which had the largest number of heavier guns, or generally heavier guns, was successful. A heavy shell obviously has far greater effect than a light shell when it hits. Its advantages in this respect do not need demonstration. It is as well, however, to make it quite clear why it is more probable that a heavy shell will hit.

And next, these actions illustrate the great advance in fire control which has been made in the last ten years, and they also show, and I think convincingly, the limitations of the systems in use. As my comments on these actions will be particularly directed towards showing the tactical developments that have followed on the advance of gunnery and towards what further tactical developments must follow from a greater advance, it is essential that the nature of the fire-control problem should be understood.

The principle of heavy guns being superior at long range is exemplified by the Sketches 1 and 2. Sketch 1 represents the manner in which a salvo of guns may be expected to spread if all the sights are set to the same range. All guns lose in range accuracy as the range increases, but light guns more than heavy. If six 6-inch guns are fired at a target at 12,000 yards the shell will be apt to be spread out as shown in the top line. Six 9.2's will fall in a closer pattern, as shown in the second line, six 12-inch in a still smaller space, and the 13.5 in one still smaller. Regarded simply as instruments for obtaining a pattern at a given range, heavy guns are, therefore, far more effective than light ones.

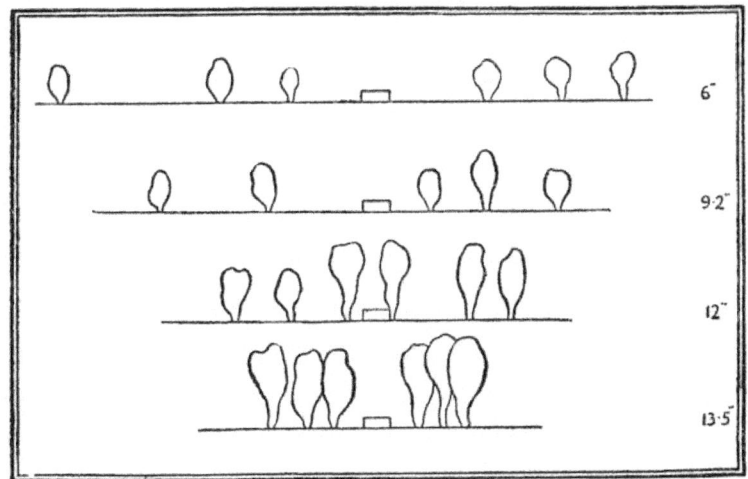

BIG GUNS MORE ACCURATE AT LONG RANGE, BECAUSE MORE REGULAR

But this is far from being the heavy guns' only advantage, as will be seen from Sketch 2. The heavier the projectile is, the longer it retains its velocity. The angle at which a shot falls from any height depends solely upon its forward velocity while it is falling. Sketch 2 shows the outline of a ship broadside on to the enemy's fire, the shell being fired from the right-hand of the sketch. A is the point where the ship's side meets the water. If the gun were shooting *perfectly* accurately and was set to 10,000 yards, all the shots would hit at this point. And clearly any shot set at a range greater than this, but one which did not carry the shot over the target, would hit the ship somewhere between the points A and X. Now if a 6-inch shot grazes the point X and falls into the water, it falls at the point B beyond the ship. But the angle at which it is falling is so steep that the difference in range between the point A and the point B is only forty yards. To hit, then, with a 6-inch gun the range must be known within forty yards. This interval is called the "Danger Space."

The 9.2 will fall at a more gradual angle, and the shot grazing on X will fall at C, which is twenty yards beyond B; and a 12-inch shell, falling still more gradually, will fall at D, which is 100 yards from A; and similarly, the 13.5 at E, which is 150 yards beyond it. Hence, at any given range, far *more accurate knowledge* of range is necessary for hitting with a 6-inch gun than with a 9.2, with a 9.2 than with a 12-inch, and with a 12-inch than with a 13.5.

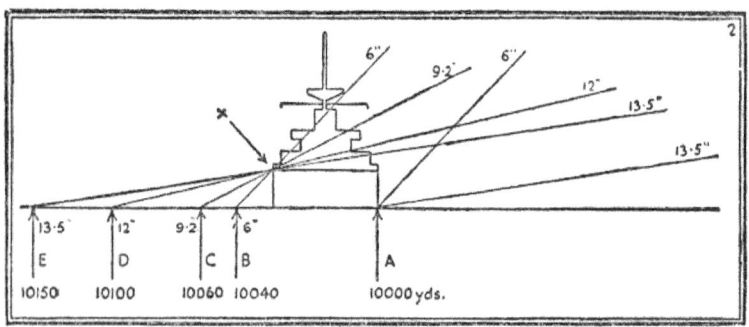

BIG GUNS NEED LESS ACCURATE RANGE-FINDING, BECAUSE THE DANGER SPACE IS GREATER

But we have seen from Sketch 1 that, in proportion as the range gets long, so does the range accuracy of the gun *decrease*, and that this loss of accuracy is greater in small guns than in bigger. To hit with it at all a more perfect fire control is necessary, and for any given number of rounds a much smaller proportion of hits will be made. The advantage of the big gun over the small, merely as a hitting weapon, is twofold. It does not require such accuracy in setting the sight, and more shots fired within these limits will hit.

FIRE CONTROL

If ships only engaged when they were stationary the range would not change, and it could be found by observation without rangefinders. And even with rangefinders it can never be found at great distances *without* observation.

But ships do not stand still, and when they move the distance between them alters from second to second. If these movements could be (1) ascertained, (2) integrated, and (3) the results impressed upon the sight, change of range would be eliminated, and we should have come back to the conditions in which ships were stationary. Fire control is successful in so far as it succeeds in doing these three things. Sketches 3 and 4 show the process by which hits are secured, when the conditions are not complicated by changes in the range, that is, if these complications have been eliminated by fire control. The second two illustrate what these complications are. The ships turn away from each other and then turn towards each other.

The rate graph (6) shows the effect of these movements on the range and the rate at which it is changing from moment to moment.

The process shown in Sketches 3 and 4 is called "bracketing." Two shots are fired at a difference of, say, 800 yards. Observation shows the first to be too short, the second to be too far. The difference is bisected by the third shot. This places the target in one of the halves of the bracket. This half is bisected by the fourth shot, placing the target in a quarter. If an eighth of the bracket is less than the danger space, then the fifth shot must hit.

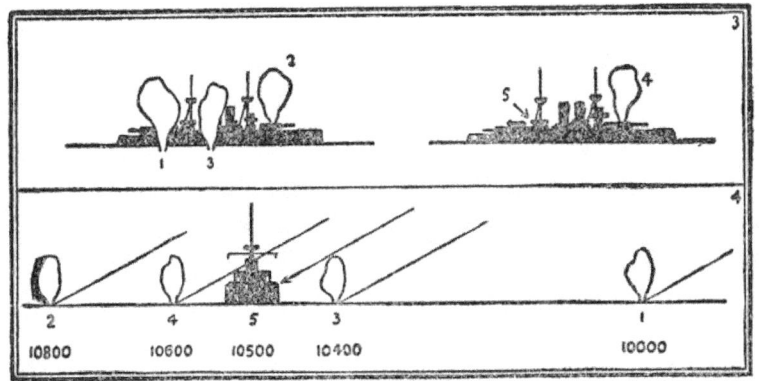

RANGE-FINDING BY BRACKET

In Sketch 5 the ships keep parallel courses for two minutes. The range does not change. The line in the graph (6) is, for these two minutes, horizontal. It is as if both were stationary. When the ships turn the range increases and the graph rises. But the graph is not a straight line but a curve. This shows that the rate also is changing. Each movement of the two ships, whether they keep steady courses or turn, alters the range and the rate. As projectiles take an interval of time to travel from the gun to the target, the range must be *forecasted*. B, then, cannot engage A unless he knows where A is going to be. He cannot know this until A has settled on a steady course.

While A is turning, then he is safe from gunfire except by a chance shot. B cannot engage while he is himself turning unless he can integrate his own movements with A's. It is this latter difficulty which largely explains the duration of modern actions. At the mean range of each engagement, with ships standing still, *Sydney* could have sunk *Emden* in ten minutes; *Inflexible* and *Invincible* could have sunk *Scharnhorst* and *Gneisenau* in fifteen. But it was ninety minutes before *Emden* was driven on the rocks, 180 before *Scharnhorst* sank, and 300 before *Gneisenau* went under.

In the ten years preceding the war, Admiralty policy, as shown by the official apology for the Dreadnought design and by the course

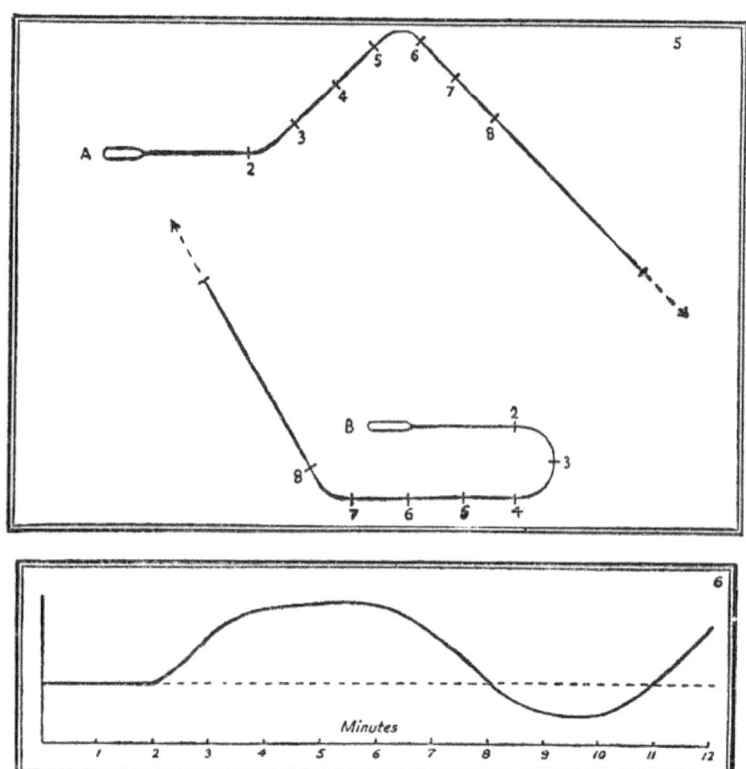

THE CRUX OF SEA FIGHTING, CHANGES OF COURSE AND SPEED PRODUCE AN IRREGULARLY CHANGING RANGE

of naval ordnance administration, had been governed by the purely defensive idea of providing ships fast enough to keep outside of the zone of the enemy's fire, armed with guns that outranged him. The professed object was to have a chance of hitting your enemy when he had no chance of hitting you. At the Falkland Islands there was given a classic example of the tactics that follow from this conception. On the assumption that twenty-five 12-inch gun hits would suffice to sink each of the enemy's armoured cruisers, it appeared that in this engagement the 12-inch gun had attained the rate of *one hit per gun per 75 minutes*.

This figure may be contrasted with the *one hit per gun per 72 seconds* attained by the *Severn* in her second engagement with the *Koenigsberg* at the Rufigi. The contrast seems to show that it was only the obsession of the defensive theory that explained contentment with methods of gunnery so extraordinarily ineffective in battle conditions. For the difference in the rate of hitting was almost completely explained by the range being *constant* at the Rufigi, and *inconstant* at the Falklands. And the methods of fire control in use were proved at the Falklands to be unequal to finding, and continuously keeping, accurate knowledge of an inconstant range.

Again at the affair of the Dogger Bank, *Lion, Tiger, Princess Royal, New Zealand*, and *Indomitable* were in action for many hours against three battle-cruisers and an armoured cruiser, and for perhaps half the time at ranges at which good hitting is made at battle practice; and although two of the enemy battle-cruisers were hit and seen to be in flames they were able, after two and a half hours' engagement, to continue their retreat at undiminished speed, and only the armoured cruiser, whose resisting power to 13.5 projectiles must have been very feeble, was sunk.

The lesson of Jutland is still more striking, and it is possible to draw the moral with a little greater precision since it has been officially admitted in Germany that *Lutzow*, Admiral von Hipper's flagship, the most modern of Germany's battle-cruisers, was destroyed after being hit by only fifteen projectiles from great guns. It is not clear from the German statement whether this means fifteen 13.5's and omits to reckon 12-inch shells, or whether there were fifteen hits in all, some of the one nature and some of the other. The latter is probably the case; for we know from Sir David Beatty's and the German despatches that it was *Invincible's* salvos that finally incapacitated the ship and compelled Von Hipper to shift his flag.

Lutzow was always at the head of the German line and so was exposed to the fire of our battle-cruisers for nearly three hours. If we assume that she was hit by ten 13.5's and five 12-inch; if we further assume that the effect of shells is proportionate to their weight; if we take the resisting power of British battle-cruisers, German battle-cruisers (which are more heavily armoured than the British), and all battleships to compare as the figures 2, 3, and 4 respectively; if we further assume that the Fifth Battle Squadron did not come into effective action till the second phase began, and went out of action at 6:30, and that the battle cruisers were in action for three hours, and omit Hood's squadron altogether, we get the following results:

Five German battle-cruisers were exposed to seventy-two hours of 13.5 gun fire and to twenty-four hours of 12-inch gun fire, and five German battleships were exposed to forty-eight 15-inch gun hours.

Similarly—omitting *Queen Mary*, *Indefatigable*, and *Invincible*, seemingly destroyed by chance shots and not overwhelmed by gunfire—four British battle-cruisers were exposed to thirty-seven 12-inch and sixty 11-inch gun hours, and the Fifth Battle Squadron was exposed to one hundred and eighty 12-inch gun hours. Had both sides been able to hit at the rate of *one hit per hour per gun*, the Germans, roughly speaking, should have sunk six British battle-cruisers, and the four ships of the Fifth Battle Squadron nearly twice over; the Fifth Battle Squadron should have sunk four German battleships; and the British battle-cruisers seven German battle-cruisers! The number of hits received by the British Fleet has not been published, but it is probably safe to say that the Germans could not have made a quarter of this number of hits, nor the British ships more than a third. It would seem, then, that at most we made one hit per gun per three hours and the Germans one hit per gun per four hours.

At no time, throughout such parts of the action as we are considering, did the range exceed 14,000 yards, and at some periods it was at 12,000 and at others at 8,000. In battle practice not only on the British Fleet but in all fleets, hits at the rate of one hit per gun per four minutes at 14,000 yards have constantly been made. How, then, are we to explain the extraordinary difference between battle practice and battle results? In the former certain difficulties are artificially created, and methods of fire control are employed that can overcome these difficulties successfully. But these methods evidently break down when it comes to the quite different difficulties that battle presents. So far, we are on indisputable ground. Whether fire control can be so improved that the difficulties of battle can be overcome, just as the difficulties of battle practice have been overcome is another matter.

The difference between action and battle practice is, broadly speaking, twofold. First, you may have to fight in atmospheric conditions in which you would not attempt battle practice. All long-range gunnery, whether on sea or on land, depends for success upon range-finding and the observation of fire, and as at sea the observations must be made from a point at which the gun is fired, the correction of fire becomes impossible if bad light or mist prevents the employment of observing glasses and range-finders.

In the Jutland despatch particular attention was directed to the disadvantages we were under in the matter of range-finding from these causes. It would appear, then, that those who, for many years, had maintained that the standard service rangefinder would be useless in a

North Sea battle, have been proved to be right.

The second great difference lies in the totally different problems which movement creates in battle. In battle practice the only movement of the target is that which the towing ship can give to it. Its speed and manoeuvring power are strictly limited, whereas a 30-knot battle-cruiser can change speed and direction at will. The smallest change of course must alter the range, and the smallest miscalculation of speed or course must make accurate forecast of range impossible. But the movements of the target are only a part of the difficulty. Those that arise from the manoeuvres of the firing ship may be still greater and more confusing. And so obvious is this that, in peace time, it used to be almost an axiom that to put on helm during an engagement—even for the sake of keeping station—should be regarded almost as a crime.

But the long-range torpedo has long since made it clear that a firing squadron may *have* to put on helm. It must manoeuvre, that is to say, in self-defence—a thing it would never have to do in battle practice. And when both target ship and firing ship are manoeuvring, it is small wonder if methods of fire control, designed primarily for steady courses by one ship and low speed and small turns by the other, break down altogether. It is undoubtedly true that the mainspring of all defensive naval ideas is *doubt as to the success of offensive action*, and as the only offensive action that a battleship can take is by its guns, it would seem as if those who disbelieve in the offensive have had far too much reason for their scepticism.

The Torpedo in Battle

It was the invention of the hot-air engine round about 1907, that converted the torpedo from a short- to a long-range weapon, and when, a year or two later, the feasibility of running one of these with almost perfect accuracy and regularity to a distance of five miles was demonstrated, it became quite obvious that a new and, as many thought, a decisive element had been introduced into naval war, the effect of which would be especially marked in any future fleet actions. Just what form its intervention would take was much discussed in three years, and the following quotation from a confidential contribution of my own on this discussion, written in December 1912, is perhaps not without interest as indicating the points then in debate:

> The tactical employment of fleets has, of course, recently been complicated, in the opinions of many, by the facts that the range of torpedoes is more than doubled; that their speed is very

greatly increased; and that their efficiency (that is, the extent to which they can be relied upon to run well) has increased almost as much as their range and speed. This advance of the torpedo has followed very rapidly on the development of the submarine, and has led, quite naturally, to the suggestion that it should be employed on a considerable scale in a fleet action either from under-water craft or by squadrons of fast destroyers. The torpedo menace has undoubtedly confused the problem of fleet action in a most bewildering manner; but, with great respect to those who attach the most importance to this menace, there are, it seems to me, certain principles that should be borne in mind in estimating its probable influence.

There is a world of difference between a weapon that can be evaded and one that cannot. You can, by vigilance, circumvent the submarine and dodge the torpedo—at any rate, in some cases. You can never double to avoid a 12-inch shell. It may yet be proved that not the least interesting aspect of modern naval warfare will be that the torpedo will thus put seamanship back to its pride of place.

In any circumstances the torpedo, however highly developed, is not a weapon of the same kind as the gun. It seems to belong to the same order of military ideas as the cutting-out expeditions and use of fire-ships in olden days and the employment of mines of more recent date. It is, of course, an element in fighting, and a most serious element; a means of offence far handier, and with a power of striking at a far greater distance than has been seen in any parallel mode of war hitherto. And yet I should be inclined to maintain that it and its employment remain more in the nature of a 'stratagem' than of a tactical weapon, truly so called.

Mines, torpedoes, a bomb dropped from an airship or aeroplane—these are all new perils of war. In the hands of a Cochrane their employment might conceivably be decisive. But it would need the conjunction of an extraordinary man with extraordinary fortune.

Both Japanese and Russians lost ships by mines and torpedoes in 1906, and ships will be lost in future wars in the same way, but I find it hard to believe that the *essential* character of fleet actions or of naval war generally can be affected by them. It seems indisputable that the future must be with the means of offence that has the longest reach, can deliver its blow with the greatest rapidity, and, above all, that is capable of being employed with the most exact precision. In these respects, the gun is, and in the nature of things must remain, unrivalled.

The two directions in which fleet-fighting seems likely to be most noticeably affected by the new weapon are in the formation of fleets and the maintenance of steady courses, and in making longer ranges compulsory.

I think there are other reasons why the tactical ideal set out above—*viz.*, that of using long lines of ships on approximately parallel courses at equal speed in the same direction—will be questioned; but even if there were not, that a mobile mine-field can be made to traverse the line of an on-coming squadron, and do so at a range of 10,000 yards, and that ships formed in line ahead offer between five and six times more favourable a target to perpendicular submarine attack than a line of ships abreast, will make it certain that sooner or later there will be a tendency in favour of smaller squadrons and, even with these, of large and frequent changes of course, and possibly of formation, so as to lessen the torpedo menace.

In other words, we must recognise that in the long-range torpedo we have a new element in naval battle, that of the *defensive* offensive. It is defensive because, if the range of the torpedo is 10,000 yards of absolute run, its range is greater if fired on the bow of an advancing squadron by the distance that squadron may travel—3,000 to 4,000 yards—while the torpedo is doing its 10,000. A very fast battle-cruiser, for instance, may have a speed only a few knots less than that of the under-water weapon. This means either keeping out of gun range of an enemy that is retreating, or taking the risk of torpedo attack. If you face the risk, you must be ready to manoeuvre to avoid it.

It looks, then, as if long-range gunnery and gunnery under helm were: the first, compulsory, and the second, inevitable.

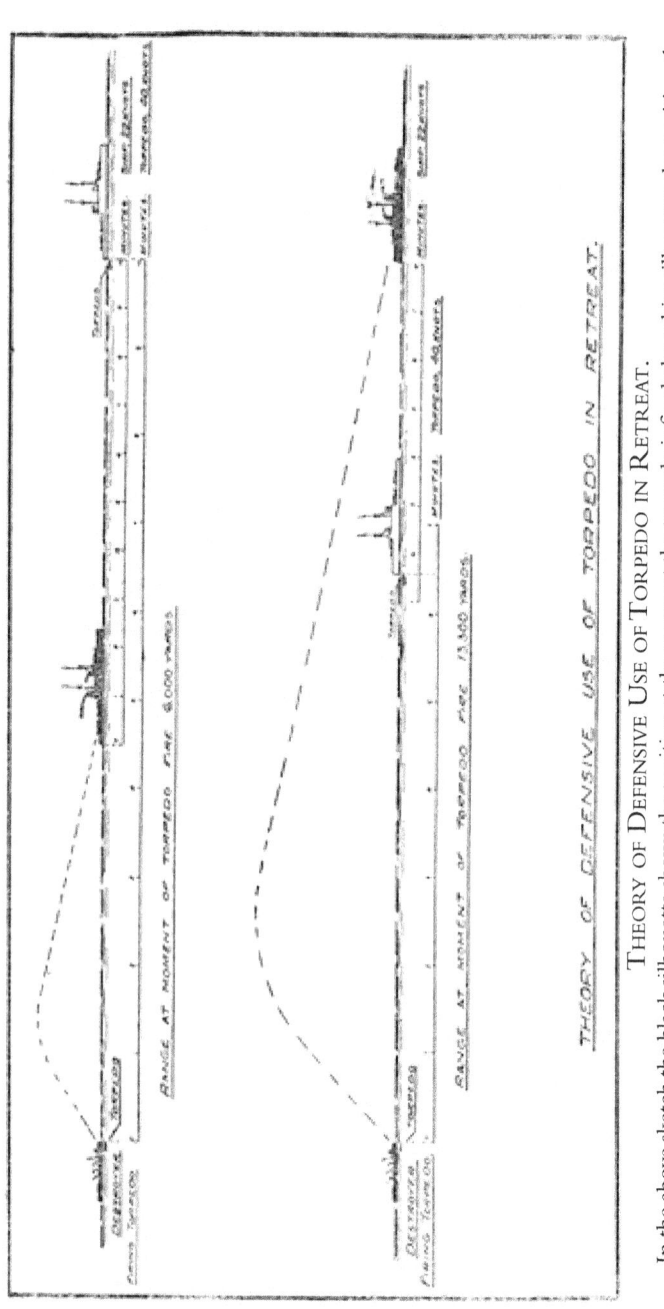

THEORY OF DEFENSIVE USE OF TORPEDO IN RETREAT.

In the above sketch the black silhouette shows the position at the moment the torpedo is fired; the white silhouette the position the ship has reached when the torpedo meets it. In the upper sketch the ship is running away from the torpedo, in the lower one coming to meet it. The distance run by the torpedo is the same in each case, but the range at the moment of firing is 6,000 yards in the upper case and 13,300 in the lower

CHAPTER 8

The Action That Never Was Fought

August, 1914.
Take it for all in all, the most remarkable thing about the naval war is that it took the Germans by surprise. They had planned the most perfect thing imaginable in the way of a scheme for the conquest of all Europe. It had but one flaw. They left Great Britain out of their calculations—left us out, that is to say, not as ulterior victims, but as probable and immediate combatants. We were omitted because Germany assumed that we should either be too rich, too frightened, or too unready to fight. So that, of all the contingencies that could be foreseen, simultaneous sea war with Great Britain and land war on two frontiers, was the one for which almost no preparations had been made. Hence to undo Germany utterly at sea proved to be a very simple business indeed.

Much has been made of this statesman or that admiral having actually issued the mandate that kept the Grand Fleet mobilised and got it to its war stations two days before war was declared. But there is here no field for flattery and no scope for praise, and the historical interest in identifying the actual agent is slender. It has always been a part of the British defensive theory that the main fleet shall be ever ready for instant war orders. Of the fact of its being the plan, we need no further testimony than Mr. Churchill's first Memorandum after his elevation to the control of British naval policy and of the British Fleet. The thing, therefore, that was done was the mere mechanical discharge of a standing order.

Once the fleet was mobilised and at its war stations, German sea power perished off the outer seas as effectually as if every surface ship had been incontinently sunk. There was not a day's delay in our using the Channel exactly as if no enemy were afloat. Within an hour of the declaration of war being known, no German ship abroad cleared for a German port, nor did any ship in a German port clear for the open sea. The defeat was suffered without a blow being offered in defence, and, for the purposes of trade and transport, it was as instantaneous as it was final.

Nor was it our strength, nor sheer terror of our strength, that made the enemy impotent. He was confounded as much by surprise as he was by superior power. In point of fact, the disparity between the main forces of the two Powers in the North Sea, though considerable, was not such as to have made Germany despair of an initial victory—and that possibly decisive—had she been free to choose her own method of making war on us, and had she chosen her time wisely. In August 1914, three of our battle cruisers were in the Mediterranean, one was in the Pacific, one was in dockyard hands. Only one German ship of the first importance was absent from Kiel. In modern battleships commissioned and at sea, the German High Seas Fleet consisted of at least two *Königs*, five *Kaisers*, four *Helgolands*, and four *Westfalens*.

All except the *Westfalens* were armed with 12.2 guns—weapons that fire a heavier shell than the British 12-inch. The *Westfalens* were armed with 11-inch guns. They could, then, have brought into action a broadside fire of 110 12-inch guns and 40 11-inch. Germany had, besides, four battle-cruisers, less heavily armed than our ships of the same class, quite as fast as our older battle-cruisers and much more securely armoured. So that if protection—as so many seem to think—is the one essential quality in a fighting ship, they were more suited to take their share in a fleet action than our battle-cruisers could have been expected to be.

On our side we had twenty battleships and four armoured cruisers. In modern capital ships, then, we possessed but twenty-four to nineteen—a percentage of superiority of only just over 25 *per cent.*, and less than that for action purposes if the principle alluded to holds good. It was a margin far lower than the public realised. At Jutland we lost two battle cruisers in the first forty minutes of the action. Had such an action been fought, with like results, in August, 1914, our surviving margin would have been very slender indeed. But the enemy dared not take the risk. He paid high for his caution. Yet his inferiority should not have paralyzed him. At Jutland he faced infinitely greater odds. His numbers were not such as to make inglorious inactivity compulsory had he been resourceful, enterprising, and willing to risk all in the attack. It certainly was a position that bristled with possibilities for an enemy who, to resource, courage, and enterprise, could add the overpowering advantage of choosing the day and the hour of attack, and could strike without a moment's warning.

If the German Government had realised from the start that in no war that threatened the balance of power in Europe could we remain either indifferent or, what is far more important, inactive spectators, then they would have realised something else as well, something that was, in point of fact, realised the moment Germany began her self-imposed—but now impossible—task of conquering Europe by first crushing France and Russia. She would have realised as then she did, that if Great Britain were allowed to come into the war her intervention might be decisive. It would seemingly have to be so for very obvious reasons.

With France and Russia assured of the economic and financial support of the greatest economic and financial power in Europe, Germany's immediate opponents would have staying power: time, that is to say, would be against their would-be conquerors. The intervention of Great Britain, then, would make an ultimate German victory impossible. In a long war staying power would make the population of the British Empire a source from which armies could be drawn. Beginning by being the greatest sea power in the world, we would necessarily end in becoming one of the greatest military powers as well. The two things by themselves must have threatened military defeat for Germany. Nor, again, was this all. For while sea power, and the financial strength which goes with sustained trade and credit, could add indefinitely to the fighting capacity and endurance of Russia and France, sea power and siege were bound, if resolutely used, to sap the fighting power and endurance of the Central Powers.

To the least prophetic of statesmen—just as to the least instructed students of military history—the situation would have been plain. And there could be but one lesson to be drawn from it. To risk everything on a quick victory over France or Russia was insanity. If the conquest of Europe could not be undertaken with Great Britain an opponent, the alternative was simple. Either the conquest of Great Britain must precede it or the conquest of the world be postponed to the Greek *Kalends*.

Was the conquest of Great Britain a thing so unattainable that it had only to be considered to be discarded as visionary? No doubt, had we been warned and upon our guard, ready to defend ourselves before Germany was ready to strike, then certainly any such scheme must have been doomed to failure. But I am not so sure that a successful attack would have been beyond the resources of those who planned the great European war, had they from the first, grasped the elementary truth that it was necessary to their larger scheme. For to win the conquest of Europe it would not be necessary to crush Great Britain finally and altogether. All that was required was to prevent her interference for, say, six months, and this, it really seems, was far from being a thing beyond the enemy's capacity to achieve.

The essentials of the attack are easy enough to tabulate. First, Germany would have to concentrate in the North Sea the largest force of capital ships that it was possible to equip. Her own force I have already enumerated. Had Germany contemplated war on Great Britain she would, of course, not have sent the *Goeben* away to the Straits. The nucleus of the German Fleet, then, would have been twenty and not nineteen ships. To these might have been added the three completed Dreadnoughts of the Austrian Fleet, the *Viribus Unitis, Tegetthof,* and *Prinz Eugen*—all of which were in commission in the summer of 1914. They would have contributed a broadside fire of 36 12-inch guns—a very formidable reinforcement—and brought the enemy fleet to an almost numerical equality with ours. A review at Kiel would have been a plausible excuse for bringing the Austrian Dreadnoughts into German waters. Supposing the British force, then, to have been undiminished, the war might have opened with a bare superiority of five *per cent.* on the British side.

But there is no reason why British strength should not have been reduced. Knowing as we now do, not the potentialities, but the practical use that can be made of submarines and destroyers, it must be plain to all that, had Germany intended to begin a world war with a blow at Great Britain, she might well have hoped to have reduced our strength to such a margin before the war began, as to make it almost unnecessary to provide against a fleet action. Most certainly a single surprise attack by submarines could have done all that was desired.

By a singular coincidence, an opportunity for such an attack—an opportunity that could hardly have failed of a most sinister success—offered itself at the strategic moment when the Central Powers had already resolved to use the murder of the archduke as a pretext for an unprovoked attack on Christendom. All our battleships of the first, second, and third lines, all our battle-cruisers commissioned and in home waters, almost all our armoured cruisers and fast light cruisers, and the bulk of our destroyers and auxiliaries were, in the fateful third week in July, gathered and at anchor—and completely unprotected—in the fairway of the Solent. There were to be no manoeuvres in 1914, but a test mobilisation instead, and this great congregation of the Fleet was to be a measure of the Admiralty's capacity to man all our naval forces of any fighting worth. The fact that this gathering was to take place on a certain and appointed date was public property in the month of March. A week or a fortnight before the squadrons steamed one by one to their moorings, a plan of the anchored lines was published in every London paper.

The order of the Fleet, the identity of every ship in its place in every line, might have been, and probably were, in German hands a week before any single ship was in her billet. From Emden to the Isle of Wight is a bare 350 miles—a day and a half's journey for a submarine—and in July 1914, Germany possessed between twenty and thirty submarines. It was a day and a half's journey if it had been all made at under-water speed. What could not a dozen *Weddigens* and *Hersings* have done had they only been sent upon this fell mission, and their arrival been timed for an hour before daybreak on the morning of July 18? They surely could have gone far beyond wiping out a margin of five big ships, which was all the margin we had against the German Fleet alone. They could, in the half light of the summer's night, have slipped five score torpedoes into a dozen or more battleships and battle-cruisers. They could have attacked and returned undetected, leaving Great Britain largely helpless at sea and quite unable to take part in the forthcoming European war.

Germany could, of course, have done much more to complete our discomfiture. A hundred merchant ships, each carrying three brace of 4-inch guns, and sent as peaceful traders astride the distant trade routes; the despatch of two score or more destroyers to the approaches of the Channel and the Western ports, and all of them instructed—as in fact, eight months afterwards, every submarine was instructed—to sink every British liner and merchantman at sight, without waiting to search or troubling to save passengers or crew—raids organised on this scale and on these principles could have reduced our merchant shipping by a crippling percentage in little more than forty-eight hours. The two things taken together—the assassination of the Fleet, the wholesale murder of the merchant marine—must certainly have thrown Great Britain into a paroxysm of grief and panic.

What a moment this would have been for throwing a raiding force, could one have been secretly organised, upon the utterly undefended, and now indefensible, eastern coast! Secretly, skilfully, and ruthlessly executed these three measures could have done far more than make it impossible for Great Britain to take a hand in the defence of France. They might, by the sheer rapidity and terrific character of the blows, have thrown us so completely off our balance as to make us unwilling, if we were not already powerless, to make further efforts even to defend ourselves. At least, so it must have appeared to Germany.

For it was the essence of the German case that the nation was too distracted by political differences, too fond of money-making, too debilitated by luxury and comfort, too conscious of its weak hold on the self-governing colonies, too uncertain of its tenure on its oversea Imperial possessions, to stand by its plighted word. The nation has since proved that all these things were delusions. But it was no delusion that Great Britain would be very reluctant to participate in any war. And we need not have fallen so low as Germany supposed and yet be utterly discomposed and incapable of further effort, had we indeed, in quick succession or simultaneously, received the triple onslaught that it was well within the enemy's power to inflict.

Even had these blows so failed in the completeness of their several and combined effects as to crush us altogether, had we recovered and been able to strike back, what would have been the situation? It would have taken us some months to hunt down and destroy a hundred armed German merchantmen. If 100,000 or 150,000 men had been landed, the campaign that would have ended in their defeat and surrender could not have been a very rapid one. Our re-assertion of the command of the seas might have had to wait until the dockyards, working day and night shifts, could restore the balance of naval power. Suppose, then, we escaped defeat; suppose these assassin blows had ended in the capture or sinking of a hundred merchantmen in the final overthrow of Germany's sea power—could these things have been any loss to Germany, if it had been the price of swift and complete victory in Europe?

In the unsuccessful attack on Verdun alone she threw away not 150,000 men but three times that number. There is not a German merchantman afloat that has been worth sixpence to her country since war was declared, nor in the first two years of war did the German Fleet achieve anything to counter-balance what the German Army lost by having to face the British as well as the French Army in the west. The sacrifices, then, would have been trivial compared with the stake for which Germany was playing. If it had resulted in keeping us out of the Continent for six months only, our paralysis, even if only temporary, should have decided the issue in Germany's favour.

Greatly as Germany dared in forcing war upon a Europe altogether surprised and almost altogether unready, yet in point of fact she dared just too little. Abominably wicked as her conduct was, it was not wicked enough to win the justification of success. If war was intended to be inevitable from the moment the Serbian ultimatum was sent, the capacity of Great Britain to intervene should have been dealt with resolutely and ruthlessly and removed as a risk before any other risk was taken. It sobers one to reflect how changed the situation might have been had German foresight been equal to the German want of scruple. Looking back, it seems as if it was but a very little thing the enemy had to do to ensure the success of all his plans.

Had any one before the war sketched out this programme as one which Germany might adopt, he would perhaps have been regarded by the great majority of his countrymen as a lunatic. But today, (1919), we can look at Germany in the light of four years of her conduct. And we can see that it was not scruple or tenderness of conscience or any decent regard for the judgment of mankind that made her overlook the first essential of success. We must attribute it to quite a different cause. I am quoting from memory, but it seems to me that Sir Frederick Pollock has put the truth in this matter into exact terms.

> The Germans will go down to history as people who foresaw everything except what actually happened, and calculated everything except its cost to themselves.

It is the supreme example of the childish folly that, for the next two years, we were to see always hand in hand with diabolical wickedness and cunning. And always the folly has robbed the cunning of its prey.

In the edifying tales that we have inherited from the Middle Ages, when simple-minded Christian folk personified the principle of evil and attributed all wickedness to the instigation of the Devil, we are told again and again of men who bargained with the Evil One, offering their eternal souls in payment for some present good—a grim enough exchange for a man to make who believed he had a soul to give. But it is seldom in these tales that the bargain goes through so simply. Sometimes it is the sinner who scores by repentance and the intervention of Heaven and a helpful saint. But often it is the Devil that cheats the sinner. The forfeit of the soul is not explicit in the bargain. There is some other promise, seemingly of plain intent, but in truth ambiguous, which seems to make it possible for sin to go unpunished. Too late, the deluded gambler finds the treaty a "scrap of paper." The story of Macbeth is a case in point.

Does it not look as if Germany had made some unhallowed bargain of this kind?—as if this hideous adventure was started on the faith of a promise of success given by her evil genius and always destined to be unredeemed? Is it altogether chance that there should have been this startling blindness to the most palpable of the forces in the game?—such inexplicable inaction where the right action was so obvious and so easy?

CHAPTER 9

The Destruction of "Koenigsberg"

The story of the destruction of *Koenigsberg* by the twin monitors *Severn* and *Mersey* in the Rufigi Delta, has an interest that far transcends the intrinsic military importance of depriving the enemy of a cruiser already useless in sea war. For the narrative of events will bring to our attention at once the extreme complexity and the diversity of the tasks that the Royal Navy in war is called upon to discharge. It is worth examining in detail, if only to illustrate the novelty of the operations which officers, with no such previous experience, may at any moment be called upon to undertake, and the extraordinary combination of patience, courage, skill, and energy with which when experience at last comes, it is turned to immediate profit.

The incident possesses, besides, certain technical aspects of the very highest importance. For it gives in its simplest form perfect examples of how guns should not and should be used when engaged in indirect fire, and by affording this illuminating contrast, is highly suggestive of the progress that may be made in naval gunnery when scientific method is universally applied. The incident, then, is worth setting out and examining in some detail, and there is additional reason for doing this, in that the accounts that originally appeared were either altogether inaccurate or so incomplete as to be misleading. First, then, to a narrative of the event itself.

Koenigsberg was a light unarmoured cruiser of about 3,400 tons displacement, and was laid down in December 1905. She carried an armament of ten 4.1-inch guns, and was protected by a 2-inch armoured deck. The Germans had begun the construction of vessels of this class about seven years before with *Gazelle*, which was followed in the next year by *Niobe* and *Nymphe*, and then by four more—including *Ariadne*, destroyed by *Lion* in the affair of the Heligoland

The German battle cruiser *Koenigsberg*

Bight—which were laid down in 1900. Two years later came the three *Frauenlobs*, and the *Bremen* class—five in number—succeeded these in 1903–4. In 1905, followed *Leipzig, Danzig*, and finally the ship that concerns us today. All these vessels had the same armament, but in the six years the displacement had gone up 1,000 tons. The speed had increased from 21½ knots to about 24, and the nominal radius of action by about 50 *per cent*. *Koenigsberg* was succeeded by the *Stettins* in 1906–7, the two *Dresdens* in 1907–8, the four *Kolbergs* in 1908–9, and the four *Breslaus* in 1911. *Karlsruhe, Grodenz*, and *Rostock* were the only three of the 1912–13 programmes which were completed when the war began.

The process of growth, illustrated in the advance of *Koenigsberg* over *Niobe*, was maintained, so that in the *Karlsruhe* class in the programme of 1912, while the unit of armament is preserved, we find that the number of guns had grown from ten to twelve; the speed had advanced from 23½ to 28 knots, and the displacement from 3,400 to nearly 5,000 tons. As we know now, in the Battle of Jutland we destroyed light cruisers of a still later class in which, in addition to every other form of defence, the armament had been changed from 4.1-inch to 6.7 guns.

Koenigsberg, on the very eve of the outbreak of war, was seen by three ships of the Cape Squadron off Dar-es-Salaam, the principal port of German East Africa. She was travelling due north at top speed, and was not seen or heard of again until, a week later, she sank the British steamer *City of Winchester* near the island of Socotra. There followed three weeks during which no news of her whereabouts reached us. At the end of the month it was known that she had returned south and was in the neighbourhood of Madagascar. At the end of the third week in September she came upon H.M.S. *Pegasus* off Zanzibar. *Pegasus* was taken completely unawares while she was cleaning furnaces and boilers and engaged in general repairs.

It was not possible then for her to make any effective reply to *Koenigsberg's* sudden assault, and a few hours after *Koenigsberg* left she sank. Sometime between the end of September and the end of October, *Koenigsberg* retreated up one of the mouths of the Rufigi River, and was discovered near the entrance on October 31 by H.M.S. *Chatham*.

From then onwards, all the mouths of the river were blockaded and escape became impossible. Her captain seemingly determined, in these circumstances, to make the ship absolutely safe. He took advantage of the high water tides, and forced his vessel some twelve or more miles up the river. Here she was located by aeroplane at the end of November. Various efforts had been made to reach her by gunfire. It was asserted at one time that H.M.S. *Goliath* had indeed destroyed her by indirect bombardment. But there was never any foundation for supposing the story to be true, and if in the course of any of these efforts the ship suffered any damage, it became abundantly clear, when she was finally engaged by the monitors, either that her armament had never been touched, or that all injuries had been made good.

The problems which the existence of *Koenigsberg* propounded were: first, Was it a matter of very urgent moment to destroy her? Second, How could her destruction be effected? The importance of destroying her was great. There was, of course, no fear of her affecting the naval position seriously if she should be able to escape; but that she could do some, and possibly great, damage if at large, the depredations of *Emden* in the neighbouring Indian Ocean, and of *Karlsruhe* off Pernambuco, had proved very amply indeed. If she was not destroyed then, a close blockade would have to be rigidly maintained, and it was a question whether the maintenance of the blockade would not involve, in the end, just as much trouble as her destruction.

Then there was a further point. Sooner or later, the forces of Great Britain and Belgium would certainly have to undertake the conquest of German East Africa. While *Koenigsberg* could not be used as a unit for defence, her crew and armament might prove valuable assets to the enemy. Finally, there was a question of prestige. The Germans thought that they had made their ship safe. If the thing was possible, it was our obvious duty to prove that their confidence was misplaced.

If the ship was to be destroyed, what was to be the method of her destruction? She could not be reached by ship's guns. For no normal warship of superior power would be of less draught than *Koenigsberg*, and unless the draught were very materially less, it would be quite impossible to get within range, except by processes as slow and laborious as those by which she had attained her anchorage. Was it worth while attempting a cutting-out expedition? It would not, of course, be on the lines of the dashing and gallant adventures so brilliantly drawn for us by Captain Marryat. The boats would proceed under steam and would not be rowed; they would not sally out to board the enemy and fight his crew hand to hand, but to get near enough to start a torpedo at him, discharged from dropping gear in a picket boat.

To have attempted this would have been to face a grave risk, for not only might the several entrances be mined, but the boats clearly would have to advance unprotected up a river whose banks were covered with bush impenetrable to the eye. The enemy, it was known, had not only considerable military forces in the colony, but those well supplied with field artillery. And there were on board *Koenigsberg* not only the 4.1-inch guns of her main armament, but a considerable battery of eight or perhaps twelve, 3-inch guns—a weapon amply large enough to sink a ship's picket boat, and that with a single shot. An attack by boats then promised no success at all, for the excellent reason that it would be the simplest thing on earth for the enemy to defeat it long before the expedition had reached the point from which it could strike a blow at its prey.

There was then only one possible solution of the problem. It was to employ armed vessels of sufficient gun-power to do the work quickly, and of shallow enough draught to get to a fighting range quickly. If the thing were not done quickly, an attack from the masked banks might be fatal. If the guns of such a vessel were corrected by observers in aeroplanes, they might be enabled to do the trick. Fortunately, at the very opening of the war, the Admiralty had purchased from the builders three river monitors, then under construction in England for the Brazilian Government. They drew but a few feet. Their free board was low, their centre structure afforded but a small mark; the two 6-inch guns they carried fore and aft were protected by steel shields. They had been employed with marked success against the Germans in their first advance to the coast of Belgium.

When the enemy, having established himself in the neighbourhood of Nieuport, had time to bring up and emplace long-range guns of large calibre, the further employment of these river monitors on this, their first job, was no longer possible. For the moment, then, they seemed to be out of work, and here was an undertaking exactly suited to their capacity. It was not the sort of undertaking for which they had been designed. But it was one to which, undoubtedly, they could be adapted. Of the three monitors *Mersey* and *Severn* were therefore sent out to Mafia Island, which lies just off the Rufigi Delta and had been seized by us early in the proceedings.

The first aeroplanes available proved to be unequal to the task, because of the inadequacy of their lifting power. The atmosphere in the tropics is of a totally different buoyancy from that in colder latitudes, and a machine whose engines enable it to mount quite easily to a height of 4,000 or 5,000 feet in Northern Europe, cannot, in Central Africa, rise more than a few hundred feet from the ground. New types of machines, therefore, had to be sent, and these had to be tested and got ready for work. For many weeks then, before the actual attack was undertaken, we must picture to ourselves the Island of Mafia, hitherto unoccupied and indeed untouched by Europeans, in the process of conversion into an effective base for some highly complicated combined operations of aircraft and sea force. The virgin forest had to be cleared away and the ground levelled for an aerodrome. The flying men had to study and master machines of a type of which they had no previous experience.

The monitors had to have their guns tested and their structural arrangement altered and strengthened to fit them for their new undertaking. And indeed, preparing the monitors was a serious matter. The whole delta of the Rufigi is covered with forest and thick bush—nowhere are the trees less than sixty feet high, and in places they rise to nearly three times this height. To engage the *Koenigsberg* with any prospect of success, five, six, or seven miles of one of the river branches would certainly have to be traversed. There was, it is true, a choice of three mouths by which these vessels might proceed. But it would be almost certain that the different mouths would be protected by artillery, machine-guns, and rifles, and highly probable that one or all of them would be mined.

The thick bush would make it impossible for the monitors to engage any hidden opponents with sufficient success to silence their fire. And obviously any portion of the bank might conceal, not only field guns and riflemen, but stations from which torpedoes could be released against them. It was imperative therefore, to protect the monitors from such gun fire as might be encountered, and to take every step possible to preserve their buoyancy if a mine or torpedo was encountered.

The *Trent* had come out as a mother ship to these two unusual men-of-war, and from the moment of their arrival, she became an active arsenal for the further arming and protection of her charges. Many tons of plating were laid over their vulnerable portions—the steering gear, magazines, navigating bridges, etc., having to be specially considered. The gun shields were increased in size, and every precaution taken to protect the gunners from rifle fire. Where plating could not be added, sandbags were employed. By these means the danger of the ship being incapacitated, or the crew being disabled by what the enemy could do from the bank, was reduced to a minimum. These precautions would not, of course, have been a complete protection against continuous hitting by the plunging fire of *Koenigsberg's* artillery. The more difficult job was to protect the ships against mines and torpedoes. Their first and best protection, of course, was their shallow draught.

But it was not left at that; and most ingenious devices were employed which would have gone a fair way to keep the ships floating even had an under-water mine been exploded beneath the bottom. At intervals, between these spells of dockyard work, the monitors were taken out for practice in conjunction with the aeroplanes. Mafia Island, which had already served as a dockyard and aerodrome, was now once more to come in useful as a screen between the monitors and the target. The various operations necessary for indirect fire were carefully studied. Gun-layers, of course, cannot aim at a mark they cannot see. The gun, therefore, has to be trained and elevated on information exteriorly obtained, and some object within view—at exactly the same height above the water as the gun-layer—has to be found on which he is to direct his sight.

The gun is now elevated to the approximate range, a shot is fired and the direction of the shot and the distance upon the sight are altered in accordance with the correction. At last a point of aim for the gun-layer, and a sight elevation and deflection are found, and his duty then is to fire away, aiming perhaps at a twig or a leaf a few hundred yards off, while the projectile he discharges falls upon a target four, five, or even six miles off.

The First Attempt

At last all was ready for the great attack. The crew had all been put into khaki, every fitting had been cleared out of the monitors; they had slipped off in the dark the night before and were anchored when, at 3:30 in the morning, all was ready. I will now let a participant continue the story:—

"I woke up hearing the chatter of the seedy boys and the voice of the quartermaster telling someone it was 3:20. I hurried along to my cabin and was dressed in three minutes; khaki shirt, trousers, shoes, and socks. A servant brought me a cup of cocoa and some biscuits, and I then gathered the waterbottle and a haversack of sandwiches, biscuits, brandy flask, glass phial of morphia, box of matches, cigarettes, and made my way up to the top.

"It was quite dark in spite of the half-moon partly hidden by clouds, and men wandering about the docks putting the last touches.

It was impossible to recognise any one as all were in khaki and cap and helmet. By 3:45 all were at general quarters and at —— we weighed and proceeded. Both motor-boats were towing, one on either side amidships. Two whalers anchored off Komo Island, and burning a single light each, acted as a guide to the mouth.

"We soon began to see the dim outline of the shore on the right hand, and —— declared he could distinguish the mouth. There were four of us in the top. We arranged ourselves conveniently, —— and —— taking a side each to look out. The Gunnery Lieutenant took the fore 6-inch and starboard battery. I had the after 6-inch and port battery. I dozed at first for about ten minutes, but as the island neared woke up completely. We had no idea what sort of reception we should have, and speculated about it. It was quite cold looking over the top. The land came nearer and nearer. We were going slow, sounding all the way. On the starboard side it was quite visible as the light grew stronger and stronger. Suddenly when we were well inside the right bank, we heard a shot fired on the starboard quarter, but could not see the flash. Then came another, but only at the third did we see where it came from. It was a field-gun on the right, but we had already passed it, and both it and the pom-pom were turned on the *Mersey* astern of us.

"At least nothing fell near us. It was still not light enough for us to judge the range, but as the alarm had been given, we opened fire with the 3-pounders, starboard side, at the field-gun. As we came up to the point on the portside, I trained all the port battery on the foremost bearing, and opened fire as soon as the guns would bear. We were now going pretty well full speed. Some snipers were hidden in the trees and rushes, and let us have it as we went past. The report of their rifles sounded quite different from ours, but we were abreast before they started, and were soon past. It was just getting light. We were inside the river before the sun rose, and went quite fast up. It was just about dead low water as we entered, neap tide. The river was about 700 yards broad. The banks were well defined by the green trees, mangroves probably, which grew right down to the edges.

"The land beyond was quite flat on the left, but about four miles to the right rose to quite a good height—Pemba Hills. Here and there were native huts well back from the river; we could see them from the top though they were invisible from the deck. On either side as we passed up were creeks of all sorts and sizes at low tides, more of them on the port side than on the starboard. As we passed, or rather before, we turned the port or starboard batteries on them and swept either side. The gun-layers had orders to fire at anything that moved or looked suspicious. We controlled them more or less, and gave them the bearings of the creeks. —— was in charge of those on deck, and the crews themselves fired or ceased fire if they saw anything or had sunk anything. We checked them from time to time as the next creek opened up.

"We were looking ahead most of the time, but I believe (from ——) we sank three *dhows* and a boat. Whether they were harmless or not, I don't know, but it had to be done as a precaution. We made a fine noise, the sharp report of the five 3-pounders and one 4.7 and the crackle of the machine-guns (four a side) must have been heard for miles. The *Hyacinth*, the tugs, the *Trent*, the *Weymouth*, and other odd craft were demonstrating at the other mouths of the Rufigi, and we could hear the deep boom of their 6-inch now and then. I believe, too, that there was a demonstration by colliers, etc., off Dar-es-Salaam at the same time.

"I had thought that the entry would be the worst part, but it was not much. A few bullets got us and marked the plates or went through the hammocks but no one was hit, and as our noise completely drowned the report of their rifles I doubt if many knew we were being sniped. The forecastle hands knew all about it later on. As they hauled in the anchor or let it go, they nipped behind any shelter there was, and could hear the bullets *zip-zip* into the sandbags. The *Mersey* astern was blazing away into the banks just as we were. There was probably nothing in most of the creeks—but we did not know it then.

"It was 6:30 o'clock by the time we reached 'our' island, where the river branches into three, at the end of which we were to anchor. We were steering straight up the middle of the stream, and then swung slowly round to port, dropped the stern anchor, let out seventy fathoms of wire, dropped the main anchor, went astern, and then tightened in both cables, so that we were anchored fast bow and stern. As soon as we steadied down a bearing was taken on the chart and the gun laid—about eight minutes' work. It was then found that, thanks to the curious run of the current, the fore 6-inch would not bear, and we had to take up the bow anchor and let it go again to get us squarer towards the *Koenigsberg*.

"We could see the aeroplane right high up, and received the signal 'open fire.' We were not quite ready, however. From the moment when we turned to port to take up our firing position to the time, we were finally ready and had laid both guns, occupied about twenty minutes. The *Koenigsberg* started firing at us five minutes before we were ready to start. Their first shot (from one gun only) fell on the island, the next was on the edge of it, and very soon she was straddling us. Where they were spotting from, I don't know, but they must have been in a good position, and their spotting was excellent. They never lost our range. The firing started, and for the next two hours both sides were hard at it. I don't believe any ship has been in a hotter place without being hit. Their shooting was extraordinarily good. Their salvoes of fire at first dropped 100 short, 50 over, 20 to the right—then straddled us—then just short—then all round us, and so on. We might have been hit fifty times—they could not have fired better; but we were not hit at all, though a piece of shell was picked up on the forecastle.

"The river was now a curious sight, as dead fish were coming to the surface everywhere. It was the *Koenigsberg's* shells bursting in the water which did the damage, and there were masses of them everywhere—mostly small ones.

"We were firing all the time, of course. I attended to the W/T, and passed the messages to the Gunnery Lieutenant, who made the corrections and passed them to the guns. —— watched the aeroplane and the banks as far as possible. —— attended to the conning tower voice pipe. We got H.T. fairly soon, and the *Koenigsberg's* salvoes were now only four guns. We heard the boom; then before it had finished came *whizz-z-z-z* or *plop, plop, plop, plop*, as the shells went just short or over. They were firing much more rapidly than we, and I should think more accurately, but if I had been in the *Koenigsberg* I should, probably, have thought the opposite!

"All this time the 3-pounders had occasional outbursts as they saw, or thought they saw, something moving. Occasionally, too, the smoke and fumes from our funnel drifted across the top, and it was unpleasant for a minute or two. We could see now where the *Koenigsberg* was, and the smoke from her funnels, or that our shells made. She was firing salvoes of four with great rapidity and regularity, about three times a minute, and every one of them close. Some made a splash in the water so near that you could have reached the place with a boat-hook.

"At 7:40 (so I am told, as, though I tried I lost all count of time) a shell hit the fore 6-inch of the *Mersey* and a column of flame shot up. Four were killed and four wounded. Part of the shield was blown away. Only one man remained standing, and after swaying about he fell dead. One had his head completely blown off. Another was lying with his arm torn out at the shoulder, and his body covered with yellow flames from a lyddite charge which caught. The R. N. R. Lieutenant in charge was knocked senseless and covered with blood, but had only a scratch on the wrist to show for it. The gun-layer had an extraordinary escape, and only lost three fingers. Two men escaped as they had just gone forward to weigh the anchor. A burning charge fell into the shell room below, but was fortunately got out. Another shell burst in the motor-boat alongside the *Mersey* and sank it.

"One burst in the water about a foot from the side, and we thought she was holed. The *Mersey* captain then wisely moved and went down river, taking up a position of 1,000 yards down, by the right bank (looking at the *Koenigsberg*). She started in again with her after gun, the other being disabled. For an hour and twenty minutes we went on, and the *Koenigsberg's* salvoes came steadily and regularly back, as close as ever. It seemed as if it could not go on much longer. We registered four hits, and the salvoes were reduced from four to three, and later to two, and then to one gun. Whether we had reduced them to silence or whether the *Koenigsberg's* crew left them and saved ammunition it is impossible to say.

"The aeroplane spotting had been fair, but now someone else started in and made the signals unintelligible. Then we got spotting corrections from two sources—both differing widely. Finally, the aeroplane made "W. O." (going home). We weighed and took up station again by the *Mersey*. She moved to get out of our way, and when another aeroplane came, we started it again. The replies from the *Koenigsberg* were not so frequent, and nothing like so accurate. It was as if they could not spot the fall of shot. The aeroplane soon disappeared, and as we could see the mast of the *Koenigsberg* (I could only see one personally) and a column of smoke which varied in thickness from time to time, we tried to spot for ourselves. It was useless as, though we saw the burs (or thought we did) in line with the masts, we did not know whether they were over or short. Finally, we moved up the river nearer, still keeping on the right side, and set to work again.

"There were two cruisers—*Weymouth* and *Pyramus*, I think—at the mouth. The *Weymouth* did a good deal of firing at Pemba Hill and a native village close to us, where there might be spotters.

"When we reached W/T corrections now they were of no use. Most were 'did not observe fall of shot,' or 600 short. We went up 1,000, but still received the same signal—whether from the aeroplane or the *Koenigsberg*, I don't know. It was most confusing. We crept up the scale to maximum elevation. Finally, we moved up the river again, but put our nose on the mud. We were soon off, and moved over to the other side and continued firing, spotting as well as we could (but getting nothing definite) till four o'clock, when we packed up and prepared to come out. We swept the banks again on both sides, but only at the entrance was there opposition.

We made such a noise ourselves that we drowned the report of any shots fired at us. Two field-guns made good practice at us from the right bank (looking at the *Koenigsberg*). "One came very close indeed to the top—so much so that we all turned to look at each other, thinking it must have touched somewhere. One burst about five yards over us. Another burst fifteen yards from the *Mersey*, and a second hit her sounding boom. We could see the white smoke of the discharge and fired lyddite, but the object was invisible.

"It was getting dusk as we got outside at full speed. The secure was sounded at about 4:45. We had been at general quarters for thirteen hours, and eleven of them had been under fire. Outside the other ships were waiting for us near Komo Island, and we went straight alongside the *Trent*. Each ship cheered us as we passed. The *Mersey* put her wounded on the *Trent*, and then pushed off to bury the dead.

"Tuesday, July 6, was the day of the first attempt, and one of the worst I ever had or am likely to have. We were at our stations from 3:45 a.m. till 4:45 p.m., and eleven hours of that were under fire. The engine-room people were not relieved the whole time, and they were down there the whole time in a temperature of 132°-135°! It was hot up in the top—but child's play to the engine room."

Success

On July 11 the second attack was made, but made in a very different manner from the first. Once more let us allow the same writer to complete the story:—

"We went to General Quarters at 10:40 a.m. and were inside the entrance by 11:40. How well we seemed to know the place! I knew exactly where the beastly field guns at the mouth would open fire and exactly when they would cease—as we pushed in, and so if their shots went over us, they would land on the opposite bank among their own troops. Very soon came the soft whistle of the shell, then again and again—but we were nearing the entrance and they turned on the *Mersey*. They hit her twice, wounding two men and knocking down the after 6-inch gun crew—none was hurt, however. I spotted a boat straight ahead making across the river for dear life—they may only have been natives, but we fired the 6-inch at them till they leapt ashore and disappeared.

"Up the river we went. I knew each creek, and almost each tree, and as before we blazed into them just before we passed.

"We left the *Mersey* at the place where we anchored last time in the hope that she would draw the *Koenigsberg's* fire and leave us a free hand. The *Koenigsberg*, however, fired one salvo at her and then for the rest of the day concentrated on us. She was plugging us for seventeen minutes before we could return her fire. The salvoes of four were dropping closer than ever if possible and afterwards almost every man in the ship found a bit of German shell on board as a souvenir. They were everywhere—in the sandbags, on the decks, round the engine room—but not a soul was even scratched!

"We went on higher up the river than last time and finally anchored just at the top of 'our' old island. As the after 6-inch gun's crew were securing the stern anchor two shells fell, one on either side, within three feet of the side, and drenched the quarter-deck. It was a very critical time. If she hit us, we were probably finished, and she came as near as possible without actually touching. I had bet 5*s.* that she would start with salvoes of four guns, and I won my bet. They did not last long, however, once we opened fire. It was a near thing, and had to end pretty quickly one way or the other. We had received orders that she must be destroyed, and the captain, the night before, had told all hands assembled on the quarter-deck that we had to do it. We intended to go up nearer and nearer, and if necessary, sight her. Of course, we could not have gone through it—but there is no doubt that on the 11th it was either the monitors or the *Koenigsberg*.

"We had no sooner anchored and laid the guns (the chart proved to be one mile out in the distance from us to the *Koenigsberg*!) than the aeroplane signalled she was ready to spot. Our first four salvoes, at about one minute interval, were all signalled as 'Did not observe fall of shot.' We came down 400, then another 400 and more to the left. The next was spotted as 200 yards over and about 200 to the right. The next 150 short and 100 to the left. The necessary orders were sent to the guns, and at the seventh salvo we hit with one and were just over with the other. We hit eight times in the next twelve shots! It was frightfully exciting. The *Koenigsberg* was now firing salvoes of three only. The aeroplane signalled all hits were forward, so we came a little left to get her amidships.

"The machine suddenly signalled 'Am hit: coming down; send a boat.' And there she was about half way between us and the *Koenigsberg* planing down. As they fell, they continued to signal our shots, for we, of course, kept firing. The aeroplane fell into the water about 150 yards from the *Mersey* and turned a somersault; one man was thrown clear, but the other had a struggle to get free. Finally, both got away and were swimming for ten minutes before the *Mersey's* motor-boat reached them—beating ours by a short head. They were uninjured and as merry as crickets!

"We kept on firing steadily the whole time, as we knew we were hitting—about one salvo a minute. The *Koenigsberg* was now firing two guns; it is hard to be certain, as there was much to do and a good noise going on. Still, within seventeen minutes of our opening fire I noticed and logged it down that she was firing two. She may have been reduced to that before, but she never fired more after.

"In a very short time there was a big explosion from the direction of the *Koenigsberg*, and from then on, she was never free from smoke—sometimes more, sometimes less; at one moment belching out clouds of black smoke, then yellow, with dull explosions from time to time. We kept on firing regularly ourselves, one salvo to the minute—or perhaps two salvoes in three minutes, but the gun-layers were told to keep cool and make sure of their aim. There was one enormous explosion which shot up twice as high as the *Koenigsberg's* masts, and the resulting smoke was visible from our deck. The men sent up a huge cheer.

"For some time now, we had had no reply from the *Koenigsberg*. At 12:53 I fancy she fired one gun, but I was not certain. She certainly did not fire afterwards. As our guns were getting hot, we increased the range from 9,550 to 9,575, and later to 9,625—as when hot the shots are apt to fall short. Fine columns of smoke, black, white, and yellow, and occasional dull reports rewarded us, but we were making no mistake and kept at it. The aeroplane was not available, and we had no one to spot for us, remember; still we could see the *K.'s* masts from our foretop, and the smoke, etc., told its own tale.

"Another aeroplane turned up, and we now signalled the *Mersey* to pass on upstream and open fire nearer. She gave us a great cheer as she passed.

"We raised our topmast and had a look at the *Koenigsberg*. She was a fine sight. One mast was leaning over and the other was broken at the maintop, and smoke was pouring out of the mast as out of a chimney. The funnels were gone, and she was a mass of smoke and flame from end to end. We had done all the firing which had destroyed her. The *Mersey* only started afterwards. That was part of the plan. *Only one ship was to fire at a time, and then there could be no possible confusion in the spotting corrections*; it was a lesson we learned on the Tuesday before! We started.

"The *Mersey* was then to move up past her and fire for an hour and so on. Fortunately, it was not necessary, and as it turned out would have been impossible. If we had gone on, we should probably be there now! When the *Mersey* passed us, she struck a bar about 1,000 yards higher up, and after trying to cross in two different places 100 yards apart, anchored for firing. There was only eight feet of water on the bar and the tide was falling. If we had got up, we should probably have had to wait twelve hours for high tide, and probably the Germans would have annoyed us from the banks!

"The *Mersey* fired about twenty salvoes and made several hits, and as the aeroplane had signalled 'O. K.' (target destroyed) we prepared to leave the river. Before we went the Gunnery Lieutenant and myself went to the top of the mast to get a better view, and I took a photo of the smoke, resting the camera on the very top of the topmast! The captain came up too, and there were the three of us clinging to the lightning conductor with one arm, glasses in the other, and our feet on the empty oil drum we had fixed up there as a crow's-nest.

"Just as we were starting back, we saw some telegraph poles crossing a creek behind us. It was undoubtedly the communication used by the German spotters. We let fly with everything and smashed them up. A pole is not an easy thing to hit, and I expect the destruction of those two cost the government about £300 in ammunition.

"All the way down we swept the banks and made up our minds to knock out the field guns at the mouth if we possibly could. We tried our best, but I don't think we touched them. They fired on us till we were out of range. They did not hit—but I saw one fragment about six inches by one inch picked up on the boat deck.

"Two tugs were waiting over the bar, and after giving us a cheer took us on tow to help us back to *Trent*. The *Weymouth*, with the admiral on board, came round and then passed us at speed; all hands lined the ship and, led by the small white figure of the admiral on the bridge, gave us three splendid cheers. It was one of the finest sights I have ever seen. We answered back—and what a difference there was to our cheers of Tuesday last. We made about three times the noise. . . .

"I went to the captain's cabin for half an hour to copy out the notes I had taken. From the very first shot we fired I kept a record of every shot fired by the 6-inch guns, and all I could see or hear round about, writing something every minute, i.e. 12:37 2 guns. H.T. J.M. 12:38 2 guns. H.T. 12:38½ (*Koenigsberg* firing 2). Column of smoke; aeroplane hit and coming down, etc.

"I ought to explain that 'J.M.,' 'B.F.,' 'F.20,' 'G.15,' 'H.T.,' and so on are signals from the aeroplanes. 'H.T.' means 'a hit.' In order to make sure of the right letters having passed the man shouts not 'H.T.' alone, 'H. for Harry, T for Tommy,' and then there can be no confusion. The man at the voice pipe in the conning tower simply roared out 'H. for Harry, T. for Tommy,' each time it was signalled. Well, when I was making my copy in his cabin on the way back, the captain came in for a moment. He leaned his hand quietly on my shoulder and with a huge sigh said, 'If ever I live to have a son, his name shall be Harry Tommy!' I firmly believe he meant it too, at the time!"

If the people in *Severn* and *Mersey* had had a narrow squeak for it, not once but a dozen times, from *Koenigsberg's* salvoes, the spotting party in the aeroplane must have had just as exciting a time. And, as we have seen from the foregoing account, with them *Koenigsberg* was more fortunate. On July 11th everything was against Lieutenant Cull, the first pilot to go up, and Flight-Sub-Lieutenant Arnold, who was acting as observer. To begin with it was a cloudy day, and the machine had to be kept dangerously low if the observer was to do his work. The aeroplane got over the target at about 12:20, while *Mersey* was firing hard. But this fire of the *Mersey* had nothing to do with the organised effort to destroy the enemy. It was merely a blind—an effort to get the enemy's observer on land to deflect the fire on that ship on to *Mersey*, while *Severn* got ready for the real work.

The aeroplane, therefore, paid no attention to *Mersey's* fire and telegraphed no observations. Ten minutes later *Severn* opened fire and *Mersey* ceased. *Mersey's* diversion did for a time bring *Koenigsberg's* guns in her direction. But no sooner did *Severn* open fire than she got the full benefit of *Koenigsberg's* salvoes of four, which followed each other at intervals of about a minute. Five minutes after *Severn* opened at 12:30, *Koenigsberg's* salvoes began to straddle her. Nine minutes after *Severn* opened fire the aeroplane signalled first hit. And less than ten minutes after that Lieutenant Arnold telegraphed:

We are hit; send boat.

In point of fact, it is probable that the aeroplane's engine had been slightly injured earlier.

For, dangerously low as the machine had to fly at the beginning, it was found impossible to keep even at that height, and as it got lower and slower, it obviously became an easier mark for the *Koenigsberg's* 12-pounders. At 12:46 a terrific bump was felt in the machine, and shortly afterwards the engine broke up with a rattle and a crash, and there was nothing for it but to start sliding down. Imagine the situation! The machine, between 3,000 and 4,000 feet in the air, nearly three miles from the monitors; the only possible hope of safety to make this long glide and then to land—if the bull may be permitted—in a narrow strip of river bordered by impenetrable bush—the bush dotted with lofty trees! If the machine missed the river and hit the trees, it was certain death wherever it landed. If it missed the trees and hit the river, there was palpably no safety unless it was within a very short distance of the monitors. For nowhere else did the pilot and observer stand the faintest chance of rescue. A situation more absolutely desperate could hardly be imagined.

It was certainly not one in which the seemingly doomed occupants could have been blamed if they had thought of their safety and of nothing else. But while the pilot was, quite properly, concentrating his attention on performing as nice a feat in flying as can be imagined, Flight-Lieutenant Arnold, content to leave this matter in the skilled hands of his comrade, continued imperturbably to carry on his duties.

Severn, having got the range, naturally continued firing. Flight-Lieutenant Arnold, having been sent up to observe, continued observing, and each shot that he observed, on what must have seemed his last glide to certain death, was signalled to the control parties on board the monitor. The gist of this was that six out of ten shots were hitting, and apparently were hitting steadily, but all were striking *Koenigsberg* in the bows. Arnold's last achievement as an observer was to deflect this fire amidships and to the stern.

And he had hardly succeeded before the 'plane crashed into the water 500 yards from the *Mersey*. *Mersey* had her motor-boat ready and it was sent full speed to the rescue. Arnold had no difficulty in getting himself free, but Lieutenant Cull was not so fortunate. In the excitement of his task he had forgotten to loosen the straps that held his belt and feet, and was fairly under water before he realised his predicament. How he wrenched himself free of these impediments is somewhat difficult to understand, and it is not surprising that his apparel suffered somewhat severely from his efforts. When he came to the surface, he found Arnold scrambling about the wrecked machine in search of him, and both were got safely into the boat. The machine, smashed and waterlogged in the river, was of course past saving, and there was nothing for it but to demolish it. Take it all in all, few prettier pieces of work in the air—whether we look at the flight craftsmanship of the thing, or the practical use that the last moments of flight were put to—have yet been recorded.

A Problem in Control

There are several features in these operations that are of great interest. To begin with, the destruction of a ship by the indirect fire of another ship had not, so far as I know, been systematically attempted before. There was indeed a story of *Queen Elizabeth* having sunk a Turkish transport by a shot fired clean over the Gallipoli peninsula. In the case of the *Queen Elizabeth's* victim the target was not only incredibly far off but actually under way. But this must be regarded as amongst the flukes of war, if indeed that may be called a fluke when the right measure had been taken to ensure success. Still, it was more probable that the attempt might be made a hundred times without a hit being made than that the first shot fired should have landed straight on the target. But here on the Rufigi the monitors had gone up after making ample preparations and after full practice, to achieve a particular object. It was to destroy a very small ship at a range which, for the gun employed, must be considered extraordinarily great.

Ten thousand yards is relatively a longer range for a 6-inch gun than is, say, 18,000 for a 15-inch. But while in this respect the task proposed was extraordinarily difficult, there was one element present that would distinguish it from almost any other known use of naval guns. In engaging land forts, both on the Belgian coast and off Gallipoli, there had been ample experience with a stationary target engaged by a stationary ship.

But here the firing ship was not only stationary in the sense that it was moored, but was practically at rest in that it was lying in smooth water with no roll or pitch to render the gun-layers' aim uncertain. The current did cause a certain veering, but not a sufficient movement to embarrass laying. But if in this respect the conditions were easy, they were extraordinarily difficult in every other. The monitors, for instance, were as much exposed to *Koenigsberg's* fire as was *Koenigsberg* to that of the monitors, and whereas *Koenigsberg's* guns could be spotted from a position on shore the monitors' fire had to be spotted by aeroplane.

The whole of the operations of *Severn* and *Mersey* then were not only carried out under fire, but under an attack that on the second day as well as the first was extraordinarily persistent and extraordinarily accurate. That in the course of two days only one of our ships was hit, and that one only once, must be considered a curiosity, for so good were the gunnery arrangements of *Koenigsberg* that each monitor when under fire was straddled again and again by salvoes, and when not straddled had the 4.2 shells falling in bunches either just short or just over them. The explanation of her having failed to get more hits than she did, while ultimately *Severn's* was completely effective, does not lie in any inferiority of skill, but almost entirely in the fact that the range, if exceptionally great for a 6-inch gun, was almost fabulous for a 4.2, and next that *Koenigsberg* was a much larger target than either *Severn* or *Mersey*.

Koenigsberg was probably aground, and therefore showing from three to four feet more of her side than she would at sea. Monitors are a craft with a very, very low freeboard, with a comparatively small central house built up amidships. As a point-blank target *Koenigsberg* would probably be more than twice the superficial area that either *Mersey* or *Severn* would present. The contrast between them as virtual targets, that is, the target that would be presented to the shell as it descended from a height upon the ship, would not, of course, be so great, because the monitors were each of them wider than the German cruiser, but even as a virtual target the *Koenigsberg* was much more favourable for the British guns.

But the master difficulty of the situation was for the men on the spot, without previous experience of indirect fire, and unaided apparently by any advice from headquarters as to the result of service experiments elsewhere, to extemporize all the processes for finding and keeping the range of a target invisible from the ship. The two essential elements in these processes were (1) for the observer in the aeroplane to note where each shot fell, and (2) to *inform the ship that fired it* exactly what the position of the impact was, whether to the right or to the left, over or short, and an approximate measurement in yards of its distance from the target.

No one of those concerned had ever engaged in any similar operation. The aviators had not only never carried observers to spot naval gunfire, they had none of them ever even flown in the tropics, where the conditions of flight differ altogether from those in more temperate zones. The observers were even more new to the work than the aviators. Apparently, some of them had never been in flying machines before. They not only had to learn the elements of spotting, they had to become familiar with the means of sending communications. There seems at one time to have been considerable doubt as to the best means to employ for communication.

The means would have to include not only a system of sending messages, whether by wireless, by lights flashing a Morse code or otherwise, but the production of a code as well. When these points were settled, the preliminary practices of Mafia Island gave what appeared to be sufficient experience to show that right principles were being followed. Only when this practice had given satisfactory results was the first attempt of July 6th made.

In the course of that day's firing the observers reported eight possible hits during the first phase of the firing, and none afterwards. Once or twice smoke was seen to issue from *Koenigsberg* and in the course of the day the number of guns in her salvo fell from five to three, and ultimately, she was employing only a single gun. The monitors had fired approximately 500 rounds to obtain these hits, and had probably double this number fired at them. Opinions differed as to the result, but that some thought *Koenigsberg* had finally been destroyed is apparent from the character of the rear-admiral's message to the Admiralty. Reflection, however, appears to have made it clear that *Koenigsberg* was very far indeed from being really out of action, and it became necessary to inquire why there should have been any uncertainty in the matter. The crux of the position was this.

Fire had opened at seven in the morning and continued till nearly half-past four in the afternoon. But when the character of the messages transmitted by the observers came under critical examination, it seemed almost certain that no hits were made at all after the first hour. Every kind of explanation for so indecisive and disappointing a result was examined. It was disappointing because it had been shown that it was quite practical to make hits, and it seemed as if there must be something wrong if the hitting could not be continued. Every possible cause of breakdown was put under examination. Had there been anything wrong with the wireless transmitters in the aeroplanes? Had the receiving gear in the monitors broken down? Were the observers too inexperienced, hasty, or unreliable? Had the guns become worn or too hot? Were the sights at fault?

But when it came to the point each of these criticisms broke down. There was no reason to distrust the observers, and as all the ships in the offing had received the messages, the transmitting gear must have been above suspicion. Then the monitors' records tallied with the ships' records, so that there was nothing wrong with the receivers. When the observers themselves were put through their paces, it seemed that over an area of at least half a mile, say 600 yards short of the target and 200 over, there was really no possibility of making mistakes about where the shots fell, for in this area it was all either open water or dry sand. But outside of this comparatively narrow area there was thick bush, and to an observer at the height of between 3,000 and 4,000 feet even a bursting shell falling in a forest whose trees ran from between 70 to 150 feet high, affords a very uncertain mark.

And after 8 p.m. it seemed that only very few shells fell in the belt where their impact was visible, and that sometimes, for very considerable periods, every shot seemed to go into the forest. Could the guns have suddenly become absolutely unreliable? But tests were made, and the guns proved to be quite as accurate as they were before the firing began, and indeed the exactitude of the results precluded this form of error from explaining the failure to complete the business.

At last, when the firing times of the two ships were compared with the observers' records of the pitching of the shell, the true explanation leapt into sight. The whole show had broken down over the old difficulty of the identification of shots. The people in the aeroplanes could not tell whether a particular shot had been fired by *Mersey* or *Severn*, and as both ships got the message, neither could tell whose shot had been observed. It followed therefore that the consequent correction was often put on to the wrong gun. Thus, for example, suppose *Mersey* had fired a shot 300 yards over the target that fell in bush and was invisible to the observers, while *Severn* had fired one that was 200 yards short and visible.

The observers would wireless 200 short, whereupon the *Mersey* would think that this message was intended for her, and raise her sight by this amount. Her next round, of course, would go still farther into the bush, and suppose this was visible or partially visible to the observer, who might perhaps have missed *Severn's* next round, he might telegraph back 500 or 600 over, a correction that *Severn* might take to herself, and lose her next shot in the bush short of the target. The men on the Rufigi in short discovered for themselves, by their experiences on this first arduous day against the *Koenigsberg*, that the problem of correcting the fire of two separated batteries by the work of a single observer is so exceedingly difficult of solution as to make it hardly worth attempting.

The lessons so painfully brought home were put to immediate and most successful use. It was resolved on the second attempt that only one monitor should fire at a time. This was not of course the only experience of value obtained in the first day's operation for when all the results were collated and compared, a pretty exact knowledge of the actual range from the chosen anchorage to the target was obtained, so that on the second day there were fewer initial rounds lost before shell began to fall in the immediate surroundings of the enemy, where the position of each could be verified. When all ambiguity as to the meaning of corrections was removed, the process of finding the target and keeping the range became exceedingly simple.

As will be seen from the narrative, the serious work of the second day began when *Severn* opened fire about half-past twelve. Nine minutes later, after quite deliberate fire, she obtained her first hit, and from then on continued hitting with great regularity. But before she had been firing ten minutes the spotting aeroplane was disabled and came down. Though the *Koenigsberg* herself was invisible, the columns of lyddite fumes and smoke sent up by the hits could be seen over the trees, and such columns indicated that hits were being made very frequently.

Within a quarter of an hour of the first hit, *Koenigsberg* ceased her return fire, and shortly after this a huge volume of smoke of a totally different colour from that sent up by lyddite indicated that there had been a great explosion in the ship. When the second aeroplane came out to resume the work of spotting, *Mersey* took up the work of firing in *Severn's* place. *Severn* had ceased fire at 1:35 and *Mersey* opened at a quarter past two. But it soon became clear that it was unnecessary for her to proceed with the work, and that with the explosion at 1:15 the business of the *Koenigsberg* was finished.

What two ships firing continuously for eight hours on July 6th had failed to achieve, a single ship had accomplished in probably fifteen minutes. It was the most perfect exemplification imaginable of the difference in results that wrong and right systems of gunnery produce. The skill shown on the second day was no better than on the first. It was a change of method that made the difference.

What is of special interest is this. Up to the year 1909, it appeared quite premature to discuss methods of concentrating the fire of several ships on a single distant target, until right methods had been discovered for making sure of hitting it with the guns of a single ship. But by the winter of 1909, there seemed to be sufficient experience to show that a complete solution of the simpler problem was assured, and that the time had come for considering how two or more ships could combine their armament. The difficulty of the matter was soon made obvious. While great guns do not all shoot exactly alike, it is possible to ascertain by experiment the individual differences of all the guns in a single ship, and to vary the sight scales so that, at all critical ranges, they should give identical results. But what can be done for a single battery of eight or ten guns cannot be done by experiment for two units of such batteries.

If then two ships are to be employed at the same target, it was the very essence of the matter if two processes were carried on simultaneously to obtain one result, that each process should be so organised as to run as if the other were not going at all. Now ships' guns at sea can be corrected only from positions high up in the masts. It therefore became clear that if the firing ship allowed a fixed interval, say three or four seconds, to elapse after a sister ship had fired, before sending her own salvo at the enemy, it would be quite easy, by keeping a record of the time of flight of the projectiles, to pick out her own amongst the salvoes falling in rapid succession on the target, so that there should be no possibility of her mixing up her own shells with her neighbours'.

It is now many years since it was suggested that gongs driven by a clockwork device, which could be set to the time of flight, would simplify this method of identification. Suppose the time of flight to be twelve seconds, the gong would be set to this interval and the clockwork started into motion simultaneously with the firing of the salvo. The observers watch the target and pay no attention to any shots that fall, except those whose incidence coincided with the ringing of the gong.

The essence of this system was the ear-marking, so to speak, of each separate salvo as it went away. But it was manifestly not a principle on which observers placed at a distance from a ship could work. If they were to do their work, they must employ some totally different means of identification. Else indirect firing could only be carried on by one ship at a time.

My correspondence in 1909, and 1910, shows that these principles were fully grasped by many gunnery officers in the navy in these years. And I must confess I was extremely astonished when our proceedings at the Dardanelles in March and February and April showed that there was no common practice in the matter throughout the navy. At last, in the month of May 1915, I set out these elementary *principia* of indirect firing in *Land and Water*.

> The difficulty in correcting the fire of a multitude of ships is, it may be added, twofold, because each salvo must be identified as coming from a particular ship, and then that ship be informed of the correction. There is apparently no escape from the necessity of having a separate spotter for each ship. If the spotter is in an independent position, the obstacles in the way of this double task are considerable. And aeroplanes are not a satisfactory substitute. *At best an aeroplane can help one ship only.*

It will be observed that, in July, the officers at the Rufigi had to work them all out again for themselves!

Nothing could better illustrate the curious individualism which governs the organisation of our sea forces. Each ship, each squadron, each fleet seems to come to the study of these things as if they were virgin problems, entirely unaided by advice or information from the central authorities, so that there is not only no uniformity of practice—in itself a not unmitigated evil—but what is really serious, a total absence of uniformity of knowledge. I am the last person in the world to suggest that all naval affairs should be regulated in every petty detail from Whitehall. There are quite enough forces at work to repress freedom of thought or restrict liberty to investigate and experiment in the fullest possible way. But there is surely the widest possible difference between a restraining tyranny and an intelligent system of communicating proved principles and the results of successful practice.

CHAPTER 10

Capture of H.I.G.M.S. "Emden"

On November 11, 1914, the Secretary of the Admiralty issued a statement which, after referring to the self-internment of *Koenigsberg* in the Rufigi River, and the measures taken to keep her there, proceeded as follows:

> Another large combined operation by fast cruisers, against the *Emden*, has been for some time in progress. In this search, which covered an immense area, the British cruisers have been aided by French, Russian, and Japanese vessels working in harmony. His Majesty's Australian ships *Melbourne* and *Sydney* were also included in these movements.
> On Monday morning news was received that the *Emden*, which had been completely lost after her action with the *Jemchug*, had arrived at Keeling, Cocos Island, and had landed an armed party to destroy the wireless station and cut the cable.
> Here she was caught and forced to fight by His Majesty's Australian ship *Sydney* (Captain John C. T. Glossop, R.N.). A sharp action took place, in which the *Sydney* suffered the loss of three killed and fifteen wounded.
> The *Emden* was driven ashore and burnt. Her losses in personnel are reported as very heavy. All possible assistance is being given the survivors by various ships which have been despatched to the scene.
> With the exception of the German squadron now off the coast of Chile, the whole of the Pacific and Indian oceans are now clear of the enemy's warships.

The material news was that *Emden* had been caught and sunk. She was one of Germany's small fast cruisers, armed like the rest with

4.2 guns, and therefore no very formidable match for the ship that met and encountered her. The work of her destruction, we afterwards learned, had been done by Captain Glossop of *Sydney*, with a rapidity and neatness unsurpassed in any naval engagement of the war before or, indeed, since. But at the moment when the news came, the method of the thing was of far less importance than the thing itself, for it is no exaggeration to say that at the end of the first week of November the spirits of the nation were at an exceedingly low ebb. There was a marked uneasiness as to the naval position. The successes of the Fleet had been achieved without fighting, and it looked as if, in the naval war, we were not only watching, almost abjectly, for the initiative of the enemy, but that we were unable to defeat that initiative when it was taken.

The public therefore forgot that 98 *per cent.* of our trade was carrying on as before, that our sea communications with our armies were under no threat, that the enemy's battle force was keeping completely within the security of its harbours. There had been but one active demonstration of British naval strength—the affair of the Bight of Heligoland. But a dropping fire of bad news had made our nerves acutely sensitive. It was submarines people feared most. Writing at the time, I summarised the general attitude of the public as it appeared to me:

> Long before the war began the public had been prepared by an active agitation to believe that the submarine had superseded all other forms of naval force, so that when one cruiser after another was sent to the bottom, almost within hail of the English coast, people really began to believe that no ship could be safe, and that (under a form of attack that was equally impossible to foresee, evade, or resist) our vaunted strength in Dreadnoughts must in time dwindle altogether away. Then there were not wanting circumstances that, superficially at least, looked as if the Admiralty's war plans and distribution of the fleet were not adequate to their purpose. In at least one conspicuous instance, the resources of our enemy had been too great either for the means or the measures of our admirals.

> War had not been declared more than a day or two before the *Goeben* and *Breslau* made their way through the Mediterranean and escaped unengaged to the Dardanelles. The public knew that we had two powerful squadrons of ships in these

The *Emden* under attack

waters, one overwhelmingly stronger than the German force; the other, on almost every conceivable train of reasoning, at least a match for it. (I should not say this now.) It seemed utterly humiliating that, with the French Fleet as our allies, and with Germany having none, so important a unit as the *Goeben* should have got away scot-free. Then it was not long before we heard of the depredations of the *Emden*, and of British ships being chased and threatened in the North and South Atlantic by other German cruisers.

Against all these things could be set more cheering incidents. Twice the North Sea was swept from top to bottom by the British Fleet, the first resulting in the sinking of three, if not four, cruisers and one destroyer, and in the driving off, apparently hopelessly crippled, of two other cruisers and a great number of smaller craft. The second sweep seemed to show that the entire German Fleet had sought safety in port. Then the *Carmania* sank the *Cap Trafalgar*, and the *Undaunted*, with a small flotilla of destroyers, ran down and sank an equal flotilla of the enemy's. But these were not sufficient to outweigh the anxiety which the German submarine successes had caused nor did they restore public confidence in the dispositions of the Admiralty in distant seas, where there were still two powerful armed cruisers, a large number of light cruisers, and an unknown number of armed merchantmen still at large.

The whole thing culminated in a series of very disturbing events. First it was announced that German mines had been laid north of Ireland, and that the *Manchester Commerce* had been sunk by striking one. Were any of our waters safe for our own battle squadrons, if the enemy could lay mines with impunity right under our noses? This was swiftly followed by our hearing that the *Good Hope* and *Monmouth* had been sunk by the *Gneisenau* and *Scharnhorst* off Coronel. Then came the sinking of the *Hermes* and the *Niger*, one in mid-Channel, the other lying in the anchorage at Deal. And just when nervous people were wondering whether the mine and submarine had really driven the English Fleet off the sea, only to find that ports were not safe, there came the startling news that a German squadron had appeared off Yarmouth. . . . To many it looked as if this was the last straw.

We had sacrificed four cruisers to patrol the neutral shipping in these waters, and when, almost too late, it was discovered that our methods made them too easy targets for submarines, we announced the closing of the North Sea. The public undoubtedly understood by this that, if we closed the North Sea to neutrals, we had closed it to the German Fleet also, and the appearance of this squadron so soon after the announcement was made, and its escape back to its own harbours without being cut off and brought to action, made people ask if the closing of the North Sea had not really meant that Great Britain had resigned its possession to the enemy.

It is difficult, this being the situation, to overrate how cheering was the news of *Emden's* destruction. (*Vide The Kaiser's Raider! Two Accounts of the S. M. S. Emden During the First World War by One of its Officers* Hellmuth von Mücke; Leonaur 2012.)

If the Canadian naval contingent were the first of our Colonial subjects to shed their blood in this war, then certainly the Australian ship *Sydney* was the first to assert Great Britain's command over distant seas, by the triumphant destruction of a ship that dared to dispute it. We began our debt to the Colonies early.

Captain Glossop's despatch was not published till January 1, but a good many other accounts had been published before, and some have become available since the action.

A very interesting letter from an officer of the *Sydney* was printed in *The Times* of December 15. With this account was also published, later on, a plan of the action which, with certain corrections which I have reason to believe are required, is reproduced here. A second account, by another officer in the *Sydney*, has been sent to me so that it is possible to add some not uninteresting or unimportant details to Captain Glossop's story. But of all of the accounts Captain Glossop's is at once the most interesting and the most complete, and I print it in full, because it is in every respect a model of what a despatch should be:—

"H.M.A.S. *Sydney*, at Colombo,
"15th November, 1914.

"Sir:—I have the honour to report that whilst on escort duty with the convoy under the charge of Captain Silver, H.M.A.S. *Melbourne*, at 6:30 a.m., on Monday, 9th November, a wireless message from Cocos was heard reporting that a foreign warship was off the entrance. I was ordered to raise steam for full speed at 7:0 a.m. and proceed thither. I worked up to 20 knots, and at 9:15 a.m. sighted land ahead and almost immediately the smoke of a ship, which proved to be H.I.G.M.S. *Emden* coming out towards me at a great rate. At 9:40 a.m. fire was opened, she firing the first shot. I kept my distance as much as possible to obtain the advantage of my guns. Her fire was very accurate and rapid to begin with, but seemed to slacken very quickly, all casualties occurring in this ship almost immediately. First the foremost funnel of her went, secondly the foremast, and she was badly on fire aft, then the second funnel went, and lastly the third funnel, and I saw she was making for the beach of North Keeling Island, where she grounded at 11:20 a.m. I gave her two more broadsides and left her to pursue a merchant ship which had come up during the action.

2. "Although I had guns on this merchant ship at odd times during the action, I had not fired, and as she was making off fast, I pursued and overtook her at 12.10, firing a gun across her bows and hoisting International Code Signal to stop, which she did. I sent an armed boat and found her to be the S.S. *Buresk*, a captured British collier, with 18 Chinese crew, 1 English steward, 1 Norwegian cook, and a German Prize Crew of 3 officers, 1 warrant officer and 12 men. The ship unfortunately was sinking, the *Kingston* knocked out and damaged to prevent repairing, so I took all on board, fired 4 shells into her and returned to *Emden*, passing men swimming in the water, for whom I left two boats I was towing from *Buresk*.

3. "On arriving again off *Emden* she still had her colours up at mainmast head. I inquired by signal, International Code, 'Will you surrender?' and received a reply in Morse, 'What signal? No signal books.' I then made in Morse 'Do you surrender?' and subsequently 'Have you received my signal?' to neither of which did I get an answer. The German officers on board gave me to understand that the captain would never surrender, and therefore though reluctantly, I again fired at her at 4:30 p.m., ceasing at 4:35, as she showed white flags and hauled down her ensign by sending a man aloft.

4. "I then left *Emden* and returned and picked up the *Buresk's* two boats, rescuing 2 sailors (5:0 p.m.), who had been in the water all day. I returned and sent in one boat to *Emden*, manned by her own prize crew from *Buresk*, and 1 officer, and stating I would return to their assistance next morning. This I had to do, as I was desirous to find out the condition of cables and Wireless Station at Direction Island. On the passage over I was again delayed by rescuing another sailor (6:30 p.m.), and by the time I was again ready and approaching Direction Island it was too late for the night.

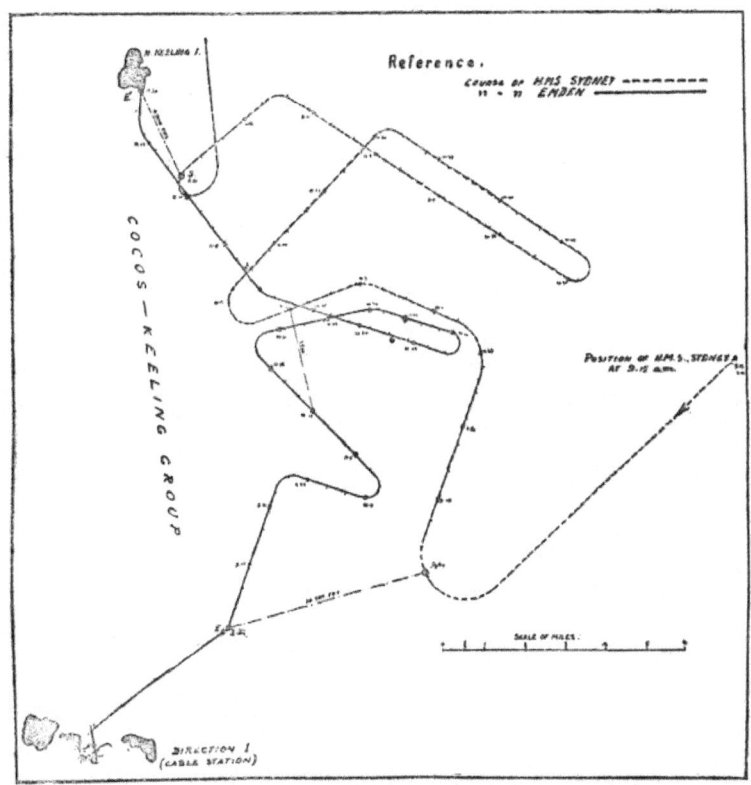

PLAN OF *SYDNEY* AND *EMDEN* IN ACTION

5. "I lay on and off all night, and communicated with Direction Island at 8:0 a.m., 10th November, to find that the *Emden's* party consisting of 3 officers and 40 men, 1 launch and 2 cutters had seized and provisioned a 70-ton schooner (the *Ayesha*), having 4 Maxims, with 2 belts to each. They left the previous night at six o'clock. The Wireless Station was entirely destroyed, 1 cable cut, 1 damaged, and 1 intact. I borrowed a doctor and 2 assistants, and proceeded as fast as possible to *Emden's* assistance.

6. "I sent an officer on board to see the captain, and in view of the large number of prisoners and wounded and lack of accommodation, etc., in this ship, and the absolute impossibility of leaving them where they were, he agreed that if I received his officers and men and all wounded 'then as for such time as they remained in *Sydney* they would cause no interference with ship or fittings, and would be amenable to the ship's discipline.' I therefore set to work at once to

tranship them—a most difficult operation, and the ship being on the weather side of the island and the send alongside very heavy. (*I. e.* the rise and fall of the sea.) The conditions in the *Emden* were indescribable. I received the last from her at 5:0 p.m., then had to go round to the lee side to pick up 20 more men who had managed to get ashore from the ship.

7. "Darkness came on before this could be accomplished, and the ship again stood off and on all night, resuming operations at 5:0 a.m. on 11th November, a cutter's crew having to land with stretchers to bring wounded round to embarking point. A German officer, a doctor, died ashore the previous day. The ship in the meantime ran over to Direction Island to return their doctor and assistants, send cables, and was back again at 10:0 a.m., embarked the remainder of wounded and proceeded for Colombo by 10:35 a.m., Wednesday, 11th November.

8. "Total casualties in *Sydney*: killed 3, severely wounded (since dead) 1, severely wounded 4, wounded 4, slightly wounded 4. In the *Emden* I can only approximately state the killed at 7 officers and 108 men from captain's statement. I had on board 11 officers, 9 warrant officers, and 191 men, of whom 3 officers and 53 men were wounded, and of this number 1 officer and 3 men have since died of wounds.

9. "The damage to *Sydney's* hull and fittings was surprisingly small; in all about 10 hits seem to have been made. The engine and boiler rooms and funnels escaped entirely.

10. "I have great pleasure in stating that the behaviour of the ship's company was excellent in every way, and with such a large proportion of young hands and people under training it is all the more gratifying. The engines worked magnificently, and higher results than trials were obtained, and I cannot speak too highly of the Medical Staff and arrangements on subsequent trip, the ship being nothing but a hospital of a most painful description!

"I have the honour to be, Sir,
   Your obedient Servant,

John C. T. Glossop,
Captain."

The first point of interest in this engagement is the rapidity with which the gunfire on both sides became effective. *Emden* made no attempt to get away, and opened fire before *Sydney* did, and at a range of 10,500 yards. One account says "her first shots fell well together for range, but very much spread out for line. They were all within twenty yards of the ship." Either the gun range-finders were marvels of accuracy, or else they had great luck in picking up the range so quickly. This account proceeds:

> As soon as her first salvo had fallen, she began to fire very rapidly in salvoes, the rate of fire being as high as ten rounds per gun per minute, and very accurate for the first ten minutes.

I draw the reader's attention particularly to this phrase, because it reproduces almost *verbatim* Commodore Tyrwhitt's comment on the fire of the German cruisers in his third action of the Heligoland affair. We find the same phenomenon at the destruction of *Koenigsberg*, whose guns both throughout the first and second day of that affair seem to have had the exact range of the monitors. This testimony to the accuracy of the enemy's fire must be read in connection with Captain Glossop's statement, that in all about ten hits seem to have been made. All accounts agree that no hits were made after the first ten minutes. But if the rate of *Emden's* fire is correctly given, she must have fired 500 rounds in this phase of the action. Ten hits to 500 rounds gives 2 *per cent.* of hits only!

The explanation, both of the Rufigi monitors and of *Sydney's* comparative immunity, is undoubtedly the extreme range at which each action was fought. At such ranges a gun of so small a calibre as the 4.2 would have to be raised to a very high elevation. The projectiles, therefore, would fall very steeply towards the target. In conditions like these salvoes may fall just short and just over, and even straddle the boat fired at, without a single hit being made.

But of the excellence of the *Emden's* shooting and of her control of fire—so long as the fire was controlled—there can be no shadow of doubt whatever. It was obvious that if the battleships were equally good, the German Fleet would prove a serious foe. We must certainly esteem it one of the fortunate chances of this war that when Germany was building her Fleet, her naval authorities were convinced that all fighting would be at short range. Their calculation was that at short range a rapid and accurate fire of smaller pieces should prove just as effective as the slower fire of larger pieces. Her cruisers therefore were armed with 4.2's when ours were being armed with 6-inch, and her battleships with 11-inch guns when ours were being fitted with 12-inch and 13.5's.

In the case of battleships and battle-cruisers, the German constructors had their eye upon a further advantage in the adoption of lighter pieces. The weight saved could be put, and in fact was put, into a more thorough armoured protection. Von Müller, the captain of *Emden*, when he was congratulated, after the capture, on the gallant fight put up, was at first seemingly offended.

> He seemed taken aback and said 'No,' and went away, but presently he came to me and said, 'Thank you very much for saying that, but I was not satisfied; we should have done better. You were very lucky in shooting away my voice pipes in the beginning.'

But if the Germans lost their voice pipes, *Sydney* lost her rangefinder in the opening salvoes. The German fire control had not survived the derangement of its communications. It was not possible to extemporise anything to take their place. We do not hear that the accuracy of *Sydney's* fire lost anything when the rangefinder went.

Both ships appeared, in this action, to have employed, or at least to have attempted to employ, their torpedoes. In an interview with Von Müller reported from Colombo, he is said to have explained that his intention in closing *Sydney* at the opening of the engagement was not to lessen the range so as to bring the ballistics of his guns to an equality with ours, but to get *Sydney* within torpedo range. *Sydney* seems certainly to have fired a torpedo rather less than half-way through the action when the range was at its shortest. But as in the Heligoland affair, so here, the difficulties in getting a hit were insuperable. That *Emden* did not fire a torpedo at the same time is explained by the fact that the action had not proceeded twenty minutes before not only was her steering gear wrecked, so that she had to steer by her screws, but her submerged torpedo flat also was put out of action.

All accounts of the action agree upon the excellent conduct of the men and boys on board *Sydney*. A letter published in *The Times* gives us many evidences of this.

> The hottest part of the action for us was the first half-hour. We opened fire from our port guns to begin with. I was standing just behind No. 1 port, and the gun-layer (Atkins, 1st class Petty Officer) said, 'Shall I load, sir?' I was surprised, but deadly keen there should be no 'flap,' so said, 'No, don't load till you get the order.' Next, he said, '*Emden's* fired, sir.' So, I said 'All right, load, but don't bring the gun to the ready.' I found out afterwards that the order to load had been received by the other guns ten minutes before, and my anti-'flap' precautions, though they did

not the slightest harm, were thrown away on Atkins, who was as cool as a cucumber throughout the action.

It was the boys' quarters on board that suffered most from *Emden's* fire. The same writer says:

Our hits were not very serious. We were 'hulled' in about three places. The shell that exploded in the boys' mess deck, apart from ruining the poor little beggars' clothes, provided a magnificent stock of trophies. For two or three days they kept finding fresh pieces.

They were probably consoled for the lost wardrobe by this treasure of souvenirs.

There are lots of redeeming points in the whole show. Best of all was to see the gun's crew fighting their guns quite unconcerned. When we were last in Sydney, we took on board three boys from the training ship *Tingira*, who had volunteered. The captain said, 'I don't really want them, but as they are keen, I'll take them.' Now the action was only a week or two afterwards, but the two out of the three who were directly under my notice were perfectly splendid. One little slip of a boy did not turn a hair, and worked splendidly. The other boy, a very sturdy youngster, carried projectiles from the hoist to his gun throughout the action without so much as thinking of cover. I do think for two boys absolutely new to their work they were splendid. (The—slightly modified—plan of this action is reproduced by the kind permission of the editor of the *Times*.)

CHAPTER 11

The Career of Von Spee

At the beginning of hostilities, the strategic position in the Pacific and Indian oceans should have been one that could have caused no possible naval anxiety to the Allies. Japan had at once thrown in her lot with us, and as we had squadrons in the China Seas, in the Indian Ocean, and in Australasia there was, when the forces of our eastern allies are added to them, a total naval strength incalculably greater than that at the disposal of the enemy. But this fact notwithstanding, there was for some months extraordinary uncertainty, and the arrangements adopted by the Admiralty permitted a serious attack to be made on our shipping and involved a tragic disaster to a British squadron. The facts of the case are far from being completely known, but the main features of the original situation and its development make it possible to draw certain broad inferences, which are probably correct.

In the summer of 1914, the German sea forces at Tsing-Tau consisted of two armoured cruisers, two light cruisers, certain destroyers and gun-boats. Leaving the destroyers and gun-boats behind, Von Spee in the month of June abandoned his base at Tsing-Tau, and, after calling at Nagasaki, made for the German possessions in the Caroline Islands. His flag flew in *Scharnhorst*, and this ship with her sister vessel *Gneisenau* constituted his main strength. He had the two light cruisers, *Leipzig* and *Emden*, in his company, and on July 20, when the situation was becoming acute, he ordered *Nürnberg*, which was at San Francisco, and *Dresden*, which was at Vera Cruz, at the other side of the American continent, to join him. *Nürnberg* reached him in a couple of weeks; *Dresden* not till the end of October.

By mid-August, then, his force consisted of two armoured cruisers, each with a broadside of six 8-inch and three 6-inch guns, and three light cruisers armed only with 4-inch. Of the light cruisers *Emden* and

Nürnberg had a speed of between 25 and 26 knots; *Leipzig* of about 23 or 24. The fighting value of the armoured cruisers was approximately equal to that of *Minotaur* and *Defence* and probably superior to that of the *Warrior* class. The German 8-inch guns fired a projectile only slightly lighter than the British 9.2, so that, gun for gun, there should have been little to choose between them; while from the point of view of the control of fire, the broadside of six homogeneous guns could probably be used quite as effectively as a mixed armament of four 9.2's and five 7.5's, and more so than one of four 9.2's and two 7.5's. To engage such a squadron with the certainty of success, therefore, at least three British armoured cruisers of the latest type would have been required.

Neither of the British squadrons in eastern waters possessed the combination of speed and power that would have made them superior to Von Spee's force. Vice-Admiral Jerram, in the China station, had under his command *Triumph, Minotaur, Hampshire, Newcastle*, and *Yarmouth*. But *Triumph* was not in commission at the outbreak of war, and, though armed with 10-inch guns, she was three knots slower than the German cruisers. Sir Richard Peirse's command in the East Indies consisted of *Swiftsure*, a sister ship of *Triumph*; *Dartmouth*, a cruiser of the same class as *Newcastle*; and *Fox*, a cruiser of old and slow type. Neither squadron, then, could have sought for Von Spee with any hope of bringing him to action, if he choose to avoid it, or with any certainty of defeating him, if he accepted battle.

Australia possessed a navy of her own of vastly greater force than either of these outpost forces of the mother-country. Of ships finished, commissioned, and ready for sea, it consisted of *Australia*, a battle-cruiser of the *Indefatigable* class; two protected cruisers of the *Dartmouth* type, *Sydney* and *Melbourne*; and *Encounter*, a sister ship of *Challenger*, with destroyers and submarines. A fast light cruiser, *Brisbane*, and some destroyers were building. In the Japanese Navy the Allies had, of course, resources out of all proportion to the enemy's strength.

When war became imminent Admiral von Spee, as we have seen, left his base for the Polynesian islands. He did this because it was obvious that he could not keep Tsing-Tau open in face of the strength that the combined Japanese and British forces could bring to bear against it, and to have been trapped would have been fatal. The same reasons that made him abandon Tsing-Tau forbade his trying to keep possession of Rabaud in the Bismarck Archipelago. He faced his future, then, without a base—just as Suffren did in 1781. There were several elements peculiar to the situation that made this possible. In the coast towns of Chile and Peru the Germans had a very large number of commercial houses and agents, and there were German ships in every South American port. Their trade with the islands was considerable and, no doubt long before war, it had been arranged that, on receiving the right warning, a great deal of shipping should be equipped and mobilised to supply the German squadron.

The widely scattered German outposts afforded also a service hardly less valuable than coal and food. They constituted an intelligence organisation that was indispensable. Having no base, and no source of supply other than these German houses in South America and the islands, it was inevitable that Von Spee should look to the east, and not to the west, in any operations that he undertook, if those operations were to be extended and made by a squadron, and not by detached ships. In discussing, then, the strategy which the German Admiralty pursued, these facts must not be lost sight of.

Of warlike policies he had a choice of two. He might either keep his ships together and embark on a war of squadrons, or he could scatter his ships and devote himself to commerce destruction. In the first case, as we have seen, he could only look for objectives in the east. In the alternative the greatest fields of his operations were either north of the Carolines, where the Chinese trade could be attacked; or northwest, where the Asiatic and Australian trades converge to Colombo; or still farther to the west, where the whole eastern trade runs into the mouth of the Red Sea. To the eastward there was no focal point of trade where great results could have been achieved—unless indeed he took his ships round the Horn to attack the River Plate trade or, better still, the main route that passes Pernambuco.

It was an obvious truth of the situation that, according as the attack on trade promised great results, so would that attack encounter the greatest dangers, for it seemed to be a certainty that the focal points would be the best protected. The most frequented of these, the approaches to the Red Sea, were also the furthest from his source of supply, and had he in fact resolved upon commerce destruction, his ships would have had to maintain themselves, as did *Emden*, by coaling and re-victualling out of the prizes that they took.

The advantage of scattering and going for the trade ruthlessly would have been the virtual certainty of inflicting very formidable damage indeed of an economic kind. The advantage of keeping his squadron together was the chance of some *coup* that would turn the scale—even if only for a time—in his country's favour. The disadvantages of the first policy were that there was the certainty that each ship would ultimately be run down and destroyed by superior force, and grave risk that one or more ships would be paralyzed by want of supplies, before a sufficient destruction of trade could justify the sacrifice. The weakness of the second was that, as a squadron, his ships might accomplish nothing at all.

I have so far discussed the German admiral's alternatives as if they had been debated at the time when war became certain. But it can be taken for granted that the principles on which he acted were not solely his own, but had determined German policy in this matter long before. And, in the main, the decisive arguments probably arose from the character of his force.

Writing in 1905, Admiral Sir Reginald Custance exposed the whole tissue of fallacies on which the policy of building armoured cruisers had been based. The main duties of cruising ships are, first, to assist in winning and maintaining command of the sea, by acting as scouts and connecting links between the battle squadrons, and, secondly, to exercise command, once it has been established by the attack on and defence of trade. For the successful discharge of these functions the essential element is that the cruisers should be numerous. So long as their speed is equal, or superior, to that of the enemy cruisers, there is no reason why their individual strength should be greatly or at all superior.

The armoured variety represents, roughly speaking, the value of three cruisers of ordinary type, and is manned by a crew almost proportionately larger. When first designed, it was possible to build these large cruisers of a speed superior to that of the smaller vessels, and having this monopoly, the French invented the type in pursuance of the idea that a sea war that consisted chiefly of attacks on commerce, promised brighter prospects than one which could not succeed unless based on battle-fleet supremacy. But this monopoly vanished nearly twenty years ago. For cruising purposes proper, then, this bastard type, while individually enormously more powerful than the light cruiser, was slower and so could not cover even one-third of the ground of its equivalent value in the smaller vessels. Over nine-tenths of the field of cruising, then, it represents a loss of between 60 and 70 *per cent.* of war efficiency, and this merely from its size.

But because size means cost and because cost has certain definite influences on the human appreciation of values, it was confidently prophesied that no one in command of a number of units of this value could fail to give an undue consideration to the importance of conserving them. Armoured cruisers, in short, would never be treated as cruisers at all, but would be kept in squadrons, just as capital ships are kept, partly to ensure a blow of the maximum strength, if to strike came within the possibilities of the situation, much more, however, for the protective value of mutual support, for fear of an encounter with superior force. This protective tendency would obviously have a further and much more disastrous effect upon the cruising value of such vessels.

It would simply mean that, instead of each doing one-third of what three smaller cruisers of the same value might have done, they would really do no cruising, properly so called, at all; and not only this, but would probably monopolize the work of two or three small cruisers to act as special scouts of a squadron so composed, so diverting these units in turn from their proper duties. If anyone will take the trouble to read the chapter in Barfleur's *Naval Policy* dealing with this topic, he will find in Von Spee's conduct an exact exemplification of what that accomplished and gallant author suggested must happen. Von Spee's policy, in other words, was probably settled for him by the logic of the situation and the doctrine which prevailed to create it.

Von Spee actually did, then, what it was fully anticipated he would do. He kept his ships together and travelled slowly eastward, maintaining himself in absolute secrecy from the outbreak of war until November 1. What were his exact hopes in the policy pursued, and what the consideration that led him to adopt it? His hopes of achieving any definite strategic result can only have been slender.

The composition of his force was so well known that he could hardly have supposed it possible that he would ever meet a squadron of inferior strength. He cannot, then, primarily have contemplated the possibility of any sort of naval victory. Failing this, he may have had various not very precisely defined ideas in his mind. There was to begin with the possibility of picking up a sufficient number of German reservists off the South American coast to have made it possible, not only to attack and seize the Falkland Islands, but actually to have occupied them by an extemporized military force.

This, as we know, he did attempt. He might further have contemplated crossing the South Atlantic to the Cape, with a view to supporting an insurrection of the Boers, if that materialised, or in any event of backing up the German colonists, who would be open to attack. Or, having struck a blow at the Falkland Islands, he might have sent his ships on a final mission in raiding the Atlantic trade. So long as his squadron was afloat, there were many possibilities—and always a certainty that it would force counter concentration on his opponents and thereby embarrass them in the task of searching for him.

But one thing was certain. He could not combine squadron war with commercial war. *Emden* he detached in August to attack the trade in the Indian Ocean. But the only support he could lend her was such immunity from pursuit as would result from the concentration he forced upon the British forces. It is highly probable that, had he sent all his ships on the same mission, he would have had at least a month's run before effective measures could be taken, if only for the fact, possibly unknown to him, that so large a part of the Allied forces were being devoted to convoying the Australian troops.

Coronel

But whatever the risks and difficulties of trade war, the uncertainties of doing anything at all as a squadron were really greater, and the final fate of his ships more certain. Whatever his hopes of striking a blow for his country's profit or prestige, he could hardly, even in his most sanguine moments, have anticipated anything so extraordinary as Admiral Cradock's attack on him on November 1.

The full story of this ill-fated British force is still to be told. Nor can what we know be made fully intelligible until we have at least the actual words of Admiral Cradock's instructions. But certain inferences from his actions show that whatever those instructions were, his own understanding of them is not in doubt at all. Briefly, the facts of the case are these:

Shortly after the outbreak of war Admiral Cradock transferred his flag from *Suffolk* to *Good Hope* and made his way round the Horn, taking *Monmouth*, *Glasgow*, and the liner *Otranto* with him. The old battleship, *Canopus*, was despatched from home to join his flag, and actually caught him up some time before the action. The *Canopus* needed time either for refitting, to coal, or to re-provision, and the admiral, instead of waiting for her, pursued his way north with his original three ships.

Before *Canopus* joined the flag the last letters written by the officers and men of the squadron were posted, and in one of these a member of his staff stated that the general feeling was that the ships were inadequate to the task set before them, and so far, at least, as their mission was concerned, the naval supremacy of Great Britain was not being employed to any useful purpose.

Certain truths with regard to the force that Cradock took north, and of the force that he attacked, should be borne in mind. *Good Hope*, *Monmouth*, and *Glasgow* were as a squadron, markedly faster than Von Spee's squadron. Whether the *Otranto* was capable of more than 22 or 23 knots I do not know; but the three warships certainly had the heels of the Germans. It is, then, obvious that if Admiral Cradock's staff regarded themselves and their ships as inadequate or in danger, it cannot have been because, had the enemy attacked them, they would have been unable to escape. It is next equally obvious that had the Admiral kept *Canopus* with him, while the pace of the squadron would have been brought down from 23 knots to 15, its fighting value, as measured by broadside power, would have been very much greater than Von Spee's. That Von Spee at least thought so is clear from his published letters.

Without *Canopus*, then, Cradock would have been safe if he had run away. With *Canopus* he would have been reasonably safe if he had awaited the enemy's attack. The significance of the letter which I have alluded to is that it was written by a man to whom neither of these contingencies seemed to be open. The superiority in speed which would always have made it possible for Cradock to evade Von Spee was also the one quality of his ships that gave him capacity to attack the Germans if they showed any signs of avoiding action. No doubt, if the Germans would have awaited action by a squadron which included the *Canopus* Admiral Cradock's chances might have been brilliant. But if he started out to look for Von Spee with a 15-knot squadron, his chances for acting swiftly on any information that came his way would have been greatly reduced; and to have limited his advance to 15 knots would have been handing over the initiative in the matter entirely to the enemy.

Bearing these elements in mind and noting first that the British admiral deliberately left *Canopus* behind; next, that at two o'clock in the afternoon of November 1, when the presence of an enemy was suspected to the north, he at once ordered all ships to close on *Good Hope*, and continued when the squadron was formed, to advance against the enemy, and that then, when he saw him, in spite of the bad weather and bad light, at once announced that he intended to attack him, the inference is irresistible that he thought it his duty to find and attack the enemy, and that he refused to interpret the sending of *Ca-*

nopus to mean that he could judge for himself whether or not he was in sufficient force to attack. He acted, that is to say, as no man would act unless he believed his mission to be of a peremptory and quite unmistakable kind.

So much, I think, is clear from the few known facts of the case. Whether Admiral Cradock was right in so interpreting his orders is, of course, another matter. Of that no one can judge until the orders themselves are published, and then only those who are familiar with the precise meaning of the phrases employed. Of the instructions themselves, then, I express no opinion. I am only concerned with the light that Admiral Cradock's actions throw on his own interpretation of them.

Two official descriptions of the action have been published, Captain Luce's, and the Graf von Spee's despatches. There are further the private letters of the German Admiral, of his son Otto, and that of a lieutenant of the *Glasgow*. All of these are in substantial agreement in their statement of the facts—an unusual thing, to be explained perhaps quite simply. The British officers naturally told the truth about the fate of the squadron; and the German success was so complete that there was no reason for the government to exaggerate or garble the straightforward and not ungenerous statements of the German sailors. It is to Von Spee's credit that he declined any public rejoicings by the German colony at Valparaiso, when he visited that port directly after the action to secure the internment of *Good Hope*, of whose fate he was uncertain.

The story of the fight is simple enough. Admiral Cradock formed his ships in line with *Good Hope* leading, then *Monmouth*, then *Glasgow*. *Otranto* he ordered away as soon as battle became imminent, and *Glasgow* shortly afterwards. Von Spee criticizes the British admiral for not attacking the two armoured cruisers during the half hour that elapsed between the formation of the fleet while *Nürnberg* and *Dresden* were coming up full speed to join the line. At 6:30 the two lines were on nearly parallel and southerly courses at a distance of about 14,700 yards. Twenty minutes later Von Spee had closed the range about 1,200 yards, and he then altered course a point towards the enemy, and this, in a quarter of an hour, brought the range to about 11,000 yards. He then opened fire and, five minutes later, got his first hit with a salvo on *Good Hope*.

He had the best of the light, and it was obvious to him that the British gunnery suffered more from the heavy seas than did his own.

As in neither squadron could any but the upper-deck guns be used, the Germans had an overwhelmingly superior armament in action— their twelve 8-inch guns having nothing opposed to them except the two 9:2 of *Good Hope* and the upper-deck 6-inch guns of *Good Hope* and *Monmouth*. Inferior metal and the more difficult conditions soon told their tale. In the quarter of an hour during which the German admiral closed the range from 11,000 yards to less than 7,000, he says:

> Both the British cruisers were practically covered by the German fire, whereas *Scharnhorst* was hit only twice, and *Gneisenau* only four times.

The German admiral now sheered off, and it looks as if Admiral Cradock had then begun to close. An English account supposes that *Good Hope* was drifting and not under control. Anyhow, the range, in spite of the German change of course, was reduced by another 1,200 yards, and the Germans thought that the British admiral contemplated a torpedo attack. About fifty minutes after the action commenced there was an enormous explosion in *Good Hope* which had been on fire some time. The people in *Glasgow* for a time thought it was the German flagship that had gone, so short had the range become. Neither of our armoured cruisers fired after this, and the Germans seem to have lost sight of *Good Hope* altogether, in spite of her proximity. *Monmouth*, listing badly and on fire, turned to keep bows on to the sea, and Von Spee sent his light cruisers in pursuit of her. She kept her flag flying to the last and was sunk, an hour and a half after *Good Hope* blew up, by a short-range attack by *Nürnberg*.

Both ships could, of course, quite honourably have saved themselves once their case had become hopeless, had their officers chosen to surrender. But it was with no thought of surrendering that they had engaged, and the stoic heroism of their end is the noblest legacy they could have left to their fellow countrymen. *Glasgow* kept with *Monmouth* as long as she could; but her orders from the admiral had been explicit, and it was obvious that she could not single-handed engage the undamaged German squadron, nor be of the slightest service to *Monmouth* had she attempted to do so. Captain Luce, quite rightly therefore, retreated from the scene.

A private letter, written a day after the action by the German admiral, throws an interesting light on the situation. After recounting the unimportant character of the damage suffered by his ships, he adds:

> I do not know what adverse circumstances deprived the en-

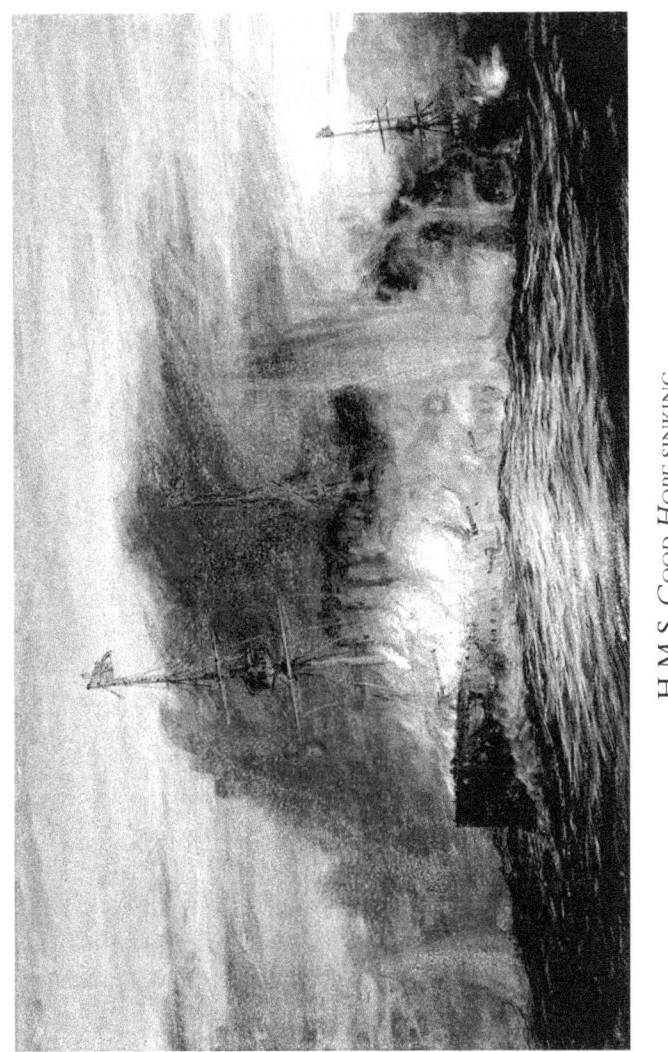

H.M.S. G*OOD* H*OPE* SINKING

emy of every measure of success. . . . If *Good Hope* escaped, she must, in my opinion, make for a Chilean port on account of her damages. To make sure of this I intend going to Valparaiso tomorrow with *Gneisenau* and *Nürnberg*, and to see whether *Good Hope* could not be disarmed by the Chileans. If so, I shall be relieved of two powerful opponents. *Good Hope*, though bigger than *Scharnhorst*, was not so well armed. She mounted heavy guns, but only two, while *Monmouth* succumbed to *Scharnhorst's* as she had only 6-inch guns.

The English have another ship like *Monmouth* hereabouts and, in addition, as it seems, a battleship of the *Queen* class carrying 12-inch guns. Against the latter we can hardly do anything. Had they kept their force together, we should probably have got the worst of it. You can hardly imagine the joy which reigned among us. We have at least contributed something to the glory of our arms, although it may not mean much on the whole and in view of the enormous number of English ships.

Viewing this action apart from the circumstances that led up to it and the magnificent spirit and self-sacrifice displayed, its technical and historical interest lies chiefly in the fact that it is the only instance in the war in which an inferior force has sought action with one incomparably stronger. The weaker, not only sought battle, but apparently executed no defensive manoeuvres of any kind whatever. We shall find, for instance, no parallel in Coronel to the tactics of Von Spee at the Falkland Islands, or to those of Admiral Scheer at Jutland. (*Vide The Naval War of 1914 Two Actions at Sea During the Early Phase of the First World War—The Action off Heligoland August 1914* by L. Cecil Jane and *Coronel and the Falkland Islands* by A. Neville Hilditch; Leonaur 2011.)

And it is perhaps remarkable that the British admiral, once having determined on action which he must have known would be desperate, did not either at once attempt to close the enemy at full speed, so as to give his very inferior artillery and his torpedoes a chance of inflicting serious damage on the enemy while daylight lasted, or delay closing until bad light would make long-range gunnery impossible, in a *mêlée* at point blank. Anything might have happened, and it was to the weaker side's interest to leave as much as possible to chance.

It is hardly conceivable that the total result of the action could have been different so far as the British squadron is concerned. But it is permissible to speculate as to whether the Germans might not have suffered more, had either of the above plans been followed. The reasoning which dictated Admiral Cradock's tactics can, of course, never be known.

A matter of considerable technical interest is, that though two armoured cruisers kept firing for a considerable period, it is quite clear from Von Spee's despatch that their fire was completely ineffective. Everyone has agreed in explaining this largely by the extreme difficulty of gunnery conditions, but it is surely highly probable that the chief cause is to be found in the fire of the German ships having, so far as the power of offence is concerned, put *Good Hope* and *Monmouth* out of action within very few minutes of action beginning. All accounts agree in the *Scharnhorst's* salvo having found *Good Hope* within five minutes, and it is not likely that *Monmouth* fared any better at the hands of *Gneisenau*. What seems to me remarkable is the length of time the ships kept afloat after being militarily useless.

The explosion in *Good Hope* took place after she was in action fifty minutes, and it is not known when she sank. The *Monmouth* survived the opening salvoes by two hours and twenty minutes, and to the last seemed to have her engines in perfect working order. It is impossible, I think, to resist the inference, that all the German hitting, except the shell that caused the explosion in *Good Hope*, was done in the first few minutes of action, while the light was at its best, though the range was at its longest.

CHAPTER 12

Battle of the Falkland Islands (1)

THE CAREER OF VON SPEE (2)

The Battle of the Falkland Islands was fought on December 8th by a squadron under Vice-Admiral Sir F. Doveton Sturdee, K.C.B., C.V.O., C.M.G., against the German China Squadron—less *Emden*, but strengthened by the addition of the cruiser *Dresden*. Admiral Sturdee's despatch was not published until about three months after the action, but in the meantime several accounts appeared in various newspapers, and since the despatch was published others have been printed in different magazines. Of no other action in the war have we such various or full information as about this. It will perhaps be a convenient way of dealing with this extremely instructive and important engagement to reproduce the Vice-Admiral's despatch textually, and to supplement it by explanatory notes, and incorporate in these what is most material of the additional information which is available.

The despatch begins with the tabulation of the sections into which the despatch is divided:

A. Preliminary Movements.
B. Action with the Armoured Cruisers.
C. Action with the Light Cruisers.
D. Action with the Enemy's Transports.

The squadron, consisting of H.M. ships *Invincible*, flying my flag, Flag Captain Percy T. H. Beamish; *Inflexible*, Captain Richard F. Phillimore; *Carnarvon* flying the flag of Rear-Admiral Archibald P. Stoddart, Flag Captain Harry L. d'E. Skipwith; *Cornwall*, Captain Walter M. Ellerton; *Kent*, Captain John D. Allen; *Glasgow*, Captain John Luce; *Bristol*, Captain Basil H. Fanshawe; and

Macedonia, Captain Bertram S. Evans—arrived at Port Stanley, Falkland Islands, at 10:30 a.m. on Monday, the 7th December, 1914. Coaling was commenced at once, in order that the ships should be ready to resume the search for the enemy's squadron the next evening, the 8th December.

The account previously given of the Graf von Spee's movements leading up to and subsequent to the action off Coronel, will have made the general strategic position in the Eastern Pacific and Southern Atlantic more or less plain. Of his ships, however, this should be added. The clear light and prevalence of smooth water on the China Station has always proved an incentive to good gunnery, and indeed the performances of the *Terrible*, when Vice-Admiral Sir Percy Scott commanded her as captain, may be regarded as the starting point of all modern gunnery skill. It is not surprising, therefore, that both of Von Spee's ships should have stood, as they in fact did, at the head of the German Fleet in order of gunnery merit.

And it was clear from their performances that their skill was not merely limited to good gun-laying. Both at Coronel and at Falkland Islands they gave conclusive evidence of being perfect masters of such fire control as they possessed, and on the first occasion shot superbly in very rough weather. They therefore constituted an extremely formidable combination. The German 8.2 shell of the latest type—with which these ships were armed—fired a projectile very nearly as heavy as did the British 9.2's—the actual weights are 320 pounds and 380. The percentage is roughly 8.4 to 10. These two ships had as scouts and auxiliaries the *Leipzig*, *Nürnberg*, and *Dresden*, cruisers of similar design; but *Dresden* was considerably faster than either of her consorts.

After the destruction of the *Good Hope* and *Monmouth*, Von Spee cruised for a short time in the Eastern Pacific, and then made his way in leisurely fashion round the Horn with the intention of crossing to South Africa. In a fatal moment he decided to attack the British Colony at Falkland Islands first, and it was this that brought him within reach of Admiral Sturdee's guns. It is clear enough from his conduct—let alone admissions made by prisoners afterwards—that he had no idea whatever of the strength of the force that had been sent out to attack him. He fully expected to find *Canopus* at Port Stanley, and he thought it possible that *Carnarvon* and *Glasgow* might be there also. And these ships he was quite prepared to engage. It was quite a different thing, however, to take on two battle-cruisers that under any bearing could bring between them a dozen 12-inch guns into action and, on certain bearings, four more. As will be seen from the despatch, the moment he realised the strength against him, he adopted what seemed the only possible course, namely flight. (*Vide The Battle of the Falkland Islands 1914* by H. Spencer-Cooper; Leonaur 2011.)

A. Preliminary Movements

At 8 a.m. on Tuesday, the 8th December, a signal was received from the signal station on shore:—

'A four-funnel and two-funnel man-of-war in sight from Sapper Hill, steering northwards.'

At this time, the positions of the various ships of the squadron were as follows:—

Macedonia: At anchor as look-out ship.

Kent (guardship): At anchor in Port William.

Invincible and *Inflexible*: In Port William.

Carnarvon: In Port William.

Cornwall: In Port William.

Glasgow: In Port Stanley.

Bristol: In Port Stanley.

The *Kent* was at once ordered to weigh, and a general signal was made to raise steam for full speed.

At 8:20 a.m. the signal station reported another column of smoke in sight to the southward, and at 8:45 a.m. the *Kent* passed down the harbour and took up a station at the entrance.

The *Canopus*, Captain Heathcoat S. Grant, reported at 8:47 a.m. that the first two ships were eight miles off, and that the smoke reported at 8:20 a.m. appeared to be the smoke of two ships about twenty miles off.

At 8:50 a.m. the signal station reported a further column of smoke in sight to the southward.

The *Macedonia* was ordered to weigh anchor on the inner side of the other ships, and await orders.

Here the signal, it will be observed, says "a four-funnel and two-funnel man of war." The ships were probably end on when they were seen, and in the *Nürnberg* there was a considerable gap between the after-funnel and the two forward funnels. Seen from a point a little off the direct keel line, she would seem therefore to have two funnels only.

Port William and Port Stanley are two inlets with a tongue of land between them, and opposite this tongue of land is the channel to the sea. Port Stanley is in the more southerly division of the harbour, which is also the larger of the two. *Canopus* was anchored to the eastward of the town of Port Stanley, so that her guns could fire over the low-lying land between her and the sea. The land rises to the north as it creeps round towards the mouth of the harbour, and on this higher land there was an observation station where arrangements had been made by which the fire of *Canopus* could be directed out to sea at any squadron that threatened to attack.

The reader is therefore to imagine the *Macedonia* lying in the outside mouth of the harbour; *Kent* anchored in the channel half way between *Macedonia* and where the harbour divides Port Stanley to the south and Port William to the north; with *Inflexible*, *Invincible*, and *Carnarvon* anchored in line in Port William; the *Bristol* and *Glasgow* in the southern bay, with Port Stanley behind them to the westward, and *Canopus* behind them to the east.

The vice-admiral wasted no time. As a fact, all his ships were then coaling. And the officers not engaged in this were making plans for a day's shooting over the rough moors in the neighbourhood of the town—where hares and partridges were to be found—and were many of them in mufti, and most of them at breakfast when the startling and welcome news of the advent of the enemy came to them. Everything, of course, gave way to the necessity of getting out of harbour with the utmost speed. Colliers were cast off. The furnaces were fed, and all hands were started to clean first the ships and then themselves. At eight the first ships seemed to be probably twenty miles off. Twenty minutes later, a further detachment came into sight; half an hour later than that, the last of the Germans were seen upon the horizon.

Round about 9 o'clock *Kent* was outside the harbour, while *Gneisenau* and *Nürnberg* were approaching at about twenty knots.

3. At 9:20 a.m. the two leading ships of the enemy (*Gneisenau* and *Nürnberg*), with guns trained on the wireless station, came within range of the *Canopus*, who opened fire at them across the low land at a range of 11,000 yards. The enemy at once hoisted their colours and turned away. At this time the masts and smoke of the enemy were visible from the upper bridge of the *Invincible* at a range of approximately 17,000 yards across the

low land to the south of Port William.

A few minutes later the two cruisers altered course to port, as though to close the *Kent* at the entrance to the harbour, but about this time it seems that the *Invincible* and *Inflexible* were seen over the land, as the enemy at once altered course and increased speed to join their consorts.

The *Glasgow* weighed and proceeded at 9:40 a.m. with orders to join the *Kent* and observe the enemy's movements.

The Germans, as we have seen, expected possibly to find *Canopus* at the Falkland Islands, but not that she would be concealed from their fire behind the low-lying ground. Their astonishment then to find themselves under the fire of 12-inch guns at twenty minutes past nine was considerable. They therefore turned, not with the intention of running away but clearly to throw out the fire control that was directing the big guns at them, for it must have been about this time that they saw the county cruiser *Kent* in the offing, and their first thought was to go in and finish her off. But a very few moments after there opened up over the line of vision the tripod masts of the two battle-cruisers, and the *Gneisenau* and *Nürnberg*, that had been coming due north for the attack, now turned round to the east, and went full speed to join their approaching consorts, who were cutting off the corner made by the first two ships.

Two quite important questions arise at this point. Was it good policy on the part of Admiral Sturdee to allow *Canopus* to open fire and so drive the Germans away? If, indeed, it was *Canopus* that drove them off. He knew, of course, that it would take him at least half an hour to forty minutes before all his squadron could be clear of the harbour, and ready to begin the chase. Would it have been wiser if he had allowed the Germans to come right up and so to have made sure of having them within easy range when he did come out? The answer to this criticism is obvious. *Gneisenau* was a great deal more than a match for *Kent*, and no British ship could have got out to her assistance in time to prevent her destruction if *Gneisenau* had been allowed to close.

The speed of Admiral Sturdee's battle-cruisers was such—he had certainly a five, if not a six knot advantage over the armoured cruisers—that he knew he had it well within his power with the whole day before him, to give the Germans forty minutes' start, and catch them and finish them off before evening. And it was his business to do this, if he could, with the smallest possible loss of life and the least possible damage to his ships. That is the first point. But next, it was quite within the possibilities of the case that *Canopus's* guns would make a hit either on *Gneisenau* or *Nürnberg*. Indeed, so close did the fourth and fifth rounds go that it was thought on shore that there had been a hit; but this was afterwards proved to be a mistake. There was a good chance then of laming one of them and so making a quick capture certain. Finally, it was not altogether the fire of *Canopus* but the sight of the battle-cruisers' masts that decided Von Spee, or rather the Captain of *Gneisenau*, to retreat.

It is more pertinent to ask whether it would not have been better policy on the part of the Germans to have got inside the range of *Canopus*—for obviously if she had fired over the hills she would not be able to use her guns at short range—and then bring the British squadron under an accurate bombardment just when they were coming out of harbour and unable to use their armament to effect. The same considerations that weighed with Admiral Sturdee in deciding to allow *Canopus* to open fire with the possible result of driving them off, should have weighed with the German captain and made him realise that once the battle-cruisers were out of harbour, there was no possible escape either for his ship or for the flagship.

And it is undoubtedly certain that whether they could have succeeded in sinking and destroying any British ships before being destroyed themselves, they must have done vastly greater damage than they were, in fact, able to inflict in an action which, as we shall see, the British admiral was able to fight on his own conditions from first to last. The main features of the final issue—that is, the destruction of the two armoured cruisers—could certainly not have been prevented, but had they closed the range, and fought the British ships as they came out, the complete escape of the light cruisers could have been assured, and it is certain that they could have done very great damage before being destroyed themselves.

4. At 9:45 a.m. the squadron—less the *Bristol*—weighed, and proceeded out of harbour in the following order: *Carnarvon, Inflexible, Invincible,* and *Cornwall*. On passing Cape Pembroke Light, the five ships of the enemy appeared clearly in sight to the southeast, hull down. The visibility was at its maximum, the sea was calm, with a bright sun, a clear sky, and a light breeze from the northwest.

At 9:45, when the squadron got clear of the harbour and was

working up to full speed, the Germans, whose main squadron was about 8½ sea miles off at 9:30, while *Gneisenau* and *Nürnberg* were three miles closer in, were probably about twelve or thirteen miles off. There was then a gap of five or six miles to be made up before action range could be reached, and to make this good in three hours the British squadron would have to produce a speed greater by some two knots.

> At 10:20 a.m. the signal for a general chase was made. The battle-cruisers quickly passed ahead of the *Carnarvon* and overtook the *Kent*. The *Glasgow* was ordered to keep two miles from the *Invincible*, and the *Inflexible* was stationed on the starboard quarter of the flagship. Speed was eased to twenty knots at 11:15 a.m. to enable the other cruisers to get into station. At this time the enemy's funnels and bridges showed just above the horizon.

It will be observed that the British admiral was carrying on his chase on a wide front and at full speed—probably twenty-four knots. Only *Glasgow*, *Kent*, and the two battle-cruisers could maintain this, which meant that *Carnarvon* and *Cornwall* were falling very much behind. The admiral therefore, after an hour, dropped his speed to twenty knots to enable his two cruisers to catch up. Why did he do this?

In the first place, his burst at full speed had probably shown him that instead of having an advantage of only two knots in speed over his enemy, he could beat him by at least five knots when he chose. And he reasoned that if he drove at the five German ships with only four of his own, it was possible for the German ships to scatter and so for one or more of them to escape. It was of the essence of his tactics that the enemy should keep his fleet together as long as possible, and it was a vital matter that when the dispersion took place the pursuit of the light cruisers should be undertaken by his own light cruisers with the best possible prospects of bringing all of them to action. As we shall see by the next paragraph, this measure did not attain its desired end.

> The enemy were still maintaining their distance, and I decided at 12:20 p.m. to attack with the two battle-cruisers and the *Glasgow*.
> At 12:47 p.m. the signal to 'Open fire and engage the enemy' was made.
> The *Inflexible* opened fire at 12:55 p.m. from her fore turret at the right-hand ship of the enemy, a light cruiser; a few minutes later the *Invincible* opened fire at the same ship.

The deliberate fire from a range of 16,500 to 15,000 yards at the right-hand light cruiser, who was dropping astern, became too threatening, and when a shell fell close alongside her at 1:20 she (the *Leipzig*) turned away, with the *Nürnberg* and *Dresden*, to the southwest. These light cruisers were at once followed by the *Kent, Glasgow*, and *Cornwall*, in accordance with my instructions.

The action finally developed into three separate encounters besides the subsidiary one dealing with the threatened landing.

It is plain from this that when the speed was limited by that of its slowest ship, that is, the *Carnarvon*, the squadron was unable to gain on the Germans at all. The time, therefore, had come to force the enemy to a decision, and full speed was once more ordered. The British squadron from now until the next decisive move was taken, must be pictured in this way—the two battle-cruisers and *Glasgow* racing along at twenty-six or twenty-seven knots; *Cornwall* and *Kent* following along at their best speed—probably a knot and a half or two knots less—and *Carnarvon* bringing up the rear. She must soon have been left considerably behind. For an hour then the two squadrons had probably been keeping about twenty-one knots at a distance of about 19,000 yards. Half an hour's chase at twenty-five knots brought the range to 17,000 and twenty-five minutes later, to something less than 15,000.

The German squadron was now under fire and Von Spee made the signal:

> I intend to fight the battle-cruisers as long as I can, the light cruisers are to scatter and to escape if possible.

The reader will of course realise that up to this moment *Leipzig, Nürnberg*, and *Dresden* had been limiting their speed by the speed of *Scharnhorst*. This was undoubtedly Von Spee's second mistake, if we assume he was wrong in not attacking the British squadron as it issued from the harbour. By keeping his light cruisers with him until the British were within ten miles of him, he brought their chance of escape to a very low ebb indeed. It is clear that Admiral Sturdee's drop in speed at 11:20 completely deceived him. He probably thought that none of the British cruisers could exceed the speed the vice-admiral then ordered.

We now have to treat of the rest of the day's work as three separate actions, though it is really more correct to call it four, because the actions between *Kent* and *Nürnberg*, *Cornwall* and *Glasgow* with *Leipzig* had, after the first phase, no influence one upon the other. We will deal first, as the vice-admiral does, with the action with the armoured cruisers.

CHAPTER 13

Battle of the Falkland Islands (2)

B. ACTION WITH THE ARMOURED CRUISERS

The fire of the battle-cruisers was directed on the *Scharnhorst* and *Gneisenau*. The effect of this was quickly seen, when at 1:25 p.m., with the *Scharnhorst* leading, they turned about seven points to port in succession into line ahead and opened fire at 1:30 p.m. Shortly afterwards speed was eased to twenty-four knots, and the battle-cruisers were ordered to turn together, bringing them into line ahead, with the *Invincible* leading.

The range was about 13,500 yards at the final turn, and increased until at 2 p.m. it had reached 16,450 yards.

The moment Von Spee found himself under the effective fire of the battle-cruisers, he took the only course open to him. To delay the finish by sheer flight would do no good. It was his duty to inflict some reciprocal injury on his opponent. He was under the fire of at least eight if not twelve 12-inch guns, and he only had six 8-inch guns bearing on Admiral Sturdee. To do anything at all effective he had to turn broadside on. He therefore turned seven-eighths of a right angle to port, that is, to the left—his course now being almost at right angles to Admiral Sturdee's—and six minutes afterwards, when both his ships were on a steady course, he opened fire.

Three minutes after he began his turn, and therefore three minutes before he opened fire, Admiral Sturdee turned his ships to port also, but his turn was not quite so big as the enemy's, and for about twelve minutes the range was steadily closing. The effect of these changes of course was to bring the battle-cruisers to within 11,000 or 12,000 yards of *Scharnhorst* and *Gneisenau*. The Germans took full advantage of this opportunity, and before they had been firing five minutes, they had salvo after salvo straddling the battle-cruisers.

As we have seen, both in the stories of the *Koenigsberg* and of the *Emden*, there has been no feature of any gunnery action more regularly reproduced than the rapidity with which the Germans find the range at the beginning of an action, or the regularity with which the projectiles of every broadside fall together. It was strikingly exemplified in the present instance, so much so indeed that Admiral Sturdee thought it wise to make a further turn to port, thus increasing the range, and as he says in this despatch, by the time his total turn was completed, he brought the range out again to about 13,500 yards. At this distance the 12-inch guns would have a marked advantage over the 8.2's. But for all that the German fire continued surprisingly accurate, and many hits were made on our ships.

The British admiral held to his new course and the German ships theirs. This involved the lengthening of the range. But Von Spee doubtless preferred this to the confusion of a changing rate. He held on then till he could reach the British ships no longer. The consequence was that in twenty minutes the range had increased by a further 2,500 yards, which was far beyond the capacity of 8.2's, and a range at which the shooting of even the 12-inch guns might be irregular. Accordingly, at about 2 o'clock the British squadron began a gradual turn towards the enemy, which in about seven minutes' time brought them on a course at right angles to their previous course, and therefore a little less than right angles to the course which the Germans were steering.

> The enemy then (2:10 p.m.) turned away about ten points to starboard and a second chase ensued, until, at 2:45 p.m., the battle-cruisers again opened fire; this caused the enemy, at 2:53 p.m., to turn into line ahead to port and open fire at 2:55 p.m. The *Scharnhorst* caught fire forward, but not seriously, and her fire slackened perceptibly; the *Gneisenau* was badly hit by the *Inflexible*.

In the seven minutes of the beginning of Admiral Sturdee's turn he reduced the range by considerably over 1,000 yards, and Von Spee perceiving the change of course of the British ships, turned about half a right angle to starboard, that is to the right, as if undecided whether to go right across the bows, and then a few minutes afterwards turned much more than a right angle to the right again. This brought the British squadron dead astern of him and showed that his only anxiety at this moment was to escape our fire as long as possible. It appears from various accounts that firing had ceased on both sides for some little time before Admiral Sturdee began his turn at 2 o'clock, and Von Spee wished to make the lull in the fighting as long as possible. There were doubtless many wounded to carry off, damages to be made good, and so forth. The whole of the first phase of the gunnery engagement, then, beginning just after half-past one on the German side, may be supposed to have ended round about ten minutes to two.

At ten minutes past two the enemy began his new flight, necessitating a reproduction by the British squadron of their tactics of two hours before. It was a chase, not on the direct track of the Germans, but on a course parallel to them and coming round on their port or left-hand side. Von Spee's retreat had naturally increased the range, carried it out indeed considerably beyond 16,000 yards, but by a quarter to three it had been reduced once more to 15,000 yards, and when the British ships reopened fire, after less than ten minutes of it the enemy turned to bring his broadside into action, just as he had done at 1:25.

> At 3:30 p.m. the *Scharnhorst* led round about ten points to starboard; just previously her fire had slackened perceptibly, and one shell had shot away her third funnel; some guns were not firing, and it would appear that the turn was dictated by a desire to bring her starboard guns into action. The effect of the fire on the *Scharnhorst* became more and more apparent in consequence of smoke from fires, and also escaping steam; at times a shell would cause a large hole to appear in her side, through which could be seen a dull red glow of flame. At 4:4 p.m. the *Scharnhorst*, whose flag remained flying to the last, suddenly listed heavily to port, and within a minute it became clear that she was a doomed ship; for the list increased very rapidly until she lay on her beam ends, and at 4:17 p.m. she disappeared.

There was this difference between the enemy's manoeuvres on this occasion and that of an hour and a half before. At 1:25 he simply turned sufficiently to bring his broadside to bear. This time he turned not less but much more than a right angle, and Admiral Sturdee was considerably behind him when he opened fire at a quarter to three. Had the British squadron not turned shortly afterwards, the Germans could have closed the range to collision point. As a matter of fact, immediately after the Germans turned, Admiral Sturdee turned too, but not so large an angle, and the consequence was that at 3 o'clock the range had been reduced to 12,000 yards, and at one time it had shortened down to about 9,000. It was apparently Von Spee's intention at this stage to shorten the range to an extent that would give his guns the opportunity of doing some real damage to our ships. This is of course the proper policy to adopt if a squadron has inferior gun-power and is unable to escape by flight.

But it will be observed that Von Spee did not persist in this manoeuvre, and it is obvious that he adopted it too late. He missed his first opportunity of inflicting serious and possibly decisive injury, when he failed to engage the British ships as they were coming out of harbour. He missed the second when, on Admiral Sturdee turning away from him at 1:45, he held on his course and allowed the range to be increased. He missed it again when at 2:10, instead of holding on his course and going across Admiral Sturdee's bows, he began his second and necessarily futile flight. When the fourth chance came it was probably too late.

Both ships had been hit and *Scharnhorst* seriously. But for about twenty minutes the German admiral did now close the range and come in almost direct pursuit of the British. So much so that shortly after a quarter past three Admiral Sturdee turned away from him, and describing a kind of circle with his ships from left to right, brought his squadron round so as to be directly behind the German ships. He had two reasons for making this turn. His course was straight up wind, so that gunnery conditions were bad, and the turn brought him to the most favourable possible position for concentrating fire upon the enemy, while they had only a minimum number of guns bearing.

This position Von Spee found intolerable. Both his ships were suffering, and one of the *Scharnhorst's* funnels was carried away. It must have been evident to him that the end was not far off when he turned at half past three. Never since the first twenty minutes had the enemy's fire been really good, and now the thing was assuming the dimensions of a military execution. The second phase of gunfire between a quarter to three and half past had been decisive as far as the *Scharnhorst* was concerned.

A curious incident in this interval should be noted. Just as the firing began in this second phase, a full-rigged sailing ship was observed about four miles off to the southeast from the leading British ship. She is not identified in any of the reports of the action that I have seen, nor has any account appeared that I know of, of what those on board saw. But it must have been an astonishing experience for a peaceful trading sailing vessel, beating down quietly towards the Horn, to find herself suddenly in the middle of so grim a business as this. Those on board saw a thing at that time unprecedented in the history of the world. A sea battle in which ships as fast as the swiftest Atlantic liners were using an armament twice as powerful as that carried by any battleship that had ever been used in war before.

The last moments of *Scharnhorst* were curiously dramatic. Till now she had led *Gneisenau* throughout the fight. Just before she sank she turned a half circle past *Gneisenau* in the reverse direction, and before anybody in the British ships could guess whether this was an intentional manoeuvre or purely involuntary, she turned over on her side, her bows plunged downwards, and after standing upright for a second or two with her screws whirring high in the air, vanished from sight. It is probable that coincident with one shot inflicting such injuries that she was flooded, another had smashed up her steering gear, and jammed her helm hard a-port.

The *Gneisenau* passed on the far side of her late flagship, and continued a determined but ineffectual effort to fight the two battle cruisers.

> At 5:8 p.m. the forward funnel was knocked over and remained resting against the second funnel. She was evidently in serious straits, and her fire slackened very much.
>
> At 5:15 p.m. one of the *Gneisenau's* shells struck the *Invincible*; this was her last effective effort.
>
> At 5:30 p.m. she turned towards the flagship with a heavy list to starboard, and appeared stopped, with steam pouring from her escape pipes, and smoke from shell and fires rising everywhere. About this time, I ordered the signal 'Cease fire,' but before it was hoisted the *Gneisenau* opened fire again, and continued to fire from time to time with a single gun.
>
> At 5:40 p.m. the three ships closed in on the *Gneisenau*, and, at this time, the flag flying at her fore truck was apparently hauled down, but the flag at the peak continued flying.
>
> At 5:50 p.m. 'Cease fire' was made.
>
> At 6 p.m. the *Gneisenau* heeled over very suddenly, showing the men gathered on her decks and then walking on her side as she lay for a minute on her beam ends before sinking.
>
> The *Gneisenau*, at 4:17, still had all her guns in action, and seemed indeed to have suffered very little. Had the fire of both battle-cruisers

S.M.S. SCHARNHORST SINKING AT THE BATTLE OF THE FALKLAND ISLANDS

hitherto been concentrated chiefly on the flagship? If so, the effect was really rather unfortunate, for with one ship going strong, it was impossible for the vice-admiral to attempt the rescue of the people in *Scharnhorst*. Rain had set in. There were signs of mist and thick weather. At any moment the light might fail. The conditions of the morning had been ideal for the control of guns at long range. These conditions had long since vanished.

No doubt it went greatly against the grain to leave the brave fellows of the *Scharnhorst* in their hopeless struggle, but the necessities of the situation gave no choice. For that matter, when the loss of life that took place in the *Gneisenau* is considered, it is highly probable that had the British ships stopped to look for people of the *Scharnhorst* they would have found none. For she turned over and sank, not as *Gneisenau* subsequently did, so slowly that the people on board were able to muster on deck and then clamber on to the ship's sides as she heeled over, but with such fearful rapidity that it is said that a salvo which *Carnarvon* had fired at her when she was still afloat and showed no signs of immediate collapse, actually pitched in the water where she had sunk!

If this story is true, she must have turned over and vanished from sight in from ten to fifteen seconds. In this instance there can have been few if any survivors left swimming in the water, and those must have perished before help could reach them.

With the disappearance of *Scharnhorst* Admiral Sturdee made a double turn with his ships to bring them more or less into the wake of *Gneisenau* and adopted a new disposition. He followed *Gneisenau* on the starboard side himself, in *Invincible*, and sent *Inflexible* to take up a corresponding position on the port quarter. This brought both ships within a range of about 12,000 yards of the *Gneisenau*, who for the next forty minutes was subjected to a double attack, one on each side. At 5:15 she made her last effort. She hit *Invincible* amidships.

It is curious that after 5:30, when every gun but one was out of action and the ship had a heavy list, that she should still have been able to fire her last surviving piece. But such incidents are common to all naval actions. It is said that, at the Battle of Tuschima, when *Savaroff* had not only been shot to pieces, but seemed to be red hot from stem to stern, one of the 6-inch casemates kept at work quite steadily throughout, the last shot being fired when the ship was on her beam ends, in the act of sinking, so that the shell must have been shot straight up into the air.

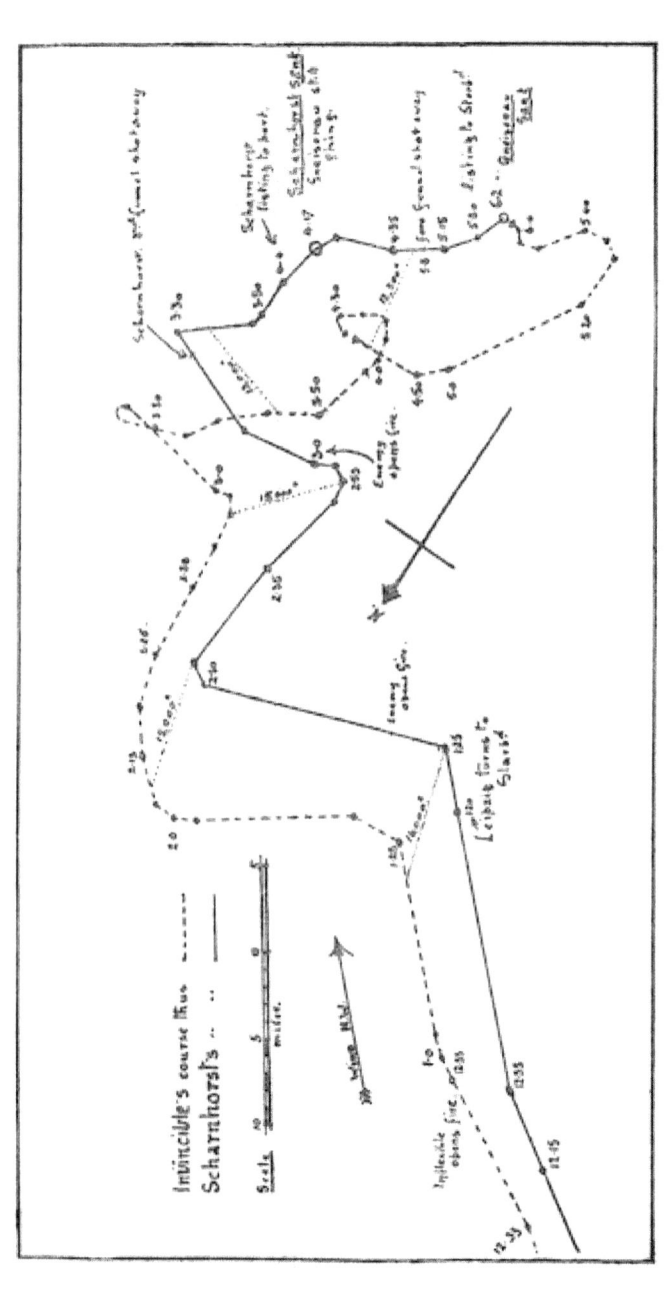

Plan of the action between the British battle-cruisers and the German armoured cruisers

The prisoners of war from the *Gneisenau* report that by the time the ammunition was expended, some 600 men had been killed and wounded. The surviving officers and men were all ordered on deck and told to provide themselves with hammocks and any articles that could support them in the water.

When the ship capsized and sank there were probably some two hundred unwounded survivors in the water, but owing to the shock of the cold water, many were drowned within sight of the boats and ship.

Every effort was made to save life as quickly as possible, both by boats and from the ships; life-buoys were thrown and ropes lowered, but only a proportion could be rescued. The *Invincible* alone rescued 108 men, fourteen of whom were found to be dead after being brought on board; these men were buried at sea the following day with full military honours.

Some of the German prisoners believed that *Gneisenau* was not sunk by gun-fire at all, and said that the commander had had the Kingston valves opened as soon as the ammunition was exhausted and there was no possibility of carrying on the fight.

CHAPTER 14

Battle of the Falkland Islands (3)

C. ACTION WITH THE LIGHT CRUISERS

At about 1 p.m., when the *Scharnhorst* and *Gneisenau* turned to port to engage the *Invincible* and *Inflexible* the enemy's light cruisers turned to starboard to escape; the *Dresden* was leading and the *Nürnberg* and *Leipzig* followed on each quarter.

In accordance with my instructions, the *Glasgow*, *Kent*, and *Cornwall* at once went in chase of these ships; the *Carnarvon*, whose speed was insufficient to overtake them, closed the battle-cruisers.

The *Glasgow* drew well ahead of the *Cornwall* and *Kent*, and at 3 p.m. shots were exchanged with the *Leipzig* at 12,000 yards. The *Glasgow's* object was to endeavour to outrange the *Leipzig* with her 6-inch guns and thus cause her to alter course and give the *Cornwall* and *Kent* a chance of coming into action.

At 4:17 p.m. the *Cornwall* opened fire, also on the *Leipzig*.

At 7:17 p.m. the *Leipzig* was on fire fore and aft, and the *Cornwall* and *Glasgow* ceased fire.

The *Leipzig* turned over on her port side and disappeared at 9 p.m. Seven officers and eleven men were saved.

At 3:36 p.m. the *Cornwall* ordered the *Kent* to engage the *Nürnberg*, the nearest cruiser to her.

Owing to the excellent and strenuous efforts of the engine-room department, the *Kent* was able to get within range of the *Nürnberg* at 5 p.m. At 6:35 p.m. the *Nürnberg* was on fire forward and ceased firing. The *Kent* also ceased firing and closed to 3,300 yards; as the colours were still observed to be flying in the

Nürnberg, the *Kent* opened fire again. Fire was finally stopped five minutes later on the colours being hauled down, and every preparation was made to save life. The *Nürnberg* sank at 7:27 p.m. and as she sank a group of men were waving a German ensign attached to a staff. Twelve men were rescued, but only seven survived.

The *Kent* had four killed and twelve wounded mostly caused by one shell.

During the time the three cruisers were engaged with the *Nürnberg* and *Leipzig*, the *Dresden*, who was beyond her consorts, effected her escape owing to her superior speed. The *Glasgow* was the only cruiser with sufficient speed to have had any chance of success. However, she was fully employed in engaging the *Leipzig* for over an hour before either the *Cornwall* or *Kent* could come up and get within range. During this time the *Dresden* was able to increase her distance and get out of sight.

The weather changed after 4 p.m. and the visibility was much reduced; further, the sky was overcast and cloudy, thus assisting the *Dresden* to get away unobserved.

Sir Doveton Sturdee's account of the two actions between the two light cruisers is almost too syncopated to be intelligible. Fortunately, however, many other records of these two encounters are available, so it is possible to describe what happened in somewhat greater detail. From 1:20 until about quarter to four, *Glasgow*, *Kent*, and *Cornwall* were engaged in a plain stern chase with the three enemy cruisers. At that time the enemy began separating out, and the three British cruisers worked into a line abreast following suit. The *Glasgow* was at the right of the line between three and four miles from *Cornwall* and about a mile to a mile and a half ahead of her. *Kent* was to the left of *Cornwall*, about two and a half miles off and about abreast of her.

Straight ahead of *Cornwall* was *Leipzig*, the centre ship of the enemy. She was about eight miles from *Cornwall* and between six and seven from *Glasgow*. To *Leipzig's* right, and two or three miles ahead of her, was *Dresden*, and to her left and about the same distance off was *Nürnberg*. There had been a certain exchange of shots before this condition was reached, for *Glasgow*, very much the fastest of the British cruisers, had more than once drawn up towards *Leipzig*, and opened fire on her in hopes of turning her towards *Cornwall* and *Kent*. And each time her attack was met by resolute and accurate fire by the

Germans. As the German ships began to separate, *Glasgow* headed off to the right towards *Dresden*, once more coming under the broadside fire of *Leipzig*.

It must be remembered that *Glasgow* only had two 6-inch guns, only one of which—the bow gun—could be employed in these conditions, and that the *Leipzig's* 4.2's completely outranged her 4-inch. It appears to be a universal practice with the Germans to mount all their guns from the largest to the smallest, so that they can be used at extreme elevation. It will be remembered how the *Koenigsberg* showed the most perfect accuracy of fire at nearly 11,000 yards with guns of a calibre that in pre-war days few in the British Service would have thought it possible to employ at greater range than 7,000 or 8,000 yards. These efforts of *Glasgow* to manoeuvre *Leipzig* into contact with Cornwall, gave *Dresden* a chance she was not slow to take. She was much the fastest of all the German craft, and managed, between four and five, to slip completely out of sight and escape.

This escape was made easier, and all the shooting throughout the two cruiser actions was made much more difficult by the sudden change in the weather that has already been noted as having begun shortly before 4 o'clock. A drizzling rain had set in, and not only had it become practically impossible to use rangefinders owing to the poor light, but it became extremely hard to detect the fall of shot and so correct the fire. In considering these two fights then, the extremely difficult conditions that prevailed must be taken into account. Let us deal first with the pursuit and destruction of *Nürnberg*.

"Kent" v "Nürnberg"

At 5 o'clock *Kent*, after a chase of nearly four hours, was getting within range of *Nürnberg*. *Nürnberg* had crept away to the eastward of *Leipzig*, so that by the time fire was opened, a considerable distance separated this from the other engagements. In point of fact, when the action began, the rain and increasing mist hid every other ship from sight. It was *Nürnberg* which was first to open fire and, so far as could be judged, the range must have been about 11,000 yards or slightly over. *Kent* held her fire for another ten minutes, as if waiting to see what the *Nürnberg's* guns could do at this range. She could of course, only use her two guns on the quarter-deck, and the after gun on the port side. To the astonishment of the *Kent* all her first salvoes were right over. The range would have been a long one for a 6-inch gun; it seemed almost fabulous for a 4.2.

Ten minutes later *Kent* opened with her bow turret, and for the next half hour an active duel was maintained. The *Kent* had sheered off a little to the left so as to bring her forward casemate guns also to bear. There was no doubt about the *Nürnberg's* shots falling over close, and the *Kent's* guns seemed from the ship to be fairly on the target. But for a considerable time, there was no evidence that they were hitting, and *Kent* was certainly not suffering from *Nürnberg's* fire, astonishingly accurate as it was. But suddenly, soon after half-past five, *Kent*, who was keeping up a speed of nearly a knot more than she had ever done before, began to gain enormously on her opponent. The range had been over 11,000 yards at 5 o'clock; by twenty minutes to six it got almost down to 7,000. It was obvious that *Nürnberg's* motive power had somehow come to grief. Had one of *Kent's* shells landed in her engine, or had one of the boilers, under the strain of so many hours' high pressure, given way?

Whatever the cause, the results were exactly what Captain Allen was looking for. If the light had been bad at five it was getting worse every minute, and if the business was to be finished it had to be finished quickly. With the shortening range, the effect of the British lyddite was soon visible, and *Nürnberg* had no alternative but to repeat the manoeuvre of Von Spee and turn broadside to for her assailant. *Kent* turned too, and not this time to lengthen the range, but to bring her whole nine broadside guns to bear.

In point of fact, she closed the range as rapidly as she could, consistently with keeping all her guns bearing, and by 6 o'clock had reduced it to 3,000 yards. *Nürnberg* was now a beaten ship. She had one topmast gone; her funnels were riddled; her speed had fallen from twenty-four knots at 5 o'clock to about eighteen at a quarter to six, and now almost to ten. Of the five guns on her port side only two were in action. Shortly after this she turned bows on to the *Kent*, and was at once caught by several 6-inch shells in the forecastle, which smashed up both the bow guns, shattering the bridge and conning-tower.

Ever since the turn at a quarter to six, *Kent* had kept ahead of her, though shortening the range, doubtless with an eye to the possibilities of *Nürnberg* using a torpedo. When, therefore, at 6:10 she was almost stopped and seemed beaten, *Kent* passed her and pushed on to about 5,000 yards to await developments. Shortly after six, *Nürnberg* ceased fire altogether, and seemed a wreck. But her colours were still flying, and it was necessary to fire at her again. Just before seven she hauled down her colours and surrendered. Both ships were now at a dead

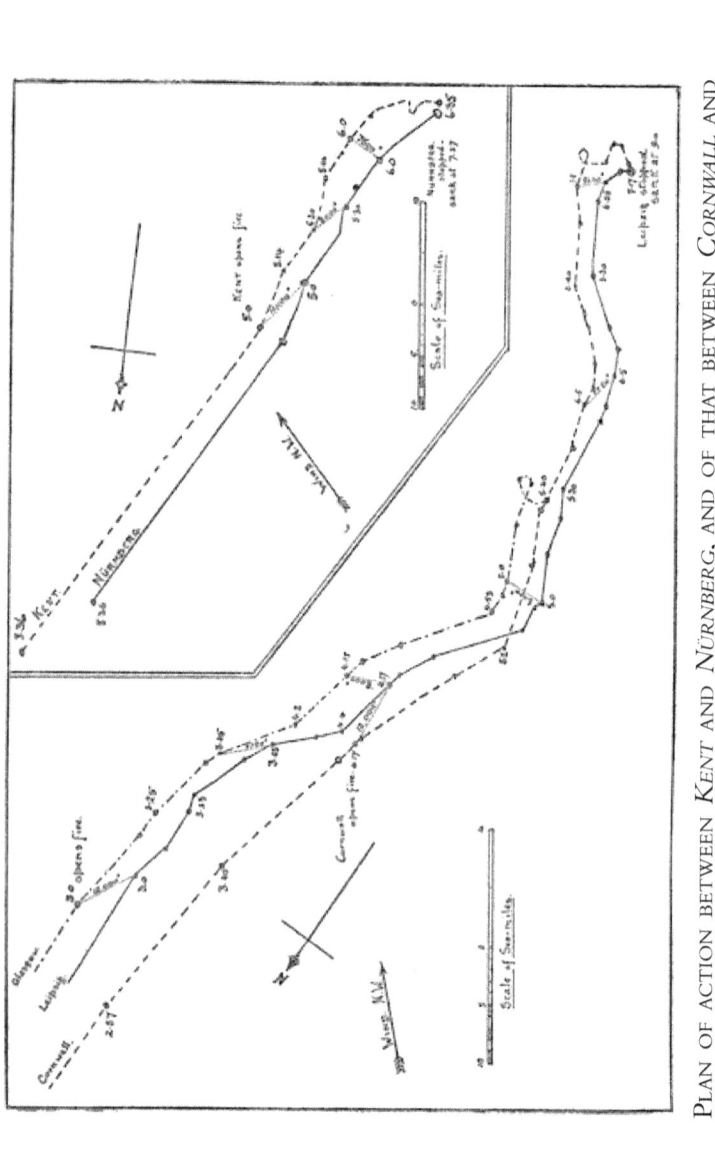

Plan of action between KENT and NÜRNBERG, and of that between CORNWALL and GLASGOW and LEIPZIG

stop, and *Kent* got out her boats as far as she could to take possession of the enemy.

But, as Captain Allen told the Association of Kentish Men in his very interesting letter about the action, the ship had received no less than thirty-six hits during the short but decisive engagement, and though she had been singularly fortunate in losing very few men—four men killed and twelve wounded—all her boats but two were in splinters, and both of these needed repairs before they could be used. They were, however, manned and lowered as quickly as possible, but they were hardly on their way towards the *Nürnberg*, some two miles off, when the enemy was seen to turn slowly on her side and sink.

As she went below the waves, some of her gallant crew were seen on the stern waving the German ensign defiantly. For an hour and a half, that is until sometime after dark, the *Kent's* two boats searched for survivors. Only seven were saved alive. Some were lashed to hammocks and gratings, and others were swimming. But in the extreme cold the great majority perished. One account of this dismal episode that has been sent to me says that the albatrosses were actually attacking the living as well as the dead in this last melancholy scene.

"CORNWALL" AND "GLASGOW" *V.* "LEIPZIG"

We have seen in the account of the *Kent* and *Nürnberg* action that up to 4 o'clock cruisers of both sides kept fairly well together, and that then the Germans opened out. It was shortly after this that they got out of sight of each other. *Kent* pursued *Nürnberg* in a more easterly direction, the *Glasgow* and *Cornwall* pursuing *Leipzig* more to the south. In order to bring the *Leipzig* to action *Glasgow* was sent forward on the *Cornwall's* left, which made *Leipzig*, while still of course retreating as fast as she could, turn slightly towards *Cornwall* and transfer her fire to her. All three ships were now firing, but the shots were falling short, until at about 4:20 *Cornwall* made the first hit on the enemy, carrying away his foremast. This made the enemy edge away to the right, a move which was followed by *Cornwall* also. The range was now shortening. When it was 8,000 yards *Leipzig* made her first hits.

Cornwall thereupon altered course still more to starboard thus bringing about two effective results. The whole broadside of guns came in play, and the change of course threw out *Leipzig's* fire control. Both ships kept on these courses, and the range increased again to nearly 10,000 yards. As we have previously seen, it was at this time that the weather began to get really thick, and as a consequence of this it became exceedingly difficult to see the fall of shot, but it is worth remembering that *Leipzig* was still hitting with her 4.2's. Shortly after 5 o'clock, however, the range reached over 10,000 yards, and it became necessary to close once more. Between five and a quarter to six *Cornwall*, that had now clearly got the speed of *Leipzig*, carried out precisely the same tactics that the vice-admiral had adopted in the case of the battle-cruisers.

Alternately, that is to say, closing the enemy at full speed, shelling him with the fo'c'sle guns, and then turning sharply to starboard to bring the whole broadside to bear. At about a quarter to six *Leipzig* landed a shell in *Cornwall's* paint room, which shook the ship but did no damage. Captain Ellerton now decided to shorten the range and use lyddite shell. In the half hour between a quarter to six and a quarter past the range was brought down to about 8,500, and by about 6:40 it was reduced to 7,000. A far better proportion of hits was now being obtained, and the effect of the lyddite became immediately apparent. First one and then another of *Leipzig's* guns ceased firing, and by ten minutes to seven a big fire started forward.

A few minutes before *Cornwall* had heard the news by wireless of the sinking of *Scharnhorst* and *Gneisenau*, and officers and men redoubled their efforts. The range was closed still more, the hitting became more intense, but the enemy in spite of his losses and damages kept every gun that could still work firing, and was actually hitting *Cornwall* frequently right up to five minutes past seven, but in another five minutes two of her funnels were gone and the ship was blazing fore and aft.

Cornwall thereupon ceased fire, expecting the enemy to strike his colours, but he did not do so. So, *Cornwall* closed about 5,000 yards and gave her a few more salvoes of lyddite. At a quarter to eight there was a loud explosion on board *Leipzig* and her mainmast went over the side. At 8:12, it was of course dark by now, she sent up signals of distress. Both *Cornwall* and *Glasgow* now lowered boats as fast as they could be repaired and manned, but they were not able to reach the enemy until after 9 o'clock, and before they did so the ship turned over and sank. Only six officers and nine men were rescued from the water. Heavy as the casualties must have been, there were in all probability more than these unwounded at the end of the action, and all of those not killed, wounded as well as unwounded, might have been saved, for the ship was not actually in a sinking condition from *Cornwall* and *Glasgow's* fire, and had been sunk by the orders of her own officers.

Cornwall was hit eighteen times, but did not suffer a single casualty.

Glasgow had one man killed and five wounded. One of the *Leipzig's* officers said that from a quarter past six till seven, that is when the range had been brought down to about 7,000 yards, some rounds out of every salvo fired hit the ship. The effect of the lyddite appears to have been appalling. Men were blown to pieces and the ship was littered with ghastly fragments and relics of humanity. When the ship could reply no more, for there was no ammunition left for such guns as might still have been worked, the captain called the survivors together and said anyone who liked could go and haul the flag down, but he would not do it. Nor did any one volunteer. About fifty jumped overboard, and when the ship sent up signals of distress there were only eighteen left alive on board. All but one of them were saved.

D. Action with the Enemy Transports

A report was received at 11:27 a.m. from H.M.S. *Bristol* that three ships of the enemy, probably transports or colliers, had appeared off Port Pleasant. The *Bristol* was ordered to take the *Macedonia* under his orders and destroy the transports.

H.M.S. *Macedonia* reports that only two ships, steamships *Baden* and *Santa Isabel*, were present; both ships were sunk after the removal of the crew.

It is not clear from this what became of the third ship. But there were persistent rumours in various South American ports that the Germans had, in the course of the autumn, collected a very considerable number of trained reservists from the different South American States and cities, and had got them on board a transport with arms, etc., so as to be ready for any military purpose the naval commander-in-chief might select. It is exceedingly probable that the reason Von Spee did not appear off the Falkland Islands till five weeks after his defeat of Admiral Cradock was that he had had to spend a considerable time in getting these reservists ready for action.

It certainly is quite clear that on December 8th he arrived off the Falkland Islands intending to attack, and it is far more probable that he intended to attack, seize, and annex the colony than merely to subdue and rob it. To seize and annex he would have needed troops, and the third transport that *Macedonia* did not find when she got *Santa Isabel* and *Baden* probably contained the men destined to hold the colony. That the British Admiralty expected some attack of this kind is shown from the fact that *Canopus*, after being ordered north, was told to return to the Falkland Islands and to do the best possible for the defence of the colony. The only military strength possessed by the colony was three hundred volunteers who had had very little training and practically no arms beyond rifles. *Good Hope* had left a field-gun when passing at the beginning of October, but of other artillery there was none.

The seizure of the island, then, by Von Spee's force of five ships, supplemented by a regiment of reservists, was a perfectly feasible project. Had it succeeded and the island been left with an adequate supply of machine and field guns, to resist a landing, it would have been an extremely difficult job to have turned them out. For with guns properly emplaced, the ships' artillery could have done very little to protect landing parties, and Admiral Sturdee's ships carried no sufficient surplus of men for it to have been practicable to incur a heavy sacrifice of life to regain the island. So far as this adventure was concerned the whole thing miscarried through being a week too late.

CHAPTER 15

Battle of the Falkland Islands (4)

STRATEGY—TACTICS—GUNNERY

Von Spee's mistakes we have seen in the course of my comment on the narrative. They were broadly fourfold. Three arose from an inability to realise from the very beginning the true character of the situation, the fourth from want of resolution to fight an unequal action on the only conditions in which any success was to be gained.

Von Spee's initial blunder was approaching the Falkland Islands with the whole of his force instead of making a *reconnaissance* by a single fast, light cruiser. It was obvious that he could gain nothing by surprise. For it was beyond the power of the colony to extemporise defence. It was equally obvious that he stood to lose everything if he was himself surprised.

And however improbable it might have seemed to him that a force superior to his had reached the Falkland Islands by this date, he should yet have realised that there was nothing impossible in such a force being there very much earlier. For from the North Sea to the Falkland Islands is only a little over 7,000 miles. He might have credited the British Admiralty with a willingness to avenge Cradock's defeat and with ingenuity enough to arrange the most secret coaling of any force that was sent out. When all allowances were made, there should have been no difficulty in battle-cruisers reaching the South Atlantic three weeks after they were despatched. Nor was there any reason why the despatch should be delayed more than two weeks after the news of the disaster.

If *Gneisenau*, instead of turning away when the tripod masts of the battle-cruisers were seen, had persisted in the advance towards *Kent*; had *Scharnhorst* joined her at top speed, it is morally certain that

Kent and *Macedonia* would have been destroyed before either of the battle-cruisers could come to their rescue. It would not have been difficult to have found dead ground that the guns of *Canopus* could not reach, and from such a point to have subjected the battle-cruisers to a most damaging succession of salvoes, as they emerged from the narrow channel, before there was any possibility of their replying. It was indeed possible that the motive power of each might have been so injured that a pursuit by the battle-cruisers would have been impossible.

At the worst, Von Spee would have paid no higher price than he ultimately paid, and he might have won an exchange entirely beneficial to German arms. Certainly, an action fought in these conditions would have given ample time for the light cruisers to make their way into the winding and uncharted fjords of Patagonia. Here *Dresden* maintained herself for many weeks, and who knows but that the others might have lasted longer still? Had it been possible for the three to keep together they would have been formidable opponents for any single cruiser in search of them. Had they scattered and been able to maintain their coal supply, they could have held up British trade for a considerable time.

Just as Von Spee missed this real opportunity, so, later on, he first of all kept his light cruisers with him far too long, and then, throughout the action, accepted battle far too much on Admiral Sturdee's conditions. But the initial mistake was the greatest.

British Strategy

The Battle of the Falkland Islands was an event of enormous importance and interest, and I propose to discuss a few of its more obvious bearings. Let us first consider its immediate direct and indirect effects upon the course of the war. The overseas naval situation at the end of October, while not in the larger sense at all threatening or dangerous, afforded nevertheless grounds for very great anxiety. *Emden* had made a series of sensational captures in the Bay of Bengal and the Indian Ocean. *Karlsruhe* was working havoc with the British trade off the northeast corner of South America. The German China squadron had evaded the Japanese and British and Allied fleets in the East, and *Australia* and her consorts had obtained no news of its whereabouts when cruising between the Antipodes and the German islands.

A few British ships had been taken by *Dresden* on her passage down to the Straits of Magellan, and the public was entirely without information which led them to suppose that either Von Spee or any of the raiding cruisers were the subject of any effective pursuit. Though the loss of ships by hostile cruisers was absurdly smaller than experts had anticipated, it was quite large enough to disconcert and alarm the public, who knew, after all, very little about the character of those anticipations. Suddenly in the first week of November came two thunderclaps.

Admiral Cradock, with a preposterously weak force, had been engaged and been defeated by the lost Von Spee. Of the four ships composing his squadron, the armed liner *Otranto* and the light cruiser *Glasgow* had escaped, but *Good Hope* and *Monmouth* had gone down, lost with all hands. Then on November 3rd came the bombardment of Lowestoft by certain German cruisers. It was the first attack of any kind on the people of these islands, and it was hastily explained to us by the Admiralty—and quite rightly—that the thing was without a military objective or military importance, and as if to forestall naval criticism, we were further told that it would not be allowed to disturb any previously made Admiralty plans. We were asked to believe that it was a mere piece of frightfulness.

But it is not certain that this was the only motive of the adventure. May it not have been done in the express hope that the British higher command, face to face with a shocked and outraged public opinion, would hesitate about diminishing those forces at home which were best calculated to intercept and bring to action the fast vessels which alone could be employed with any chance of safety on these bombarding expeditions? Is it not more than possible that the German staff, knowing the prospects of the rebellion in South Africa, was most desperately anxious to give Von Spee an added chance of crossing the Atlantic in security and lending the tremendous support of his squadron to the German forces in South-West Africa, who, with this added prestige, could be counted upon to attract all the disaffected South African sentiment to its side? Were not these bombardments, in short, undertaken solely to compel us to keep our stronger units concentrated?

Whether this was the German plan or not, let it stand to the credit of the Fisher-Churchill *régime* that no fear, either of public opinion or as to the success of future raids, stood in the way of dealing promptly with the Von Spee menace. It should undoubtedly have been dealt with long before. It was a blunder that Jerram's force was not overwhelmingly superior to Von Spee's; a blunder that he had not been instructed to shadow him from the beginning. Cradock's mission ought never to have been permitted. But now that fate had exposed these errors of policy, the right thing at last was done. Yet it must have taken some nerve to do it.

The British forces in the North Sea had certainly been greatly strengthened since the outbreak of war. *Agincourt, Erin, Canada, Benbow*, and certain lighter units had joined the Grand Fleet. *Tiger* was finished and commissioned as part of the Battle-Cruiser Fleet under Sir David Beatty. This gave him four battle-cruisers of a speed of twenty-eight knots and armed with 13.5 guns, in addition to the four of an older type—*New Zealand, Indomitable, Invincible, Inflexible*. To take two of these and send them after Von Spee reduced this force very considerably, but it was probably thought that the addition of *Tiger* left Sir David strong enough for the main purpose. After victory had been won a month later, rumours were prevalent that a third battle-cruiser had been despatched westward as well, but this has never been confirmed. But on the main point, namely, the vital importance of sending an adequate force for the pursuit and capture of Von Spee, the strategical decision was indisputably right.

Its value can be judged by the immediate results of the victory. Between November 1st and December 8th, it is almost true to say that British trade with the west coast of South America was at a standstill. On the east coast things were very little better. For if shippers were still willing to send their ships to sea, it was only on the receipt of greatly enhanced freights. Immediately after the victory Valparaiso shipping put to sea as if no war was in existence, and all Pacific and South Atlantic freight fell immediately to normal.

Even the escape of *Dresden* did not qualify the universal sense of relief. The repercussion in South Africa was equally prompt. The rebellion in the Anglo-Dutch colonies had been put down. But to embark on the conquest of German South-West Africa was a different thing altogether, and certainly one that could not be attempted so long as there was the least suspicion of insecurity in General Botha's sea communications. And while Von Spee was at large this insecurity was obvious. One of the direct results then of the despatch of Admiral Sturdee to the South Atlantic was to make the first military invasion of German territory both possible and ultimately successful.

Apart from its immediate results in the way of relieving British trade in South America and removing the last obstacle to active British military policy in South Africa, the Falkland Islands engagement was of enormous value not only in re-asserting the prestige of the British Navy, but in giving fresh heart to all the Allies after the exhausting struggles to defeat the German advances on the French capital and Calais. It was especially the first definite proof the Alliance had received that British sea-power was no vague and shadowy thing, but a real force which, rightly and relentlessly employed, must ensure the ultimate victory of Allied arms. These were its good sides.

It had one lamentable and disastrous consequence. *Emden* was captured before the battle-cruisers left their English port. *Karlsruhe* was never heard of again, and the rumours of her destruction seemed before December to be well founded, so that after the victory of December 8th, beyond the fugitive *Dresden* and two armed liner unaccounted for, there was not a German ship in the world to threaten a single British trade or territorial interest. For *Koenigsberg*, if she had escaped the guns of the two ships that had attempted her destruction in the mouth of the Rufigi, which was doubtful, was at any rate so closely blockaded that her power for active mischief was clearly at an end. German naval force was then limited to the High Seas Fleet, still of course intact, but with apparently no wish to attempt an active, and no power to make an effective, offensive.

Of this force Sir John Jellicoe seemed to have taken the measure. Four months of activity, strenuous and anxious beyond description, had made our fleet bases proof against submarine attack, so that the only offensive open to the German fleet, that embodied in the policy of attrition, was no longer a menace. The submarine attack on trade was unexpected. At a blow, then, Whitehall, which for four months had been kept on tenterhooks by its unpreparedness for cruiser or submarine warfare, suddenly found itself without a naval care in the world.

But Mr. Churchill could not be idle, and the tempter planted in his fertile brain the crazy conception that the unemployed and unemployable fleet should add to his laurels, by repeating, on the Dardanelles forts the performances of the German howitzers at Liège, Maubeuge, and Antwerp. The failure of the Naval Brigade at Antwerp was to be picturesquely avenged. In judging of the results of the Falkland Islands battle then, we must set against its immediate and resounding benefits the humiliating tragedy of Gallipoli.

The Tactics of the Battle

The Battle of the Falkland Islands, as we have seen, resolved itself into three separate engagements, and two of these may be taken as classic examples of the tactics of superior speed and armament, unconfused by the long-distance torpedo. It was this theory of tactics that held the field in England from 1904, or 1905, when the Dreadnought policy was definitely adopted, until 1912, or 1913, when the effect in naval action of the new torpedo, was first exhaustively analysed. These actions, then, taken in conjunction with the *Sydney-Emden* fight, stand entirely by themselves, and it is possible that very little naval fighting will ever take place again under similar conditions.

At the Dogger Bank and off the Jutland Reef the torpedo was employed to the fullest extent, with results that we shall see when we come to consider these actions. We have of course, no direct statement that no torpedoes were employed in the Falkland engagements. Indeed, in a modified way the torpedoes certainly had some influence. But there is the whole world of difference between torpedoes fired singly from one warship to another, and torpedoes used both in great quantities and by light craft which, under the defensive properties of their speed, can close to ranges sufficiently short to give the torpedo a reasonable chance of hitting, or, by taking station ahead, can add the target's to the torpedo's speed to increase its range. We shall be broadly right then in treating these engagements as affairs of gunnery purely, for the torpedo had seemingly no influence in the periods that were decisive.

Briefly put, what were the tactics of Admiral Sturdee with the battle-cruisers, and Captain Ellerton with *Cornwall* and *Glasgow* on December 8th? Their business was to destroy an enemy far weaker than themselves, one who had neither strength enough to fight victoriously nor speed enough to fly successfully. Both followed the same plan. They employed their superior speed, first to get near enough for their heavier guns to be used with some effect, and then, whenever the enemy tried to close, to get to a range at which his inferior pieces could be expected to get a considerable percentage of hits, they manoeuvred to increase the range so as to keep the enemy at a permanent gunnery disadvantage.

As this long-range fire gradually told, the enemy's artillery became necessarily less and less effective, until he was reduced to a condition in which he could be closed and finished off without taking any risks at all. These tactics resulted in *Gneisenau* and *Scharnhorst* being destroyed by *Invincible* and *Inflexible*, the whole crews of both German ships being either killed or captured, while the two battle-cruisers had three casualties only. *Invincible* was actually hit by twenty-two shells, *Inflexible* by only three, and it was the latter ship who had the only three men hit. *Cornwall* received eighteen direct hits and, like *Invin-*

cible, had no casualties at all, while *Glasgow* had one man killed and five wounded.

Obviously, an action could not be fought upon these lines unless time and space sufficed in which to bring about the desired result. In point of fact, when the disparity of force is considered, the time taken was extraordinary. *Inflexible* opened fire on the German cruisers at five minutes to one, *Scharnhorst* sank at seventeen minutes past four, and *Gneisenau* just after 6 o'clock. If we suppose only twelve 12-inch guns to have been bearing throughout the action, we have one hundred 12-inch gun hours! There was time therefore—at a battle-practice rate of fire—for both ships to have fired away their entire stocks of ammunition at least dozens of times over. What they did, of course, was to fire extremely deliberately when the target was within range and the conditions suitable, and to cease fire altogether when they were manoeuvring.

In the *Cornwall-Glasgow-Leipzig* action, fire was opened at about 4 o'clock, and it was not till about 7:8 that the enemy was beaten. An hour afterwards he sent up signals of distress and surrendered. Here there were eleven 6-inch guns in the two British broadsides, and five 4-inch, against a handful of 4.25. The disparity in force was perhaps not quite so great as in the battle-cruiser action, but these things are difficult to compare, and from all accounts 6-inch lyddite, once the hitting begins, does not take long to put a light cruiser of the *Leipzig* class completely out of action.

Captain Allen's action against *Nürnberg* is in very sharp contrast to this. He opened fire at 5 o'clock, some few minutes after the enemy had attacked him. The range was about 11,000 yards, and for some time no apparent damage was done. At 5:45, however, though *Nürnberg* seemed still undamaged, the range was reduced by 4,000 yards, owing to *Nürnberg's* sudden loss of speed. There then followed twenty minutes of action at ranges between 6,000 and 3,000, and these sufficed to finish the enemy off altogether. It may be objected to Captain Allen's tactics that he received twice as many hits as the *Cornwall* and had twelve men wounded and four killed. But as Admiral Sturdee points out in his despatch these casualties were almost entirely caused by a single chance shell that burst in a gun position, right amongst the crew. No one in any of the very exposed positions—control tops, rangefinder positions, etc.—was even touched.

Too much, therefore, must not be made of the casualties, for in this matter chance enters too largely for safe deductions to be made.

Invincible, for instance, received twenty-two hits without a single casualty, *Inflexible* three hits and three casualties. *Cornwall* and *Kent* were sister ships, and if the gun shields of *Kent* were unable to protect one crew, any one of the eighteen shells that hit *Cornwall* might have done equal damage to that suffered by *Kent*. The value, as it seems to me, of the *Kent-Nürnberg* example lies in this, that for all practical purposes exactly the same result was obtained, at the same cost, in one hour—of which twenty minutes was at almost point-blank range—in this action, as was got by two ships in three hours in the *Leipzig* action, and by two battle-cruisers in five hours in the battle cruiser action.

It would be a mistake to assume that we see a new contrast in methods in these engagements. *Kent* certainly followed the Nelsonian tradition. He closed with his enemy at top speed, and got not only the full artillery value of his attack, by making hitting easier and therefore more certain, but won what is hardly less valuable, the vast moral advantage of giving his enemy no breathing time at all. There are fifty parallels to this, of which Trafalgar is in fact only the supreme example. Given a superior force of guns—obtained by Nelson by the concentration of the whole of his fleet on the centre and rear of the enemy—the tactical plan is to be found in the method of bringing these guns to do their work in the shortest possible time.

We can find many exact parallels to Admiral Sturdee's tactics in the war of 1812, for the Americans employed them against us with the utmost success on several occasions. Indeed, it was these victories that led first to a practical revival of gunnery skill—brought about with such effect by Broke—and later to Sir Howard Douglas's effort to create a scientific study of gunnery in the British Navy. It is now nearly a hundred years since his historic work on naval gunnery was published. His father had been one of Howe's captains and had invented an important improvement in naval guns.

The son entered the artillery, and his education, no less than his family tradition, made him both an interested observer and a very competent critic of the naval gunnery of the period. He had, in his own words, witnessed "the triumphant and undisputed domination of the British marine," after the victories of Nelson had swept continental fleets from the sea, and then, seven years after Trafalgar, he had seen this triumphant navy utterly humiliated by the Americans in the war of 1812. He analysed the causes both of the triumph and the humiliation, and was, perhaps, the first to lay down the most important of all maxims of naval doctrine—then and still also the most neglected.

He pointed out how, in the later years of the Republic, practical gunnery amongst French seamen was so wretched that strongly manned ships were seen:

> . . . .employing batteries of twenty or thirty guns against our vessels without more effect than might easily have been produced by one or two well-directed pieces. Indeed, in some cases, heavy frigates used powerful batteries against our vessels for a considerable time without producing any effect at all.

Thus, the victories of the Nelsonian era were made possible because of the great disparity between the two forces in gunnery skill, and it was this disparity that made it possible to adopt the tactics by which the victors got their great successes. Victory was won by superior skill and tactics founded upon its employment. And in the hour of victory we forgot its conditioning cause. Douglas says:

> We became too confident by being feebly opposed, and then slack in warlike exercises, by not being opposed at all. And, lastly, in many cases inexpert for want of even drill practice. And herein consisted the great disadvantage in which, without suspecting it, we entered, with too great confidence, into a war with a marine much more expert than that of any of our European enemies. Comparative views of warlike skill, as well as of bulk and force . . . are necessary to correct analysis of naval actions.

In the course of his work he made a very detailed analysis of the actions between the *Macedonian* and the *United States*, the *Guerriere* and the *Constitution*, the *Shannon* and the *Chesapeake*, and the *Java* and the *Constitution*. In the three instances in which the Americans were victorious, they owed success to no superiority in the handling of their ships, but to a combination of longer-range guns and a much higher accomplishment in marksmanship and tactics designed to keep outside the range of British effective fire. In none of the three cases could any criticism be based upon the bravery of any of the British officers and crews. All were, in fact, honourably acquitted by court martial. But it was obvious in each case that had the gunnery skill been equal, while the difference in armament might ultimately have been decisive, the enemy would have had to pay very dearly indeed for victory. In each case, in point of fact, the victor's losses were trivial.

Amongst these, the action between *Shannon* and *Chesapeake* stands out just as the *Kent* and *Nürnberg* action stands out in the Falkland

Islands. Broke, in the first very few minutes of the engagement, established a complete fire ascendancy over *Chesapeake*, and had he chosen, could have hauled off and pounded her into submission without risking the life of a single one of his men. But, as in the first instance, he had relied upon close action, trusting with perfect confidence to the skill and marksmanship of his well-trained crew, so after he had got *Chesapeake* out of control, he chose the quickest path to victory. He ran straight alongside and boarded her without a moment's delay. As at Trafalgar, so here we see the British commander pre-occupied with one thought only—to bring the enemy to action as soon as possible and to finish the business quickly and decisively. So long as this is ensured, there is no thought of losses nor any hesitation in risking the ship.

Why was there any other tactical conception? It arose, as we have just seen, in the war of 1812, and was spontaneously reproduced in 1905, and in both cases, it was the product of a new skill in long-range gunnery. In 1812, there was the choice in armament, long range and short range that existed in 1905, but with this striking difference. The long-range gun of a century ago might be an eighteen or twenty-four pounder, but it was far heavier for the weight of shell it used than the short-range carronade. There was therefore a distinct temptation to arm ships with a lighter gun that would be more effective at close range, and the mistake was not discovered till the greater skill of the American ships made it clear that the long gun, in a ship rightly handled, could prevent the short-range gun from coming into action at all.

But in our own day the pride of length of reach goes with the heavier projectile. Not that the 12-inch guns of *Inflexible* and *Invincible* literally outranged the 8.2's of Von Spee, for the Germans have always mounted their guns, as we have seen, so that they can be elevated far more greatly than our own. It is quite possible therefore, that, speaking literally, Von Spee's 8.2's, as they were mounted, might have outranged Sir Doveton Sturdee's 12-inch. But at the extreme range of the 12-inch, it would be almost impossible for the 8.2's to hit on account of the extremely steep angle at which the shot falls, and, consequently, the high accuracy in range knowledge required and the improbability of the gun shooting with perfect precision at such extreme distances.

But both in 1812, and now, the basic idea behind seeking for a long-range decision is defensive. Captain Glossop opened up the range when *Emden* closed him and got the advantage of his heavy artillery. Admiral Sturdee kept the range as long as possible to save his ships from being hit. Captain Ellerton did his best to keep *Cornwall* and *Glasgow* out of *Leipzig's* reach. In all these cases there was a very obvious argument in favour of defensive tactics. *Sydney*, *Glasgow* and *Cornwall*, *Inflexible* and *Invincible* were all at very great distances from dockyards and possibilities of repairs. The two battle-cruisers were a considerable percentage of our total Dreadnought force. It was not a question of risking their destruction; it might at any moment be vital for them to be immediately ready for action. If possible, even the shortest period devoted to repairs and docking should be avoided. These considerations do not excuse defensive tactics; they may be said to have imposed them. But this should not blind us to the fact that they were defensive.

And this leads to another interesting question. Von Müller in *Emden* began the action by trying to close *Sydney*. Von Spee turned at right angles at one o'clock to shorten the range. *Nürnberg* finally turned round to bring her broadside to bear on *Kent*, but she was too late. *Leipzig* never turned at all. In no case did the German commanders persist in seeking a short-range action. Cradock apparently did nothing to close Von Spee at Coronel. What would have happened if Von Spee and Von Müller had stuck to their resolution to close? In all these cases, as we have seen, the weaker side accepted the stranger's conditions. But it was not necessary that it should have been so.

A resolute effort to close at full speed would no doubt throw a broadside of guns out of action, just as flight did. But would the stronger ships have run away had the weaker persisted in attacking? If they had held their course, there would have been a very considerable change of range, in itself a defensive element favouring the weaker ship. We can take it for granted that no effort to close would ultimately have saved the weaker ship in any case. But—and this seems to me to be the vital point—would not his chance of seriously damaging the stronger have been far higher? And is not this the one thing that should preoccupy the weaker force when compelled to engage?

Finally, two entirely new elements in naval fighting in our own time distinguish it from the fighting of the early days of last century. With ships dependent upon wind, if the chance of engaging was lost, it might never recur.

In all Nelson's letters, memoranda, and sayings, he is haunted by the vital importance of swift decision and rapid and resolute action. The whole spirit behind the Trafalgar Memorandum is impatience of delay. When the Allied Fleet was seen, there was no time wasted in securing symmetrical formations or order. The fleet was roughly grouped as Nelson intended it should be, and the only preliminary of action was not a race to get into station but a race to get to grips with the enemy. The cult of the close action was thus a direct outcome of the haunting uncertainty as to whether the fighting ship would be able to move or not. This has all been changed by steam. Admiral Sturdee, for instance, at 10:20, 11:15, and 12:20 knew perfectly well that he could have the Germans in his grip and finish the thing off in five minutes whenever he liked. If he played with them as a cat plays with a mouse, it was because he knew that he had time on his side.

But time will not always be on the side of what is for the moment the stronger force. The enemy may be heading for protection or may be expecting reinforcements, or the light may suddenly fail altogether. In spite of steam, therefore, the desirability of a quick decision is really as paramount in modern conditions as in the old days. So that, had the problem of action never been complicated by the long-range torpedo, we ought, as soon as we began the cultivation of long-range gunnery, to have realised that it was useless to limit our skill to conditions in which the target ship and the firing ship were keeping steady courses.

A further argument against closing the range in modern conditions has been put forward. Just as the change from sails to steam has helped the tactician of today, (1919), so the altered relation of the destructive power of the weapon and the resisting power of the ship has operated to his disadvantage. *Lion*, for instance, in the Dogger Bank affair, was knocked out by a chance shot that killed no men and did no vital injury to the ship at all. But it cut the feed pipes of an engine, and in two minutes the ship was disabled and for the purposes of that action, useless. Only small damage could be done to sailing ships by a shot amongst the masts and rigging. And when to a single shot there is added the risk of a torpedo, it must be admitted that the arguments against closing are stronger today than they were.

A Point in Naval Ethics

The conduct of Cradock and his captains at Coronel, of Von Müller in *Emden*, and of the captains of *Gneisenau*, *Leipzig*, and *Nürnberg*, raises an interesting point in the ethics of war. Captain Glossop, it will be remembered, after driving *Emden* on to the rocks at Direction Island, had to return towards Keeling Island to look for the *Emden's* tender. When he came back with certain prisoners on board, he appealed to Von Müller to surrender. No reply was given, and the prisoners on board the *Sydney* informed Captain Glossop that no surrender would be made. It therefore became necessary to open fire again. This brought about the hauling down of the German flag. *Gneisenau* had lost 600 killed out of a crew of eight or nine hundred when, at 8:40, she hauled down her flag. *Leipzig* and *Nürnberg* were in a similar case. *Bluecher* was similarly defeated long before she was sunk. Both *Good Hope* and *Monmouth* were apparently out of action within five minutes of action beginning.

Now in each instance it is obvious that fighting was carried on, and that therefore men were sacrificed, long after the ship was hopelessly beaten. But in many cases not only was the fighting carried on, so to speak, gratuitously, but the ship herself scuttled, thus ensuring the drowning of several wounded men and risking the drowning of a very large number of unwounded. In all, taking the *Emden*, *Gneisenau*, *Nürnberg*, *Leipzig*, and *Bluecher* together, it is not improbable that over 1,000 lives were thus thrown away to no immediately military purpose. The alternative was to surrender the ship.

Why is it taken for granted that no ship, however fairly defeated in action, however hopeless further resistance, may not quite honourably yield herself a prize to the enemy? It is an entirely new doctrine, unknown in an age surely not inferior in naval skill, in military spirit, or in chivalrous feeling. Does it date from the howl of execration that went up in Russia when, after the flower of the Russian Fleet had been defeated at Tsushima, Nebogatoff surrendered his archaic craft to the overwhelming force of the victors?

So far as I know it was in that war that the great break with the old tradition was made. The old tradition, of course, was that a ship that had fought till it could fight no longer could be surrendered to a victorious enemy without shame. The records of the wars of a century ago abound in courts-martial on officers who in these circumstances had yielded a beaten ship, and they were always honourably acquitted, when it was shown that all that was possible had been done. It was evidently thought to be mere inhumanity to condemn a crew that had fought bravely to death by fire or drowning. Not that there are not grim stories that tell of a sterner resolution, like that of Grenville in the *Revenge*.

But on the whole the navy that had done more fighting than any other, and in the period of its existence when its fighting was most continuous, took what is at once a rational and a Christian view of these situations. Now it seems that war at sea dooms those who have fought unfalteringly to finish the business, when they can fight no longer, by a savage self-immolation. It is the only alternative to allowing the enemy the glory of a capture. Is this, after all, an intolerable humiliation? To find it so is a break with the old tradition and is not an innovation for the better. It sets up a pagan standard, and it is not the paganism of the stoic, but the unfeeling barbarism of the Choctaw.

CHAPTER 16

The Heligoland Affair

Towards the end of August, 1914, the submarines under Commodore Roger Keyes discovered a *rôle* of quite unexpected utility. Their immediate function had been to watch the approaches to the Channel, so as to stop any attempt by the German Fleet to interfere with the transport of the Expeditionary Force into France. In doing this, they found that they had exceptional opportunities for observing the enemy's destroyers and light craft, and, as soon as the safety of the transports seemed assured, they constituted themselves the most efficient scouts possible. They soon found themselves in possession of an extensive knowledge of the habits of the Germans. It was this knowledge that led to the decision to sweep the North Sea up to Heligoland and cut off as many of the enemy's light craft, destroyers, and submarines as possible.

The expedition included almost every form of fast ship at the commander-in-chief's disposal. First the submarines were told off to certain stations, presumably to be in a position to attack any reinforcements which might be sent out from Wilhelmshaven or Cuxhaven. Then, in the very earliest hours of the morning, the two light cruisers *Arethusa* and *Fearless* led a couple of flotillas of destroyers into the field of operations. The *Arethusa* flew the broad pennant of Commodore Tyrwhitt. The *Fearless* was commanded by Captain Blount. The two flotillas, with their cruiser leaders, swept round towards Heligoland in an attempt to cut off the German cruisers and destroyers and drive them, if possible, to the westward.

Some miles out to the west, Rear-Admiral Christian had the squadron of six cruisers of the *Euryalus* and *Bacchante* classes ready to intercept the chase. Commodore Goodenough, with a squadron of light cruisers, attended Vice-Admiral Beatty, with the battle-cruisers, at a prearranged rendezvous, ready to cut in to the rescue if there was any chance of *Arethusa* and *Fearless* being overpowered.

The expedition obviously involved very great risks. It took place within a very few miles of bases in which the whole German Fleet of battleships and battle-cruisers was lying. It was plainly possible that the attempt to cut the German light cruisers off might end in luring out the whole fleet, and one of the conditions contemplated was that Admiral Beatty, instead of administering the quietus to such German cruisers as survived the attentions of the two Commodores, might find himself condemned to a rearguard action with a squadron of German battleships. That he took this risk cheerfully, well understanding the kind of criticism that would meet him, if in the course of such an action he lost any of his ships, was the first indication we got of the fine fighting temper of this admiral.

Arethusa, *Fearless*, and the destroyers found themselves in action soon after seven o'clock with destroyers and torpedo-boats. Just before eight o'clock two German cruisers were drawn into the affray, and *Arethusa* had to fight both of them till 8:15, when one of them was drawn off into a separate action by *Fearless*, which in the ensuing fight became separated from the flagship. By 8:25 *Arethusa* had wrecked the fore-bridge of one opponent with a 6-inch projectile, and *Fearless* had driven off the other. Both were in full flight for Heligoland, which was now in sight. Commodore Tyrwhitt drew off his flotillas westward. He had suffered heavily in the fight. Of his whole battery only one 6-inch gun remained in action, while all the torpedo tubes were temporarily disabled.

Lieutenant Westmacott, a gallant and distinguished young officer, had been killed at the commodore's side. The ship had caught fire, and injuries had been received in the engines. *Fearless* seems now to have rejoined, and reported that the German destroyer commodore's flagship had been sunk. By ten o'clock Commodore Roger Keyes, in the *Lurcher*, had got into action with the German light cruisers and signalled to the *Arethusa* for help. Both British cruisers then went to his assistance, but did not succeed in finding him. All *Arethusa's* guns except two had meantime been got back to working order.

At eleven o'clock *Arethusa* and *Fearless* engaged their third enemy, this time a four-funnelled cruiser. *Arethusa*, it must be remembered, still had two guns out of action. The commodore therefore ordered a torpedo attack, whereupon the enemy at once retreated, but ten minutes later he reappeared, when he was engaged once more with guns

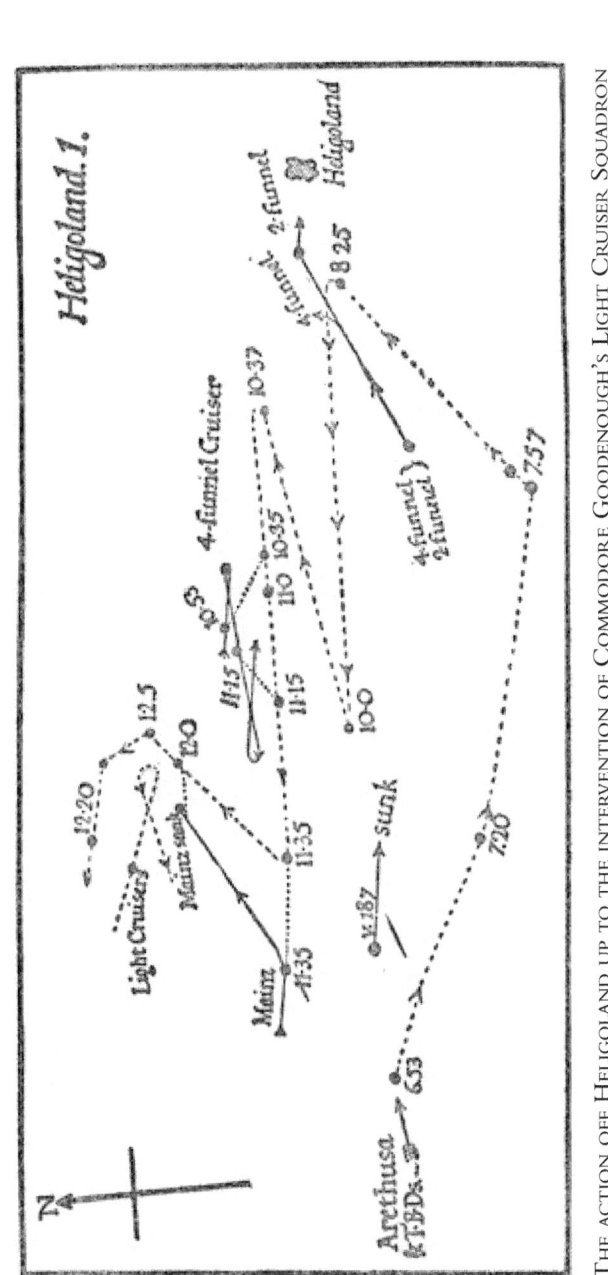

THE ACTION OFF HELIGOLAND UP TO THE INTERVENTION OF COMMODORE GOODENOUGH'S LIGHT CRUISER SQUADRON

and torpedoes, but no torpedo hit. The commodore notes an interesting feature of this cruiser's fire:

> We received a very severe and most accurate fire from this cruiser. Salvo after salvo was falling between twenty and thirty yards short, but *not a single shell* struck.

We shall find this happened several times in the different engagements. The commodore continues:

> Two torpedoes were also fired at us, being well directed but short.

At this point the position was reported to Admiral Beatty. This cruiser was finally driven off by *Fearless* and *Arethusa*, and retreated badly damaged to Heligoland. Four minutes after, the *Mainz* was encountered. *Arethusa*, *Fearless*, and the destroyers engaged her for five-and-twenty minutes, and when she was in a sinking condition Commodore Goodenough's squadron came on the scene and finished her off. *Arethusa* then got into action with a large four-funnelled cruiser at long range, but received no hits herself, and was not able to see that she made any.

It was now 12:15. *Fearless* and the first flotilla had already been ordered home by the commodore. The intervention of the battle-cruisers was very rapid and decisive. The four-funnelled cruiser that had been the last to engage *Arethusa* was soon cut off and attacked, and within twenty minutes a second cruiser crossed the *Lion's* path. She was going full speed, probably twenty-five knots, and at right angles to *Lion*, who was steaming twenty-eight. But both *Lion's* salvoes took effect, a piece of shooting which the vice-admiral very rightly calls most creditable to the gunnery of his ship. The change of range must have been 900 yards a minute. I know of no parallel to this feat, though it must be remembered that the range was short. *Lion's* course was now taking her towards known mine-fields, and the vice-admiral very properly judged that the time had come to withdraw. He proceeded to dispose of the cruiser he first attacked—which turned out to be *Köln*—before doing so.

The expedition had been a complete success. Three German cruisers had been sunk and one destroyer. Three other cruisers had been gravely damaged, and many of the German destroyers had been hit also. Our losses in men were small, and we lost no ships at all. *Arethusa* had perhaps suffered most, though some of the destroyers had been

Sinking of the *V187*, Heligoland, 1914

pretty roughly handled. But all got safely home, and none were so injured but that in a very few days or weeks they were fit again for service.

The affair was in every respect well-conceived and brilliantly carried out. The two essential matters were to begin by employing a force sufficiently weak to tempt the enemy to come out, and yet not so small nor so slow a force as to risk being overwhelmed. If something like a general action amongst the small craft could be brought about, the plan was to creep up with a more powerful squadron in readiness to rescue the van, if rescue were necessary, at any rate to secure the final and immediate destruction of as many of the enemy's ships as possible. But there was no squadron fighting at all. Goodenough's light cruisers, and Beatty's battle-cruisers did, no doubt, keep in formation, but they found no formed enemy. There were no obvious tactical lessons.

Perhaps the most interesting part of the business is to be found not in what did happen, but in what did not. The German commander-in-chief must have known long before eight o'clock in the morning that fighting was going forward within five-and-twenty or thirty miles of him. He could have got to the scene with his whole force before ten o'clock. But beyond sending in a few more light cruisers and U-boats, he appears to have done nothing either to rescue his own ships or to attempt to cut off and sink ours. It is more than probable that he suspected the trap that was indeed laid for him.

But the opportunity had been given of appearing in the North Sea in force, and the opportunity was not taken. It seemed very clear to most observers after this that the German Fleet would not willingly seek a general action, or even risk a partial action in the North Sea, except under conditions entirely of their own choosing. It seemed obvious that if such action was not sought in the early days of the war, it certainly would not be sought later, when the balance of naval power would be turning increasingly against them.

The battle-cruisers in this action had some exciting adventures with submarines. They had, for instance, to wait for some hours before the moment came for their intervention, and while at the rendezvous they were repeatedly attacked by them. From the vice-admiral's despatch, it would appear that this attack was frustrated partly by rapid manoeuvring, partly by sending destroyers to drive the U-boats off. Later in the day, when the squadron was engaged in sinking *Köln* and *Ariadne*, it was once more attacked by submarines, and *Queen Mary*

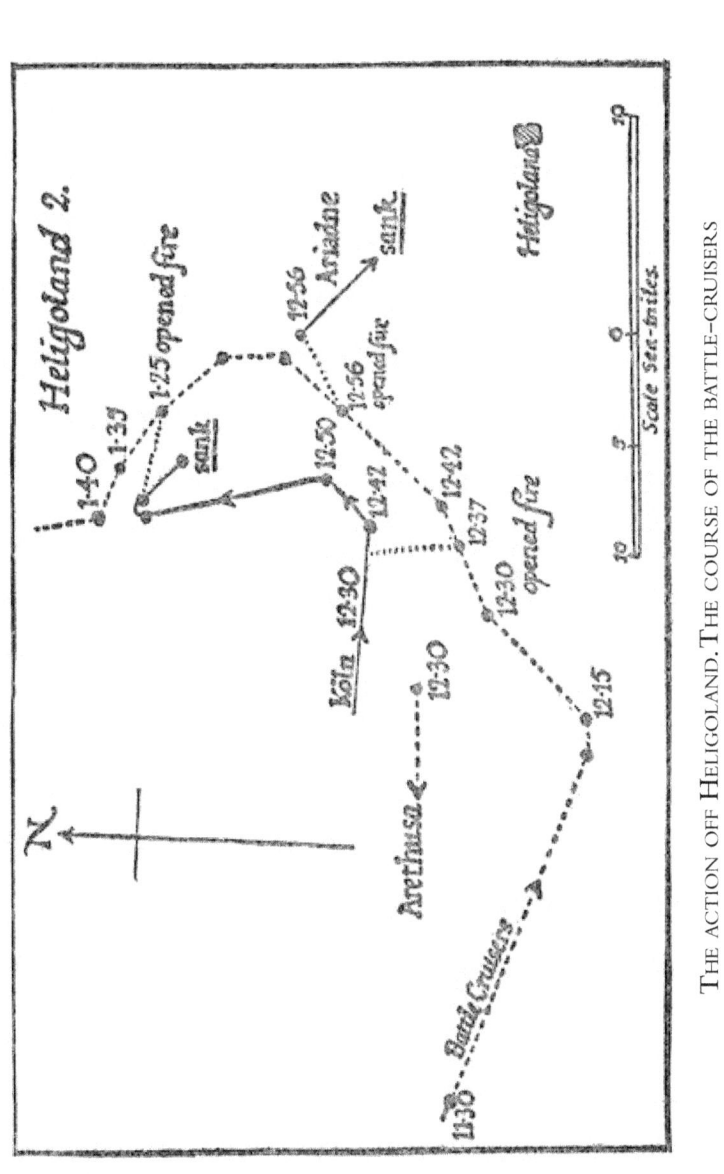

THE ACTION OFF HELIGOLAND. THE COURSE OF THE BATTLE-CRUISERS

(Captain W. R. Hall) turned his ship, not to avoid the submarine, but its torpedo, which was seen approaching. We got very early warning, therefore, of the truth of the prophecy that the first result of the employment of the torpedo in fleet actions would be compulsory movements of the attacked ships. It was a prompt reminder that if manoeuvring meant loss of artillery efficiency, that the enemy had it in his power, by submarine and destroyer onslaughts, to extinguish our gunfire from time to time.

Alone of the actions which have taken place in this war, the firing was all within comparatively short range. Six thousand yards was the limit of visibility. There are not sufficient data to judge whether the British gunnery was greatly superior to the German. But Commodore Tyrwhitt draws attention to a fact, already familiar to us, *viz.* that a German cruiser can send salvo after salvo, all within a few yards of the target, without securing a hit. It proved later to be a feature common to all engagements.

The North Sea

The engagement off Heligoland had no successor until the spring of 1916, when the attack on the island of Sylt took place. A second sweep some days after the first was made in the same waters, but nothing of the enemy was seen. Whether such sweeps were repeatedly made in 1915, without the public being informed, we do not know. By this I do not imply that no incursions into German waters were made—I mean only that we heard of none, and presumably that, if any were made, there was no result.

But two points in this connection may be borne in mind. The affair off Heligoland took place on August 28, 1914. After losing three cruisers by exposing them to Sir David Beatty's and Commodore Goodenough's forces, the Germans managed their affairs very differently. Perhaps from this time on no German craft ventured into the North Sea at all, except when the whole fleet came out in force. And they did not come out in force very often, nor at all, except at night or when the weather was clear enough for the fleet's scouts, either in the form of airships, destroyers, or cruisers, to give long warning of the presence of danger. The two raiding expeditions and Von Hipper's excursion of January 28 are undertakings of a very different character.

The Bombardments.—Whatever the explanation, there was no more fighting in home waters for exactly five months, but the Germans made two expeditions in force right across to the English shores. Early in November a squadron of cruisers appeared off Yarmouth, fired at the *Halcyon*, let off some rounds, without doing any damage, on the town, and retreated precipitately, dropping mines as they went. A British submarine unfortunately ran foul of one of these and was lost with all hands at once. *Halcyon*, perhaps the smallest and least formidable vessel that ever crept into the "Navy List", engaged the enemy imperturbably when they fled, losing one man from a fragment of shell, though practically unhurt herself. Private letters speak of salvoes falling short and over in the most disconcerting manner, and of the ship being so drenched with water as to be in danger of foundering.

The old story of the very accurate, but ineffective, fire of the German ships, was thus repeated. But no official or detailed information on this subject has been given. In December a second and much more successful raid was made. Scarborough, the Hartlepools, and Whitby were bombarded by a squadron, whose composition was never officially announced. The American papers have printed letters from Germany stating that the *Von der Tann* and *Moltke*, the *Yorck* and the *Bluecher*, with smaller cruisers, constituted the force. The visitors to Hartlepool experienced the hospitality of that flourishing port in its warmest form. The garrison artillery dealt faithfully with *Von der Tann*, and her disappearance was credibly attributed to injuries sustained in a collision, which damage to her steering gear, effected by the north country gunners, had prevented her evading.

The squadron that bombarded Yarmouth made off in the thick weather. It was obvious from the terms in which the Admiralty announced the fact that the bombardment had taken place that it was considered quite certain that they could not escape a second time. Unfortunately, however, they did; but they lost the *Yorck* by a German mine when re-entering harbour. The details of the arrangements made for anticipating them were quite properly kept secret, but it became known that a sudden fog explained why these arrangements did not succeed.

Both in the case of the Yarmouth and the Scarborough raids the enemy appeared at daylight. He had evidently crossed the North Sea during the night. From Whitby to the mine-fields off Heligoland is about 275 miles, a distance which each of the ships employed could cover quite comfortably in thirteen or fourteen hours. Had the squadron left Heligoland an hour before dark it could have fetched the English coast by daylight, hardly using more than three-quarter power. If it started for home at 8:30 it would have nine hours of daylight before it. At twenty-five knots 225 miles could be covered. This would bring them within fifty or sixty miles of the minefields, and it is probable that at some greater distance from Heligoland than this a rendezvous for submarines and destroyers had been arranged.

These raids were doubtless planned on the theory that the battle-cruiser fleet would be based on some point so far north that no difference in speed between the British and German ships would enable the former to overtake them before the mine-fields, or at least the waiting submarines and destroyers were met. And it may well have been hoped that an exasperated English Admiral, if he came up with them then, would not willingly give up the hope of an engagement. It may have seemed a very feasible operation to draw him either on to the mines themselves or within range of the submarines. It is, it seems to me, not difficult to reconstruct the German plan for both the Yarmouth and the Whitby raids.

It has often been pointed out—and with perfect justice—that in shelling open and undefended towns, and even a commercial port like Hartlepool that did have a 6-inch gun or two to defend it, the Germans were employing their fleet to no *immediate* military purpose whatever. It has been suggested that there might have been the very excellent military object of keeping our battle-cruisers in home waters and so securing Von Spee a free hand abroad. What has not been so often insisted on is that had there been any military centre, fort, or magazine worth attack, the fugitive character of the bombardments robbed them of any probable hope of hitting it.

There have been ample experiences during this war of ships bombarding distant objects on shore. And it is finally proved to be one of the most difficult operations conceivable. The case of the *Koenigsberg* was altogether exceptional. And many as were the difficulties to be faced in that action, there was yet this favourable element present, that the people in the aeroplanes could not possibly make any mistake as to the target that was to be bombarded, nor from the fact that it was a small ship lying in a considerable expanse of water could the observers, spotting all the different rounds, fail to give to the fire-control parties on board very accurate indications how to correct their sights for the next round.

At the Dardanelles when isolated forts were attacked on a point on land, where one ship could lie off nearly at right angles to the line of fire and mark the fall of shot and the firing ship correct the fire for line, exact corrections of the same character as at the Rufigi were made possible. But when it came to correcting the fire by captive balloons and aircraft, when forts and gun positions had to be picked out in the folds of the hills, and still more where forts had to be engaged with no other corrections than the men in the control tops of the firing ship could supply, it became practically impossible to ensure sustained effective firing.

When, therefore, the German ships lay off Lowestoft, Hartlepool, Whitby, and Scarborough and bombarded for half an hour or so without any attempt to select particular targets, or if such were selected, to adopt any scientific means of directing their fire on to them, it became perfectly clear that their military object was about as defined as that of midnight bombing raids with Zeppelins. One is driven to the conclusion, therefore, that the primary object of these adventures was mere frightfulness, and that perhaps the secondary object was to draw the pursuing ships into some catastrophic trap.

Chapter 17

The Action off the Dogger Bank

The two bombardments of the early winter of 1914, have been variously explained. They may have been meant to force us to keep our main forces concentrated: or simply to cheer up the Germans and depress our people. Both were organised so that the German squadron could start its race for home within an hour of daybreak.

It is more difficult, however, to explain the events of January 28. The precise point where Sir David Beatty encountered Admiral von Hipper's fleet has not been authoritatively made known, but it seems to have been on the northeastern edge of the Dogger Bank. They were encountered at seven o'clock in the morning. Von Hipper's presence at this point cannot, then, explain his being out on an expedition analogous to the former two. And I have some difficulty in understanding exactly why he took this risk. It is, of course, possible the Germans had had reports to the effect that the North Sea was clear on the 27th. It may have been so reported on several occasions, and it is possible that aircraft had verified this fact, when the weather permitted of their employment for this purpose.

The Germans, who are fond of jumping to conclusions on very insufficient premises, may have exaggerated the effect of their submarine campaign on British dispositions. We know, for instance, that the alarm undoubtedly felt by the public in September and October was very greatly exaggerated in the German press. At any rate, immediately after the battle of the Falkland Islands a good deal of rodomontade appeared about the British being driven from the North Sea, and the German seamen may have felt bound to act as if this rodomontade were true. Or a much simpler explanation may suffice. Von Hipper may have come out to look for the British ships and draw them into prepared positions and to engage them on the German terms. The defeat of Von Spee may have made a naval demonstration necessary.

Whatever the explanation of the Germans being where they were, it was only by mere chance that they escaped annihilation. Had Sir David Beatty—as it might well have happened—been to the east of them when they were sighted, not a single German ship would ever have got home. It was unlucky, too, that his squadron was temporarily deprived of the services of the *Queen Mary*. A fourth ship of a speed superior to that of *Lion*, *Tiger*, and *Princess Royal*, and armed like them with 13.5 guns might have made the whole difference in the conditions in which the fight took place. Besides, *Queen Mary* was much the best gunnery ship in the Fleet. Once more, then, the Germans had quite exceptional luck upon their side.

The moment Von Hipper's scouting cruisers found themselves in contact with Commodore Goodenough's squadron the German battle-cruisers turned and made straight for home at top speed. They had a fourteen-miles' start—say, six miles beyond effective gun range—of the British squadron, and Admiral Beatty settled down at once to a stern chase at top speed. The chase began in earnest at 7:30, the Germans, fourteen miles ahead, steering S.E., the British ships on a course parallel to them, the German ships bearing about twenty degrees on the port bow. In an hour and twenty minutes the range had been closed from 28,000 yards to 20,000. Von Hipper was evidently regulating the speed of his squadron by that of the slowest ship, *Bluecher*.

Admiral Beatty disposed of his fleet in a line of bearing, so that there should be a minimum of smoke interference, and the flagship opened fire with single shots to test the range. In ten minutes, her first hit was made on the *Bluecher* which was the last in the German line. *Tiger* then opened on the *Bluecher*, and *Lion* shifted to No. 3, of which the range was 18,000 yards. At a quarter past nine the enemy opened fire. Soon after nine, *Princess Royal* came into action, took on *Bluecher*, while *Tiger* took No. 3 and *Lion* No. 1. When *New Zealand* came within range, *Bluecher* was passed on to her. This was at about 9:35. So early as a quarter to ten the *Bluecher* showed signs of heavy punishment, and the first and third ships of the enemy were both on fire. *Lion* was engaging the first ship, *Princess Royal* the third, *New Zealand* the *Bluecher*, while *Tiger* alternated between the same target as the *Lion* and No. 4.

For some reason not explained the second ship in the German line does not appear to have been engaged at all. Just before this the Germans attempted a diversion by sending the destroyers to attack.

Meteor (Captain Mead), with a division of the British destroyers, was then sent ahead to drive off the enemy, and this apparently was done with success. Shortly afterwards the enemy destroyers got between the battle-cruisers and the British squadron and raised huge volumes of smoke, so as to foul the range. Under cover of this the enemy changed course to the northward. The battle-cruisers then formed a new line of bearing, N.N.W., and were ordered to proceed at their utmost speed. A second attempt of the enemy's destroyers to attack the British squadron was foiled by the fire of *Lion* and *Tiger*.

The chase continued on these lines more or less for the next hour, by which time the *Bluecher* had dropped very much astern and had hauled away to the North. She was listing heavily, was burning fiercely, and seemed to be defeated. Sir David Beatty thereupon ordered *Indomitable* to finish her off, and one infers from this, the first mention of *Indomitable*, that she had been unable to keep pace with *New Zealand*, *Princess Royal*, *Tiger*, and *Lion*, and therefore would not be able to assist in the pursuit of the enemy battle-cruisers.

The range by this time must have been very much reduced. If between 7:30 and 9:30 a gain of 10,000 yards, or 5,000 yards an hour, had been made, between 9:30 and 10:45 a further gain of 6,250 yards should have been possible, if the conditions had remained the same. But with *Bluecher* beaten, the German battle-cruisers could honourably think of themselves alone. Unless their speed had been reduced by our fire, while we ought to have gained, we should hardly have caught up so much as in the first hour and a half. But there had, besides, been two destroyer attacks threatened or made by the enemy, one apparently at about twenty minutes to ten, and one at some time between then and 10:40.

It is highly probable that each of these attacks caused the British squadron to change course, and we know that before 10:45 the stations had been altered. Each of these three things may have prevented some gain. Still, on the analogy of what had happened in the first two hours, we must suppose the range at this period to have been at most about 13,000 yards. At six minutes to eleven the action had reached the first rendezvous of the German submarines. They were reported to and then seen by the admiral on his starboard bow, whereupon the squadron was turned to port to avoid them. Very few minutes after this the *Lion* was disabled.

What happened from this point is not clear. We know that as Sir David stopped, he signalled to *Tiger*, *Princess Royal*, and *New Zealand* to

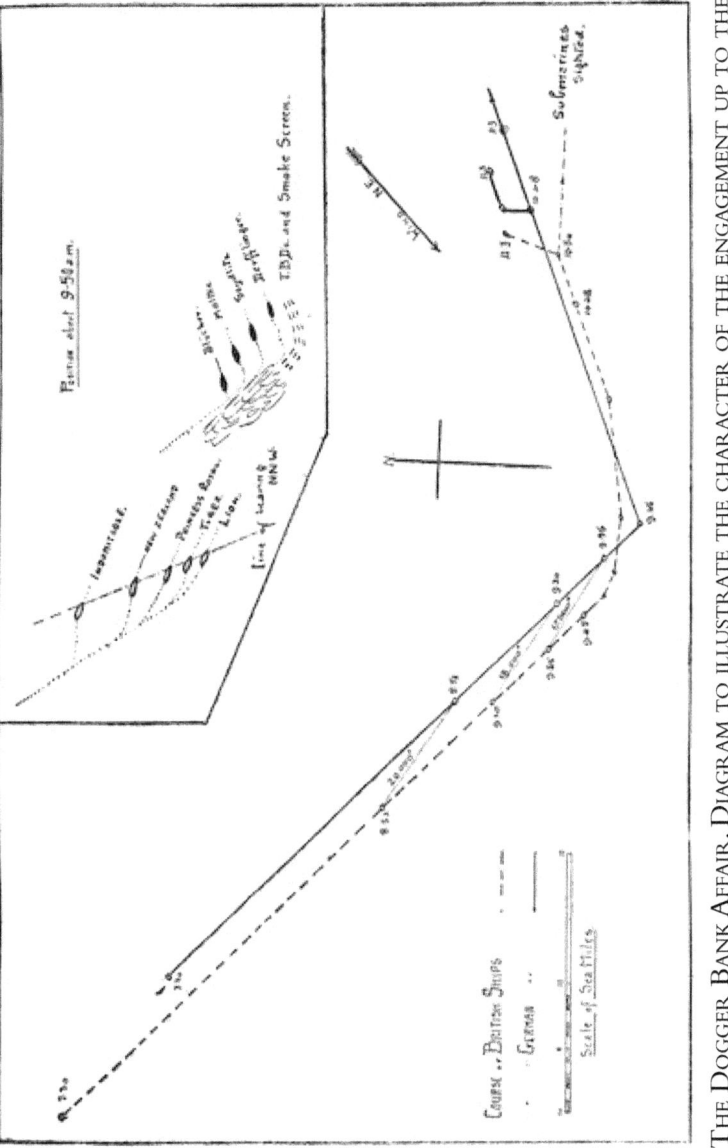

The Dogger Bank Affair. Diagram to illustrate the character of the engagement up to the disablement of *Lion*

close on and attack the enemy. *Bluecher* had been allotted to the *Indomitable* some twenty minutes before. The squadron passed from Admiral Beatty's command to that of Rear-Admiral Sir Archibald Moore. In a very few minutes it was, of course, out of sight of the vice-admiral himself. Sir David called a destroyer alongside and followed at the best pace he could and, soon after midday, found the squadron returning after breaking off the pursuit some seventy miles from Heligoland. *Bluecher* had been destroyed, but the three battle-cruisers had escaped. Of the determining factors in these proceedings we know little. Such data as there are will be examined in the next chapter.

Chapter 18

The Dogger Bank 2

There are several matters of technical and general interest to be noted about this action. In the two torpedo attacks by destroyers on Sir David Beatty's fleet, we see the first employment of this weapon for purely defensive purposes in a fleet action. It is defensive, not because the torpedo is certain to hit, and therefore to remove one of the pursuing enemy, but because if shoals of torpedoes are fired at a squadron, it will almost certainly be considered so serious a threat as to make a change of course compulsory. This is of double value to the weaker and retreating force. By compelling the firing ships to manoeuvre, the efficiency of the fire control of their guns may be seriously upset, and hence their fire lose all accuracy and effect.

To impose a manoeuvre, then, is to secure a respite from the pursuers' fire. But it does something more. By driving the pursuer off his course, he is thrown back in the race, and his guns therefore kept at a greater distance. If the pursuer has then to start finding the range, and perhaps a new course and speed of the enemy, all over again, an appreciable period of time must elapse before his fire once more becomes accurate. And if he is prevented closing, the increase of accuracy, which shorter range would give, is denied him. Apart altogether, then, from quite good chances of a torpedo hitting, the evolution is of the utmost moment to the inferior force. It was employed in this action for the first time.

Again, for the first time we find the destroyers getting between the pursuing ships and the chase, and creating a smoke screen to embarrass the pursuers' aiming and fire control. Finally, we find that Von Hipper has directed his flight to a prearranged point, where certainly submarines had been gathered and possibly mine-fields had been laid. This of course was a contingency that had always been foreseen. In an article published in the *Westminster Gazette* a week or two before the action, I dealt with Von Tirpitz's remark, that "the German Fleet were perfectly willing to fight the English, if England would give them the opportunity," and interpreted this to mean, that the Germans would be willing to fight if they had such a choice of ground and position as would give them some equivalent for their inferior numbers. And writing at that time, I naturally set out what may be called the general view of North Sea strategy. No good purpose would have been served by questioning it—even if such questioning had been permitted. Nor, in view of the very narrow margin of superiority that we possessed in capital ships, had I any wish to question it.

I began with the supposition that the enemy might attempt, on a big scale, exactly what, on a much smaller scale, we ourselves had attempted in the Bight of Heligoland five months before. I said:—

"Assuming that it is a professed German object to draw a portion of the English Fleet into a situation where it can be advantageously engaged, what would be the natural course for them to pursue? The first and perhaps the simplest form of ruse would be to dangle a squadron before the English Fleet, so that our fastest units should be drawn away from their supports, and enticed within reach of a superior German force. If we suppose the Scarborough raid to be carried out by a squadron used for this purpose, we must look upon that episode not merely as an example of Germany practising its much-loved frightfulness, but as an exercise in wiliness as well. That the Admiralty had taken every step it could think of to catch and destroy this squadron, we may safely infer from the character of the communications made to us. The measures adopted were, we also know, frustrated by the thick weather, so that no engagement actually took place.

"Is it not highly probable that the Germans, not knowing the character of the English counter-stroke, may have concluded that our failure to bring their squadron to action was brought about quite as much by prudence as by ill-luck? At any rate, it is rather a curious phenomenon that the German papers during the last two weeks have been filled with the most furious articles descanting upon the pusillanimity of the British Fleet. To our eyes such charges, of course, seem absurd, nor when we know how welcome the appearance of the German Fleet in force would be to Admiral Jellicoe and his gallant comrades can we conceive any sane man using such language; but if we interpret this as the expression of disappointed hopes, as evidence of the failure of a plan to catch a portion of our fleet, a reasonable explanation of what is otherwise merely nonsense is afforded.

"The average layman probably supposes that a fleet action between the English Grand Fleet and the German High Seas Fleet would be fought through on the lines of previous engagements in this war, and of the two naval battles of the Russo-Japanese war. They would expect the contest to be an artillery fight in which superior skill in the use of guns, if such superiority existed on either side, would be decisive; and if equality of skill existed, that victory would go to the side possessing a superior number of guns of superior power. But other naval weapons have advanced enormously in the last eight years. We not only have torpedoes that can run five and six miles with far greater accuracy and certainty than the old torpedo could go a third of this distance, but we know that Germany—almost alone amongst nations—has carried the art and practice of sowing mines to a point hitherto not dreamt of.

"When the first raid was made on Yarmouth, it will be remembered that the German ships retreated from a British submarine, and that the submarine ran into and was blown up and sunk by a mine left by the German ship in its wake. Again, after the North-Eastern raid, many ships—some authorities say over a dozen—were blown up by running into German mines left in the waters which the raiders had been through. The German naval leaders are perfectly aware that in modern capital ships they have an inferiority of numbers, and that gun for gun their artillery force is inferior to ours in an even greater degree.

"It is certain, therefore, that in thinking out the conditions in which they would have to fight an English fleet they are fully determined to use all other means that can possibly turn the scale of superiority to their side. Just as they have relied on the torpedo and the mine to diminish the general strength of the English Fleet, while it was engaged in the watch and ward of the North Sea, so as to redress the balance before the time for a naval action arrived; so, too, they have counted, when actually in action, on crippling and destroying English ships by mines and torpedoes, so that the artillery preponderance may finally be theirs.

"If we suppose that the German admirals have really thought out this problem, and we must suppose this, it is not difficult to see that with a fast advance battle-cruiser squadron engaged in mine laying, the problem of so handling a fleet as to pursue and cut off this squadron without crossing its wake must be extremely intricate and difficult. If further we imagine that this fast squadron has drawn the hostile squadron towards its own waters, where mine-fields unknown to us have been laid, we have not only the problem of the mines left in the wake of the enemy, but the further difficulty of there being prepared traps, so to speak, lying across the path which the attacking squadron would most naturally take.

"If we imagine the problem still further complicated by an attack on a battleship line by flotillas of fast destroyers firing high-speed, long-range torpedoes, to intersect the course that that squadron is taking, we have the third element of confusion. It does not need much imagination then to see that with mines actually dropped during the manoeuvres that lead up to or form part of the battle, with mine-fields scattered over the chosen battlefield, and with the possibility of a battle fleet being rendered liable at the shortest notice to a massed attack of long-range torpedo fire, a naval battle will be a totally different affair from the comparatively simple operations that took place in the engagement of August 10, or at the Battle of Tsushima.

"Such conditions as these demand extraordinary sagacity on the part not only of the commander-in-chief, but of all the squadron commanders under him. It requires insistent vigilance; but then, for that matter, such vigilance is the daily routine of the navy always. Finally, it makes demands on the art of gunnery of which we have hitherto had no practical experience at all. For reasons that hardly need discussion, all practice gunnery is carried out in conditions almost ludicrously unlike war, and quite absurdly unlike the kind of naval engagement that seems to me probable. The principal difference between the two is that it is impossible to practise with the big guns at a fast target. There is no way of manoeuvring and running a target at high speed unless it is propelled by its own power, and that power is kept supplied and is got by human agents, and obviously you cannot fire at a ship which is full of people.

"And when you fire at a towed target the differences are, first, that no target can be towed beyond perhaps a third of a battleship's speed, and next, that it cannot be manoeuvred as a ship can. Lastly, the firing ship, so far as I am aware, is never called upon to fire while executing the kind of manoeuvres, or subject to the kind of limitations, that would be incident to a modern battle.

"To sum up my argument. The present indications are that Germany, carrying out its previously expressed intentions, has made a first, and is now aiming at getting the information for a second, attempt to draw the English Fleet into fighting on ground which she can mine before we are drawn on to it, and to fight in conditions in which she can use a fast advance squadron to compel our ships to adopt certain manoeuvres, and to turn that advance squadron into mine-layers, so as to limit our movements or make them exceedingly perilous. She will try to make the battlefields as close as she can to her own ports, both so as to facilitate the preliminary preparation by mines and to surprise us with unexpected torpedo attacks. I interpret the fulminations of Captain Persius and others as expressions of their anger at the failure of their first attempt, and I interpret the air raids as attempts to get information for making a second.

"We can, I am sure, rely upon Sir John Jellicoe being at no point inferior to his enemy, either in wiliness or in resources. It is to be remembered that, so far as we are concerned, much as we should like to have all anxiety settled by hearing of the definite destruction of the German Fleet, its continued existence is nevertheless perfectly innocuous, *so long as it is unable to affect the transporting of our troops or the conduct of our trade.*"

The foregoing article, I think, fairly represents what the *Spectator*, in referring to it, called the case for "naval patience." But it did not mean, nor was it intended to mean, that it would be improper in *any* circumstances for a British ship to face *any* risks from torpedoes and mines, nor that to fight the Germans in their own waters was necessarily the same thing as fighting them on their own terms. It is indeed clear that I expected the British commanders to be more their equal to circumventing the enemy's ingenuity. But no resource can rob war of risk—and if it were made a working principle that risks from torpedoes and mines were *never* to be faced, then the clearing of the British Fleet out of the North Sea would be a very simple process. It would only be necessary for the enemy to send out a score or so of submarines to advance in line abreast when, *ex hypothesi*, the fleet would have no choice but incontinent flight.

My object was first to show the public that the problem of the naval engagement was far more complicated than was generally supposed, and that the ingenuity, resource, and vigilance of the Admiral in command would be taxed. It seemed to me important that a sympathetic understanding of these anxieties should be created in the public mind. Next, however, it was not less important to discount any extravagant expectation in the matter of naval gunnery. We had not at that time any full accounts of the Battle of the Falkland Islands;

but it seemed clear that, in this respect, the performance of the two battle-cruisers had been disappointing. If in the North Sea an action was to be fought in poor light, with the ships made to manoeuvre by torpedo attack and the enemy from time to time veiled in smoke screens, it seemed quite certain that a task would be set to the service fire-control with which it would be quite unable to deal.

And if these were the weaknesses of our fire-control, it was further highly desirable to keep before our eyes the certainty that, if the opportunity arose and a fleet action, intended to be decisive and pushed to a decision, took place, we were almost bound to lose ships by torpedoes and mines. At any rate, it seemed as if such a risk *must* be run if our own gunfire was to be made effective. And for such losses the public should be prepared.

This being the situation, it seems to me most unfortunate that the Admiralty followed the course they did in communicating their various accounts of this action to us. For there were three accounts given, and no two of the three agreed as to the reason why the pursuit was broken off! For two days we were not told that *Lion* was injured, and for four days were ignorant of the fact that the control of the British Fleet had passed out of Sir David Beatty's hands some time before the action was ended. It was not till March 3—that is, five weeks after the action—that we were told the name of the officer on whom command had devolved when *Lion* fell out of line!

This suppression was really extraordinary. To be mentioned in despatches had always been an acknowledged honour. To be ignored was a new form of distinction. How was the public to take so singular an omission? Had it ever happened before that an officer had been in command of a fleet at so grave a crisis and the fact of his being in command suppressed in announcing the fact of the engagement? No one quite knew how to take it. The discrepancies in the *communiqués* are worth noting. In the first, of January 25, was this curiously worded paragraph:

> A well-contested running fight ensued. Shortly after one o'clock *Bluecher*, which had previously fallen out of the line, capsized and sank. Admiral Beatty reports that two other German battle-cruisers were seriously damaged. They were, however, able to continue their flight, and reached an area where dangers from German submarines and mines prevented further pursuit.

H.M.S. *Lion* at the Battle of Dogger Bank on 24 January 1915

Did whoever drafted this statement suppose that the *Bluecher* was a battle-cruiser? We are now, however, more concerned with the reasons given for breaking off the action. An area was reached where "dangers from German submarines and mines prevented further pursuit." The *communiqué* of January 27 was silent on this point. On the 28th was published what purported to be "a preliminary telegraphic report received from the vice-admiral." The paragraph dealing with this matter is as follows:

> Through the damage to *Lion's* feed-tank by an unfortunate chance shot, we were undoubtedly deprived of a greater victory. The presence of the enemy's submarines subsequently necessitated the action being broken off.

In this statement the excuse of mines is dropped. In the despatch published on March 3 the end of the action is treated by the vice-admiral as follows:

> At 11:20 I called the *Attack* alongside, shifted my flag to her at about 11:35. I proceeded at the utmost speed to rejoin the squadron, and met them at noon retiring north-northwest. I boarded and hoisted my flag in *Princess Royal* at about 12:20, when Captain Brock acquainted me with what had occurred since *Lion* fell out of line, namely, that *Bluecher* had sunk, and that the enemy battle-cruisers had continued their course to eastward in a considerably damaged condition.

Here observe no mention was made of submarines necessitating the action being broken off, nor of an area being reached where dangers from submarines and mines prevented further pursuit. The whole incident is passed by the vice-admiral without comment, unless indeed the phrase about the accident to the *Lion*, in the telegraphic report, is a comment. Did the vice-admiral imply that had he remained in command he would have seen to it that his specific orders—*viz.* that *Indomitable* should settle *Bluecher* and the other ships pursue the battle-cruisers—were carried out?

A very unfortunate situation resulted from these reticences and contradictions. Naval writers in America were naturally enough amazed by the statement attributed to Admiral Beatty in the telegraphic report, for, if the presence of submarines could stop pursuit, could not submarines drive the British Fleet off the sea? These authors naturally expressed extreme astonishment that an admiral capable of breaking off action in these conditions, and publicly acknowledging so egregious a blunder, was not at once brought to court-martial. No one in his senses could have supposed that Sir David Beatty, who dealt with submarines without the least concern in the affair of Heligoland and earlier in the day on January 28, could possibly have accepted the dictum that the presence of a German submarine would justify pursuit having been broken off.

It was then quite evident that the quotation from the vice-admiral's telegraphic report could not have represented the vice-admiral's opinion on a point of warlike doctrine. What the actual facts of the case were, we do not to this day know. Rear-Admiral Moore did not continue long in Sir David Beatty's squadron after this, but there was no court-martial nor any public expression of the Admiralty's opinion by way of approval or disapproval of his proceedings. In a speech made a month after the action in the House of Commons, Mr. Churchill passed over the fact that the action had not been fought out, as if such a thing was of no exceptional importance or interest whatever. Soon afterward it became known that the rear-admiral in question had got another and very important command elsewhere, so that it became plain that his conduct had not met with Their Lordships' reprobation.

War in modern conditions undoubtedly makes it exceedingly important to keep the enemy as far as possible in ignorance of a great many things. It imposes too a continuous strain upon practically the whole personnel of the navy, and these two things taken together have been quoted to explain why the old rule of holding a public court-martial on the captain of every ship that was lost, or on every individual officer whose action in battle gave rise to uncertainty or question, has virtually been abrogated. But it is doubtful whether the navy has not lost more by the abandonment of this wholesome practice than the enemy could have gained by its Spartan application.

This point came in for a good deal of public discussion at the beginning of 1915, and I venture to quote a contribution to it. Looking back upon this controversy, it is easy enough to see now wherein lay the chief disadvantage of the suppression of courts-martial. There was no general staff at the Admiralty, representative of the best service opinion, and, deprived of court-martial, the navy had no means of expressing a corporate judgment on the vital issues as they arose. The doctrine with regard to torpedo risk, which seems to have been acted on at the close of this action, was evidently one which either the Admiralty had laid down, or at least accepted as correct. Could it have been referred to the corporate judgment of the service and had that judgment not endorsed it, the history of the war might have been altogether different.

Mr. Churchill's speech in the official reports is entitled *British Command of the Sea: Admiralty Organisation*. It would have been as well if this description had been given out before the speech was made, for, as it happened, many thought it was intended as a survey of the first epoch of the war and were disappointed that, in so eloquent and forceful a review, there was hardly a word of tribute to the incomparable services of our officers and men. There was lavish praise of the generosity of the House of Commons; of the foresight of Lord Fisher; of the excellence of the Admiralty's preparedness at every point; of the amazing scale and success of the provisioning with coal and supplies of a vast fleet always at sea; of the astonishing perfection of the work of the engineering branch.

But there was singularly little of the work of the fighting men. The officers were dismissed simply as "painstaking." No doubt the tribute will be made at another time. Is there any time, however, which is not the right time for acknowledging these services? On Tuesday we learned that between 300 and 400 officers have died for us—and over 6,000 men. Is it gracious to postpone their eulogy? And the absence of eulogy was emphasised by the forceful manner in which the First Lord asked that he and his colleagues should be entrusted with the most absolute and dictatorial powers. Indeed, he excused the departure from the Service custom of holding courts-martial whenever a ship was lost on the ground that modern conditions called for instant action, with which courts-martial were incompatible. But the court-martial, as I have before pointed out, is the palladium of the navy's liberties.

To abolish it is like suspending the *Habeas Corpus*. It is so extreme a measure because it ignores the great unwritten law of the navy, which is that, in spite of the authority of Whitehall over the navy, of an admiral over a fleet, and of a captain over a ship's company, being necessarily and in each case absolute, yet there must always be an appeal from authority to the profession itself. If this is necessary for the protection of subordinate officers and men against arbitrary action by a captain, against arbitrary and prejudiced action by an admiral in a fleet, how much more necessary is it as a protection of naval standards and traditions against arbitrary action by the Board?

For a captain is at any rate an entirely naval authority; an admiral is certainly an officer of large naval experience, acting generally with at least one other admiral. But the Board is largely a lay body. Indeed, it is now by a majority a lay body. And like all boards, it is liable to be the mouthpiece of its strongest personality. If this, as sometimes happens, is a seaman, he may be a partisan—I say it in no invidious sense—of certain policies and so prejudiced against brother officers who differ. If the stronger character is a layman, he may be ignorant of, or see no danger in waiving, naval traditions that are embodied in no statute or regulation, but are not embodied simply because their cogency has never been questioned. In other words, the autocracy of the Admiralty is a necessity of executive administration, but can only be exercised safely if its enforcement is continuously tested by professional opinion.

How many people, I often wonder, really appreciate how singular a body is that which is made up of admirals, captains, commanders, and lieutenants of the Royal Navy? The accomplishments that make the seaman confuse the landsman by their strangeness and intricacy. Indeed, if one wishes to express the extremity of bewilderment, he does so best by the metaphor which describes the sailor's normal environment. When we say we are "at sea," we do so because language expresses no greater helplessness. To master these conditions calls for forms of knowledge and proficiency that are only acquired by a lifetime's familiarity. But these conditions are not only baffling, they are incredibly dangerous. If steam has done much to lessen the perils of the sea, speed, the product of steam, has added to them. The sailor then, even in times of peace, passes his days, and still more his nights, encompassed by the threat of irreparable disaster.

An oversight that may take thirty seconds to commit—and a hundred deaths, a wrecked ship, and a shattered reputation reward thirty years of constant and unblemished devotion to duty. To face a life and responsibilities like these calls for more than great mental and physical skill, though nowhere will you find these in a higher degree or more widely diffused than in the fleet. It calls for moral and spiritual qualities, for a development of character in patience, unselfishness, and courage which few landsmen have any inducement to cultivate.

A life lived daily in the presence of death must be a unique life, and it is not surprising that men bred to these conditions—always as hard and ascetic as they are uncertain and unsafe—grow to be a body quite unlike other men, with standards and traditions of their own, and a corporate spirit and capacity that are unique, wonderful, and to most landsmen incomprehensible.

Their standards and traditions can only be maintained and can only be enforced by themselves. And the great peril that follows from excluding all reference to them of the accidents and failures of war is that, failing this reference, we have no security that naval action will be judged as it should be, solely by the highest naval standard.

Much was said in the House of Commons about the loss of ships. Mr. Churchill assumed that the only motive for asking for courts-martial was to find a scapegoat. Lord Charles Beresford only made clear that a court-martial was as much for clearing the character as for finding criminals. There was a significant phrase in Mr. Churchill's speech that raises, it seems to me, a point in this connection of far greater importance. The Battle of the Dogger Bank, he said, was "not fought out because the enemy made good their escape into waters infested by submarines and mines."

The officer who had to call off a fleet in these circumstances was necessarily faced by a grave and almost terrifying responsibility. To be too bold was to risk everything, to be too cautious was to throw away a victory. Can any tribunal, except the navy, judge whether this responsibility was rightly exercised? When we remember that in our greatest days hardly a naval battle took place that was not followed by courts-martial, it seems to me a most perilous thing to allow these tremendous issues to go by the board because unless they are adjudicated upon by the profession itself, they are not adjudicated upon at all.

CHAPTER 19

The Battle of Jutland

1. NORTH SEA STRATEGIES

The Battle off Jutland Bank, which took place on May 31, 1916, was the first and, at the time of writing, has been the only meeting between the main naval forces of Great Britain and Germany. It was from the first inevitable that we should have to wait long for a sea fight. It was inevitable, because the probability of a smaller force being not only decisively defeated, but altogether destroyed in a sea fight, is far greater than in a land battle, and the consciousness of this naturally makes it chary of the risk. Sea war in this respect preserves the characteristic of ancient land fighting, for—as is luminously explained in Commandant Colin's incomparable *Transformations of War*—it was a common characteristic of the older campaigns that the main armies would remain almost in touch with each other month after month before the battle took place. He sums up his generalisation thus:

> From the highest antiquity, till the time of Frederick II, operations present the same character; not only Fabius or Turenne, but also Caesar, Condé, and Frederick, lead their armies in the same way. Far from the enemy they force the pace, but as soon as they draw near, they move hither and thither in every direction, take days, weeks, months in deciding to accept or to force battle. Whether the armies are made up of hoplites or legionaries, or pikemen or musketeers, they move as one whole and deploy very slowly. They cannot hurl themselves upon the enemy as soon as they perceive him, because while they are making ready for battle, he disappears in another direction.

In order to change this state of affairs we must somehow or another be able to put into the fight big divisions, each deploying on its own account, leaving gaps and irregularities along the front.

This, as we have seen, is what happened in the eighteenth century.

Up to the time of Frederick II, armies remained indivisible during operations; they are like mathematical points on the huge theatres of operations in Central Europe. It is not possible to grasp, to squeeze, or even to push back on some obstacle, an enemy who refuses battle, and retires laterally as well as backwards. There is no end to the pursuit. It is the war of Caesar, as it was that of Condé, Turenne, Montecuculi, Villars, Eugène, Maurice de Saxe, and Frederick. It is the sort of war that all more or less regular armies have made from the remotest antiquity down to the middle of the eighteenth century.

Battle only takes place by mutual consent, when both adversaries, as at Rocroi, are equally sure of victory, and throw themselves at one another in open country as if for a duel; or when one of them, as at Laufeld, cannot retreat without abandoning the struggle; or when one is surprised, as at Rossbach.

And certainly today, as heretofore, a general may refuse battle; but he cannot prolong his retreat for long—it is the only means that he has for escaping the grip of the enemy—if the depth of the theatre of operations is limited. On the other hand, an enemy formerly could retire laterally, and disappear for months by perpetually running to and fro, always taking cover behind every obstacle in order to avoid attack.

But at sea a fleet has today (1919) precisely the same power of avoiding action that an army had in former days. It cannot disappear for months by "running to and fro," but it can disappear for years by burying itself in inaccessible harbours. It can, in other words, take itself out of the theatre of war altogether while yet retaining liberty at any moment to re-enter it. How, in view of these potentialities, did the rival fleets dispose their forces?

On April 25, 1916, some German cruisers made an attack on Lowestoft, similar in character but far less considerable in result to those made in the autumn of 1914, on the same small town, on Scarborough, Whitby, and the Hartlepools. As in 1914, there was considerable perturbation on the East Coast, and the Admiralty, urged to take steps for the protection of the seaboard towns, made a somewhat startling announcement. While this was going forward in England, the German Admiralty put out an inspired commentary on the raid, which dwelt with great exultation over the picture of "the Island Empire, once so proud, now quivering with rage at its own impotence." These two documents, the First Lord's and the German apology, led to a good deal of discussion, which I dealt with at the time in terms that I quote textually, as showing the general conception of naval strategy underlying the dispositions of the British Fleet:—

"The directly military employment of the British Fleet has during the last week been made the subject of discussion. Mr. Balfour has written a strange letter to the mayors of the East Coast towns, which foreshadows important developments; an inspired German apology for the recent raid on Yarmouth and Lowestoft has been published, and both have aroused comment. Mr. Balfour's letter was inspired by a desire to reassure the battered victims of the German bombardment. He realised that the usual commonplace that these visits had little military value no longer met the case, and proceeded to threaten the Germans with new and more effective methods of meeting them, should these murderous experiments be repeated.

"The new measures were to take two forms. The towns themselves would be locally defended by monitors and submarines, and, without disturbing naval preponderance elsewhere, new units would be brought farther south, so that the interception of raiders would be made more easy. But for one consideration the publication of such a statement as this would be inexplicable. If the effective destruction of German raiders really had been prepared, the last thing the Admiralty would be expected to do would be to acquaint the enemy with the disconcerting character of its future reception. Count Reventlow indeed explains the publication by the fact that no such preparations have indeed been made. But the thing is susceptible of a more probable explanation.

"When Mr. Churchill, in the high tide of his optimism, addressed the House of Commons at the beginning of last year—he had the Falkland Islands and the Dogger Bank battles, the obliteration of the German ocean cruising force, the extinction of the enemy merchant marine, the security of English communications to his credit—he explained the accumulated phenomena of our sea triumph by the splendid perfection of his pre-war preparedness. The submarine campaign, the failure of the Dardanelles, the revelation of the defenceless state of the northeastern harbours, these things have somewhat modified the picture that the ex-First Lord drew. And, not least of our disillusions, we have all come to realise that in our neglect of the airship we have allowed the enemy to develop, for his sole benefit, a method of naval scouting that is entirely denied to us. That the British Admiralty and the British Fleet perfectly realise this disadvantage is the meaning of Mr. Balfour's letter. He would not have told the enemy of our new North Sea arrangements had he not known that he could not be kept in ignorance of them for longer than a week or two, once they were made. The letter is, in fact, an admission that our sea power has to a great extent lost what was at one time its supreme prerogative, *the capacity of strategical surprise*.

"But this does not materially alter the dynamics of the North Sea position, although it greatly affects tactics. The German official apologist will have it, however, that another factor has altered these dynamics. Admiral Jellicoe, he says, may be secure enough with his vast fleet in his 'great bay in the Orkneys,' and, between that and the Norwegian coast, hold a perfectly effective blockade line, but all British calculations of North Sea strategy have been upset by the establishment of new enemy naval bases at Zeebrügge, Ostend, and Antwerp. He speaks glibly, as if the co-operation of the forces based on the Bight with those in the stolen Belgian ports had altered the position fundamentally. This, of course, is the veriest rubbish.

"So far, no captured Belgian port has been made the base for anything more important than submarines that can cross the North Sea under water, and for the few destroyers that have made a dash through in the darkness. Such balderdash as this, and that the German battle-cruisers did not take to flight, but simply 'returned to their bases' without waiting for the advent of 'superior forces,' imposes on nobody. It remains, of course, perfectly manifest that our surface control of the North Sea is as absolute as the character of modern weapons and the present understanding of their use make possible.

"The principles behind our North Sea Strategy are simple. One hundred years ago, had our main naval enemy been based on Cuxhaven and Kiel, we should have held him there by as close a blockade as the number of ships at our disposal, the weather conditions, and the seamanship of our captains made possible. The development of the steam-driven ship modified the theory of close blockade and, even without the torpedo, would have made, with the speed now attainable, an exact continuation of the old practice impossible. The under-water torpedo has simply emphasized and added to difficulties that would, without it, have been insuperable. But it has undoubtedly extended the range at which the blockading force must hold itself in readiness.

"To reproduce, then, in modern conditions the effect brought about by close blockade in our previous wars, it is necessary to have a naval base at a suitable distance from the enemy's base. It must be one that is proof against under-water or surface torpedo vessel attack, and it must be so constituted that the force that normally maintains itself there is capable of prompt and rapid sortie, and of pouncing upon any enemy fleet that attempts to break out of the harbour in which it is intended to confine it.

"The great bay in the Orkneys' may, for all I know to the contrary, supply at the present moment the Grand Fleet's main base for such blockade as we enforce. But there are a great many other ports, inlets, and estuaries on the East Coast of Scotland and England which are hardly likely to be entirely neglected. Not all, nor many, of these would be suitable for fleet units of the greatest size and speed, but some undoubtedly are suitable, and all those that are could be made to satisfy the conditions of complete protection against secret attack. Assuming the main battle fleet to be at an extremely northerly point, any more southerly base which is kept either by battle cruisers, light cruisers, or submarines may be regarded as an advance base, if for no other reason than that it is so many miles nearer to the German base.

"The Orkneys are 200 miles farther from Lowestoft than Lowestoft is from Heligoland. An Orkney concentration while making the escape of the Germans to the northward impossible, would leave them comparatively free to harry the East Coast of England. If, approaching during the night, they could arrive off that coast before the northern forces had news of their leaving their harbours, they would have many hours' start in the race home. It is not, then, a close blockade that was maintained. This freedom had to be left the enemy—because no risk could be taken in the main theatre.

"It is assumed on the one side and admitted on the other, that Germany could gain nothing and would risk everything by attempting to pass down the Channel. The Channel is closed to the German Fleet precisely as the Sound is closed to the British. It is not that it is physically impossible for either fleet to get through, but that to force a passage would involve an operation employing almost every kind of craft.

"Minefields would have to be cleared, and battleships would have to be in attendance to protect the mine-sweepers. The battleships in turn would have to be protected from submarine attack, and as the operation of securing either channel would take some time, there would be a virtual certainty of the force employed being attacked in the greatest possible strength. In narrow waters the fleet trying to force a passage would be compelled to engage in the most disadvantageous possible circumstances.

"The Channel is closed, then, for the Germans, as the Sound is closed to the British, not by the under-water defences, but by the fact that to clear these would involve an action in which the attacking party would be at too great a disadvantage. The concentration, then, in the north of a force adequate to deal with the *whole* German Fleet—again I have to say in the light of the way in which the use of modern weapons is understood—remains our fundamental strategical principle."

I then went on to reply to the critics who had said that the use of monitors for coast defence was the most disturbing feature of a very unwise series of departures from true policy, and then passed on to what seemed to me the more serious criticism, as follows:

> The attack on this part of Mr. Balfour's policy is vastly more damaging. For it asserts that the policy of defensive offence, Great Britain's traditional sea strategy, has now been reversed. The East Coast towns may expect comparative immunity, but only because the strategic use of our forces has been altered. It is a modification imposed upon the Admiralty by the action of the enemy. Its weakness lies in the 'substitution of squadrons *in fixed positions* for periodical sweeps in force through the length and breadth of the North Sea.' Were this indeed the meaning of Mr. Balfour's letter and the intention of his policy, nothing more deplorable could be imagined.
>
> But what ground is there for thinking that this is Mr. Balfour's meaning? He says nothing of the kind. He makes it quite clear that a new arrangement is made possible by *additional units* of the first importance now being ready to use. The old provision of adequate naval preponderance at the right point has not been disturbed. It is merely proposed to establish new and advanced bases from which the new available squadrons can strike. It stands to reason that the nearer this base is to the shortest line between Heligoland and the East Coast, the greater the chance of the force within it being able to fall upon Germany's cruising or raiding units if they venture within the radius of its action.

To establish a new or more southerly base, then, is a development of, and not a departure from, our previous strategy—it shortens the radius of German freedom. If there is nothing to show that the old distribution is changed, certainly there is no suggestion that the squadron destined for the new base will be 'fixed' there. If squadrons now based on the north are there only to pounce upon the emerging German ships, why should squadrons based farther south not be employed for a similar purpose?

The foregoing will make it clear that the general idea of British strategy was to maintain, to the extreme north of these islands, an overwhelming force of capital ships. It was adopted because it economized strength and secured the main object—*viz.* the paralysis of our enemy, outside certain narrow limits.

The southern half of the North Sea—say, roughly from Peterhead to the Skagerack, 400 miles; from the Skagerack to Heligoland, 250; from Heligoland to Lowestoft, 300; and from Lowestoft to Peterhead, 350 miles—was left as a kind of no man's land. If the Germans chose to cruise about in this area, they took the chance of being cut off and engaged by the British forces, whose policy it was to leave their bases from time to time for what Sir John Jellicoe in the Jutland despatch describes as "periodic sweeps through the North Sea." But the German Fleet being supplied with Zeppelins, could, in weather in which Zeppelins could scout, get information so far afield as to be able to choose the times for their own cruises in the North Sea, and so make the procedure a perfectly safe one, so long as chance encounters with submarines and straying into British mine-fields could be avoided.

Thus, for the old policy of close blockade was substituted a new one, that of leaving the enemy a large field in which he might be tempted to manoeuvre; and it had this value, that should he yield to the temptation, an opportunity must sooner or later be afforded to the British Fleet of cutting him off and bringing him to action. Meantime he was cut off from any large adventure far afield. He would have to fight for freedom. It gave, so to speak, the Germans the chance of playing a new sort of "Tom Tiddler's ground." The point to bear in mind is, that it left the Germans precisely the same freedom to seek or avoid action as the armies of antiquity possessed. Thus, no naval battle could be expected unless—as Colin says—the weaker wished to fight, or was cornered or surprised.

Now, against surprise, the German Fleet was seemingly protected by Zeppelins. It could hardly be cornered unless, in weather in which aerial scouting was impossible, it was tempted to some great adventure—such as the despatch of a raiding force to invade—which would enable a fast British division to get between this force and its base. So that the chance of a fleet action really turned upon the Germans being willing to fight one. And they could not be expected to be anxious for this. Colin says:

> A war is always slow in which we know that the battle will be decisive, and it is so important as to be only accepted voluntarily.

The state of relative strength in May, 1916, was not such as to afford the Germans the slightest hope of a decisive victory if it brought the whole British Fleet to action. Nor was the naval situation such that there was any stroke that Germany could execute if it could hold the command of some sea passage for twenty-four hours or so. There was nothing it could expect to achieve if, by defeating or at any rate standing off one section of the British Fleet, it could enjoy a brief local ascendancy.

The argument, indeed, was all the other way. The professed main naval policy of Germany, *viz.*, the blockade of England by submarine, though for the moment in abeyance, was being held in reserve until the military and political situation made the stake worth the candle. Now, deliberately to risk the High Seas Fleet in an action on the grand scale, when the chances of decisive victory were remote and the probability of annihilation extremely high, was to jeopardize not the fleet alone but also the blockade. For, with the High Seas Fleet once out of the way, the one stroke against the submarine which could alone be perfectly effective, *viz.*, the close under-water blockade by mines, immediately outside the German harbours, would at once become feasible. So far, then, as military considerations went, the arguments against seeking action were far stronger than those in its favour.

But in war it is not always reasons which are purely military that operate; and as this war got into its second year there were many forces, each of which contributed something towards driving the German Navy into action. First, and in all probability by far the most powerful, would be the impatience of a large body of brave and skilful seamen—in control of an enormous sea force—with the *role* of idleness and impotence that had been imposed upon them. The German apologist, when uttering his *paens* of triumph over the bombardments of Lowestoft, said, on May 7:

It must not be assumed that this adventure was a mere question of bombarding some fortified coast places. It would also be a mistake to think that it was only an expression of the spirit of enterprise in our young navy. The spirit is indeed just as fresh as ever, and is simply thirsting for deeds, and when one sees or talks to officers and men one reads on their lips the desire 'If only we could get out.' The sitting still during the spring and winter may also play their part in this. Only a well-considered leadership knows when it will use this thirst for action, and employ it in undertakings which keep the great whole in view. Our navy, thank God, does not need to pursue prestige policy; the services which it has already rendered us are too considerable and too important for that.

There is no occasion to quarrel with a word in this passage. The German admirals and captains in command of twenty-three or twenty-four of the most powerful ships in the world must certainly have been straining at the leash. This, then, would be a predisposing cause to a battle of some kind being voluntarily sought by the weaker force.

And in May, 1916, there were other causes as well. The German Higher Command, while ignorant perhaps of the exact points at which the Allies would attack, must have been very perfectly aware that attacks of the most formidable character, and on all fronts, were impending. It also knew that the resources of the Central Empires were to this extent relatively exhausted, that all the Allied attacks, when they came, must result in a series of successes, not of course immediately decisive, but such as no counter-attacks could balance or neutralize. Austria and Germany, in short, would be shown to be on the defensive. They would have to yield ground. It may not have seemed a situation bound to lead to military defeat. For the superiority of the Allies—at least so it may have appeared to the German command—in men and ammunition and morale, would have to be overwhelming to bring this about.

But the Higher Command had made the mistake of carrying the civil population with them in the declaration and prosecution of the war, first by the promise and then by the assertion of overwhelming victory. But the victory that was claimed did not materialize in the way that is normal to great victories. There was no submission of the enemy, and no sign of a wish for an honourable peace. What was worse, the defeated enemy had shown an almost unlimited capacity to starve and hamper their conquerors. It was bad enough that they should not acknowledge themselves beaten. It was worse that the flail of hunger should fall on those who should be fattening on the fruits of victory. What would the state of mind of the German people be if, on the top of all this, the conquered Allies were to evince a capacity for winning a few battles themselves? It was manifestly a position in which, at any cost, the morale of the German people should be braced for a new trial. Given a fleet impatient to get out and a higher command anxious for news of a victory, these are surely elements enough to explain the events that led to the action of May 31.

But the most powerful motive of all was this: Not only was German morale badly in need of refreshment, it was especially that Germany's belief in her naval power needed to be confirmed. For, in the last week in April, the emperor and his counsellors had been compelled to submit to a peremptory ultimatum despatched by President Wilson with the endorsement of both houses of Congress behind him. Towards the end of the winter 1915–16, the German people had been led to expect a decisive stroke against England by the new U-boats which the Tirpitz building programme of the previous year was reputed to be producing in large and punctual numbers. The Grand Admiral himself, amid the vociferous applause of the Jingoes and Junkers, announced that the campaign would begin on a certain day in March.

The story how more cautious counsels prevailed, how the Grand Admiral was dismissed, how an agitation was thereupon organised throughout Germany, and how, finally, the campaign was begun, though its author was out of office, are well known. The point is that the sinking of the passenger ship *Sussex* led America to define the position and to inflict a public humiliation, not only on the German Government but on the German Navy. On the top of all the other predisposing causes, then, here was a special reason why the sea forces of the Fatherland should vindicate their existence by some signal act of daring.

We must then, I think, in considering the Battle of Jutland, start with the assumption that the German Fleet came out in obedience both to policy and to its own desire. But we should be wrong if we supposed that they came out with any hopes of achieving final and decisive victory. It has never been a characteristic of German military thought to build on the possibilities of an inferior force defeating its superior.

On the other hand, it was very confident that it could not be decisively beaten. Being an inferior force, the German Navy has been driven to giving the utmost consideration to all the methods of fighting that can add to the defensive in battle. It was not slow to realise, as we have seen, the enormous advantage that the dirigible airship offered in scouting, and from the first it has devoted itself with special energy and care to the practice and development of the defensive tactics which the long-range torpedo made possible. Nor is this all. For though the Germany Navy was the last of all the great navies to cultivate long-range gunnery, it very quickly appreciated the fact that its efficiency depended upon the visibility of the target, that it should be launched at periods when the rate of change was constant.

It consequently made it a first step in its war preparations to supply itself with the finest optical instruments regardless of cost, so as to get the range and the rate with utmost accuracy and rapidity and to master all the means by which the enemy's gunfire could be made nugatory both by devices that would hide its own ships from his view, and by imposing sudden manoeuvres by torpedo attack. We have already seen, in the story of the Dogger Bank engagement, how the pursuing British battle-cruisers were hampered in their chase and indeed deflected from their course by submarines skilfully stationed for attack, and by the employment in action of destroyer flotillas. And, again, how when *Bluecher* was disabled, and two out of three battle-cruisers were on fire and their batteries useless, they were shielded in their final flight by the destroyers interposing themselves on the British line of fire and then raising huge volumes of smoke impenetrable to the eye.

Lastly, as German writers since the battle have never ceased to remind us, the German Fleet had never been built with the idea of its being able to fight and defeat the British Fleet, but with the idea of creating a force so formidable that the British Fleet would not face the risk to itself that would be involved in its destruction. That there was some justification for such a belief will become apparent when we consider the statements of various British naval authorities made after the action was over. I draw attention to it here because it was undoubtedly reliance on some hesitation of this kind that gave the Germans such confidence in the methods of evasion which they adopted when the two fleets met.

In asking ourselves why the Germans came out we must bear this extremely significant truth in mind. They believed that they could almost certainly avoid contact with the Grand Fleet, but they also believed that if contact were made, what with torpedo attacks and smoke screens, they could hold off their enemies long enough to make evasion possible. To the Germans, then, it was very far from being an irrational risk to come into the North Sea to look for the enemy, with a view to fight on the principle of limited liability.

CHAPTER 20

The Battle of Jutland (Continued)

2. The Urgency of a Decision

We can safely accept the German official statement, that their objective on May 31 was to cut off and chastise that portion of our advanced forces that had so often swept across to the Schleswig coast in the previous few months. The force they were looking for would naturally be the Battle Cruiser Fleet, for it had been this force that had always been nearest the German bases, even when the whole of both British fleets were engaged in sweeping. But it is not necessary to suppose that in every sweep both fleets took part. In coming out, then, the Germans would expect to meet the battle-cruisers, if anything, and they would count either upon the Grand Fleet not being in the field at all, or at any rate to be sufficiently far off to be of no immediate danger.

But how could the Germans expect to bring Sir David Beatty to action? The Battle Cruiser Fleet, before the Battle of Jutland, was exactly twice as numerous, and in gun power more than twice as strong, as the German fast division. In the Battle of Jutland, it was reinforced by the Fifth Battle Squadron, ships to which Germany possessed no counterparts at all. Clearly, then, if Sir David Beatty's force was to be brought to action and defeated it would be useless to rely upon Von Hipper alone. The whole German naval forces would be required.

And according to enemy accounts sixteen modern battleships appeared on May 31. None of these had a greater speed than 21 knots, and, as they were said to be accompanied by six pre-Dreadnoughts, the speed of the whole fleet could not have exceeded 18 knots. The united German forces would, of course, have a fleet speed of the slowest squadron. How can an 18-knot squadron corner and chastise a

25-knot squadron—for 25 knots was an easy speed for the slowest of the Battle Cruiser Fleet?

It is clear, then, that Von Hipper's fleet would not be able to get into action with Sir David Beatty's fleet, unless the British Admiral chose to engage. Before the news of the battle was three days old, the suggestion had been many times made that the loss of *Queen Mary*, *Indefatigable*, and *Invincible* was to be explained by their having been employed in "rash and impetuous tactics," and set to engage a superior force by the "over-confidence" of the admiral responsible for their movements. And one critic went so far as to say that the opportunity for the German commander-in-chief to overwhelm an inferior British force with greatly superior numbers was exactly what the enemy was looking for. With the justice of this as a criticism of Sir David Beatty's tactics I will deal later.

But that Admiral Scheer fully expected that if Sir David Beatty found him, he would engage him, we may take for granted. Just as he and his own officers and men were anxious for action, so must Sir David and his fleet be burning with a desire to get to grips. He banked, that is to say, on Sir David attacking. If he did, the German position and prospects were distinctly good. There would be twenty-one ships against nine or ten, and if the fast battleships were with the British vice-admiral, against fourteen or fifteen.

The preponderance in force would certainly be on the German side. It should not be difficult to escape defeat. With luck, serious loss might be inflicted on the British before it was compelled to break off battle and retreat, especially if it sought close action. It might indeed be compelled to continue the battle, if some of its units were wounded, for the vice-admiral would certainly hesitate to desert them.

As to the danger of the situation being reversed—by the Grand Fleet turning up—in the first place, Zeppelins might save him from that. If they did not, he always had the card up his sleeve, that he could stand the British Fleet off by torpedoes, and shield himself by smoke from the very long-range gunnery which the torpedo attacks would make inevitable. So much for the German plan. Now how about the English plan?

It is a little difficult to say exactly what the British plan was, if by plan we mean a definite understanding existing between the Higher Command in London and the Commander-in-Chief at sea. For as to this no information whatever has been given to the public and we can only arrive at its tenor by the fact that the Admiralty after the event

Loss of H.M.S. INDEFATIGABLE

expressed itself completely satisfied with the commander-in-chief's conduct after the fight—a matter to be gone into in greater detail later. For the moment the only indication we have of the general policy which has inspired Whitehall, is that given by Mr. Churchill in an article contributed to a popular magazine a few months after the action was fought. In this he laid down the following as the sea doctrine that should guide our naval conduct:

From the first day of the war, he said, the British Navy had exercised the full and unquestioned command of the sea. So long as it really remained unchallenged and unbeaten the superior fleet ruled all the open waters of the world. From the beginning it had enjoyed all the fruits of a complete victory. Had Germany never built a Dreadnought, or if all the German Dreadnoughts had been sunk, the control and authority of the British Navy could not have been more effective. There had been no Trafalgar, but the full consequences of a Trafalgar had been continuously operative. There was no reason why this condition of affairs should not continue indefinitely. Without a battle we had all that the most victorious of battles could give us.

This was the true starting point of any reflections on the war by sea. We were content! As for Jutland, there was no need for the British to seek that battle at all. There was no strategic cause or compulsion operating to draw our battle fleet into Danish waters. If we chose to go there it was because of zeal and strength. A keen desire to engage the enemy impelled, and a cool calculation of ample margins of superiority justified, a movement not necessarily required by any practical need. The battle must, therefore, be regarded as an audacious attempt to bring the enemy to action, arising out of consciousness of overwhelming superiority!

A little consideration will, I think, convince us that Mr. Churchill was altogether wrong in supposing that a decisive action was not highly important to us at this time. For obviously the German Fleet came out to do something, and if my suggestion is right—that its mission was to raise German morale—we had first the obvious duty of preventing the German Fleet doing anything it wished to do, and next an insistent duty to depress German morale, at least as much as Admiral Scheer wished to raise it. Apart from any material or directly military results, a second Trafalgar, had it really broken the hearts of German civilians, might have been an element decisive of the power of the German people to endure the privations that the prolongation of war inflicts upon them.

Exploding of H.M.S. Queen Mary

It might finally have broken down the whole structure of lying bluff that the emperor's government has maintained. This would have been a military object of the first value and importance. If the war is to end by the collapse, not of the German Army but of the German people, the value of such a victory and such a result can be measured by the number of days of war that it would have saved at a cost in men and treasure that it is hard to calculate.

But apart altogether from this, there were other considerations, some economic and some military, so immensely serious, as would certainly have justified Sir David Beatty in risking, not three, but all his battle-cruisers, if by so doing he could have insured the entire destruction of the German Fleet by Sir John Jellicoe's forces. To realise this point we must carry our consideration of the naval strategy of the two sides in this war a little further. We have seen that our method of disposing of our forces in the North Sea gave the German Fleet a certain limited freedom of manoeuvre in the irregular quadrilateral formed by Peterhead, the Skagerack, Heligoland, and Lowestoft. Outside of this area there was not, after December 8, 1914, a single German warship afloat that was not a fugitive or in hiding, nor has any surface ship ventured outside this area since. When the careers of *Karlsruhe* and *Emden* terminated, the period of systematic capture of our trading ships closed also. But Von Tirpitz was very far from being satisfied with the situation so created.

The Grand Admiral was wildly wrong in the kind of navy that he built for Germany, and hopelessly at sea in his forecast of the action England would take in the kind of war that Germany intended to provoke. But when the events of the first few months showed that the war would be a long one, it is not certain that he was not the first European in authority to realise to the full the *rôle* sea-power would play. In a long war, the merchant shipping of the world—and it was immaterial whether it was belligerent or neutral—would obviously be the one thing by which the Allies, by importations of raw material, and the manufactures of America, the British colonies, and Japan, could counterbalance the vastly superior organisation of the Central Powers for working their industries and factories.

Shipping was at once the source of supply of the whole Alliance and the military communications of the most formidable of them. The German submarines had had a small initial success against British warships. It was disappointing from the point of view of the attrition that Germany had hoped for. But it opened Von Tirpitz's eyes to the immense possibilities of a submarine attack on trading ships. He saw, then, both the necessity of cutting the Allies off from the sea, and the means of cutting them off. The plan was an outrageous one from the point of view of morals. But Von Tirpitz's conception of the importance of sea supplies to the Allies was perfectly correct, and in organising an attack upon it he was striking straight at the heart of our power of carrying on the war.

This campaign had a very direct bearing upon our North Sea strategy, for at the date at which the Battle of Jutland was fought, about two and a half million tons of British, Allied, and neutral shipping had been sunk by submarine and mine. Had the war imposed no other attacks upon merchant shipping, the percentage lost would not have been very formidable. In the eighteen months that had elapsed since the first organised submarine attack on trade, it represented a rate of sinking of less than a million and three-quarter tons a year, a loss which the Allies and neutrals could easily have counteracted by more energetic building.

But more than half of Great Britain's ocean-going shipping had been commandeered for various war purposes and already in 1916 it had become obvious that the remaining stock of ships could not seriously be diminished without grave embarrassment, either to civil supply, to our financial position, to our military power abroad, or to all three. What was much more serious was this: It was a well-known fact that immediately after the German Government decided to blockade by submarine, a very large building programme was put in hand. The programme, as we have seen, had begun to materialise at the beginning of 1916, and it was Germany's resources in new ships that was Tirpitz's justification for risking a quarrel with America, so certain did the ruin of England seem, were ruthlessness of method combined with the employment of larger and larger numbers.

The Higher Naval Command, then, in this country were fully aware of the extreme importance of being able to deal drastically with this menace, should it once more arise to threaten our sea communications. They also knew that it was certain to arise. And, again, they knew that the underwater threat could only be completely met by an underwater antidote. In the nature of things, as we have seen, there could be no complete reply to the submarine except by mines laid in continuous barrage outside the German harbours, and this in turn was a thing that could not be done unless the German Fleet were destroyed.

Whatever reason there may have been in 1914, and 1915, for holding the Churchill doctrine that a victory was unnecessary, the brief submarine campaign of 1916, must have undeceived the blindest. For this campaign had not only shown that ruthlessness could double the rate of sinking, it had also shown that our stock counter-measures were ineffective to thwart it. It was, then, a matter of the very highest military importance to the cause of the Alliance that the German Fleet should be disposed of, so that the renewal of the German submarine campaign should be virtually impossible.

Had this indeed been the result, it is difficult to calculate the profound influence it must have had upon the course of the war, for within a year of the Battle of Jutland over five and a half million tons of shipping were destroyed and throughout that year a very high percentage of British shipbuilding capacity had necessarily to be devoted to purely military purposes.

The continued existence of the German Fleet made it impossible to curtail, made it indeed obligatory to increase and accelerate, the building of war ships of all sizes. The effect of this on the capacity to build merchant ships was felt immediately. In pre-war days the shipyards of Great Britain had turned out over a million and a quarter tons of merchant shipping and a quarter of a million tons of naval shipping. The same yards, had their industry been organised as a national activity, could under the pressure of war undoubtedly have produced two and a half million tons a year. The complete destruction of the German Fleet at Jutland, then, would have made the difference of nearly eight million tons of shipping before another year was out. What would this have meant in the saving of treasure, in man-power, in every other form of military strength to the Allies? But apart from these, there were further military objects of a very striking kind that might well have been within reach.

We have just seen, in discussing the North Sea strategy, that the kind of blockade we have maintained over the Germans was a long-range sort, leaving the German fleets an area of, say, 60,000 square miles in which to manoeuvre. If there had been no fleet of German battleships something very like the old close blockade could have been maintained. It is well known that it is not mines and submarines that close the Channel and the Sound to the German and British fleets. It is the fact that the operation of clearing these things away must expose the force doing it to battleship action.

The converse also holds true. If there were no German battleships the operation of confining the German cruisers, destroyers, as well as the German submarines, within waters of comparatively narrow limits, by mines, nets, &c., might not have been impossible. Certainly, the opening of the battle would have been comparatively simple. There are many kinds of operations in which it would be folly to risk a battle-fleet so long as the enemy's battle-fleet was in being. But with no hostile enemy fleet in existence a whole vista of new possibilities is opened up to naval and amphibious force. It is unnecessary to enumerate them.

We may take it, then, as axiomatic that, if any chance of bringing the German Fleet to action was offered, it was the first business of the British Navy, and on purely military grounds, no less than those of economic and moral advantage, to force it to decisive action, and that very heavy losses indeed would be justified by complete success.

But a further word must be added. If every admiral at every juncture is to regulate his action by nice calculation of policy and chance, is there not a risk that the balancing of pros and cons may be pushed so far as to confuse the main issue? It is not on these principles that, when it comes to fighting, brave men with an instinct for war do in fact act. It is almost true to say that the example of Hawke and Nelson, no less than those of the light cruiser and destroyer captains in the battle we are about to consider, prove that the best way of diminishing the risk of loss is to take the risk as boldly and as often as you get the chance. Something seems to be due to fighting for fighting's sake. What was it that Nelson said about no captain could go far wrong who laid his ship alongside an enemy's! or as Napoleon has it, "the glory and honour of arms should be the first consideration of a general who gives battle!"

In summing up the situation on May 31, the elements appear to be as follows: The German Government was in double need of a stroke to restore the *moral* of its people. A Russian revival was possible, the British Army in France and Flanders was growing to formidable dimensions, the blow at Verdun had failed. The German Government, and particularly the Imperial Navy, had been humiliated by the surrender to America, so that everything pointed to a stroke at sea, if one could be planned that did not involve too great a risk. Admiral Scheer and his officers of the High Seas Fleet were full of eagerness to justify themselves to their force. They believed the British naval strategy to be such that it would be possible for them to inveigle the fast division of the British Fleet into an action with greatly superior numbers, when serious damage might be inflicted on them. They counted, and with confidence, on Sir David Beatty's eagerness to fight, and they trusted to being able to defeat him before he could break off action or could be supported by forces with whom engagement would be hopeless. They relied upon their air scouts to save them from surprise, and had no intention of coming into contact with Sir John Jellicoe if it could possibly be avoided.

At the same time, however, they recognised that the defensive tactics which smoke screens and the new torpedo made possible would not only prevent contact with superior numbers being disastrous, they believed here, too, either that the British would avoid the risk of torpedo disaster, or that the keenness of the British Fleet for action must expose them to very formidable losses by under-water attack, while their gun-fire could be rendered harmless by the obscuration of the target and the manoeuvres the torpedo could force upon them. And in these conditions the evasion of an artillery fight at decisive range should present no difficulties. Finally, such risks as were involved were well worth the incalculable enhancement of German prestige that would follow if a not-too-untruthful claim could be made to a naval victory. The world that has a natural sympathy with the weaker force would be inclined to regard even the escape of the German Fleet as something very like a German success.

It was the manifest duty of the British Fleet first to thwart any German naval design, whatever it might be, and, secondly, to remove from the theatre of war the only formidable sea force that the enemy possessed. For to do this would make a close investment of his ports possible, would to a large extent cut down the possibility of his submarine successes by mining them into their harbours and channels instead of netting them out of ours, would open the Baltic to British naval enterprise, and would set the whole resources of the Clyde and the Tyne free to produce merchant shipping.

CHAPTER 21

The Battle of Jutland (Continued)

3. THE DISTRIBUTION OF FORCES

In the afternoon of May 31, the main sea forces of Great Britain and Germany were all in the North Sea. The Grand Fleet, under the command of Sir John Jellicoe, accompanied by a squadron of battle-cruisers, two of light cruisers, and three flotillas of destroyers, were to the north; the Battle Cruiser Fleet—of two squadrons—three squadrons of light cruisers, and four destroyer flotillas, supported by the Fifth Battle Squadron, all under the command of Sir David Beatty, were scouting to the southward.

The British Fleet was out "in pursuance of the general policy of periodical sweeps through the North Sea." The disposition of the forces and the plan of operations were the commander-in-chief's own. Neither was dictated from Whitehall. The despatches describing the operation do not—as some of those relating to the events off Heligoland in August, 1914—say that the ships were following Admiralty instructions. The fact has considerable importance in view of the fears expressed earlier in the spring that Whitehall was interfering with the commander-in-chief's dispositions. Note also that the fleet was here in pursuit of the general policy followed since the early days of the war. This hunting for the enemy is not described as taking place at regular intervals, but as "periodic." These searching movements would be made at the times when there was a greater likelihood of there being an enemy to find.

There was a considerable interval between the forces—just how great we do not exactly know. But at the point at which the story in the despatches opens, Sir David Beatty's force was steering northward, that is, toward the Grand Fleet. At 2:20 *Galatea*, the flagship of Com-

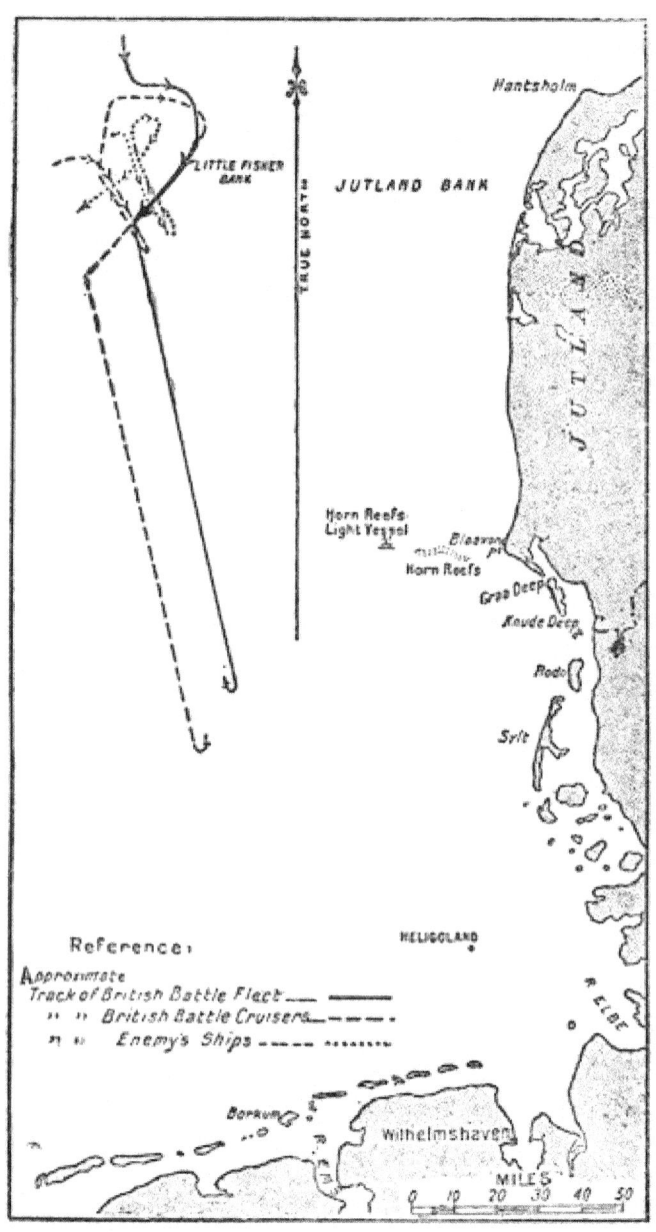

THE OFFICIAL PLAN OF THE BATTLE OF JUTLAND.
Note that the course of the Grand Fleet is not shown to be "astern" of the battle-cruisers, but parallel to their track

modore Alexander Sinclair, reported the presence of enemy vessels. The light cruisers were spread out on a line east and west, ahead of the battle-cruisers. When Sir David Beatty got news that the enemy had been sighted on the extreme right of his line of cruisers, he at once altered course from north to S.S.E., that is, rather more of a right angle and a half, steering for the Horn Reefs, so as to place his force between the enemy and his base. It is to be noted that the vice-admiral at once adopted not the movement that would soonest bring the enemy to action, but that which would compel him to action whether he wished it or not. Observe he does not wait to do this till he has ascertained the enemy's strength.

A quarter of an hour later smoke was seen to the eastward—that would be on the port bow—which would confirm the *Galatea's* account that the enemy was still to the north of the line that Sir David Beatty was steering. The distance of the battle-cruisers from the Horn Reefs was such that the enemy's escape from action would still be impossible, even if he altered course to cut him off sooner. This, accordingly, he did, steering first due east and then northeast and, in less than an hour, sighted Von Hipper's force of five battle-cruisers, probably almost straight ahead.

When, at 2:20, the battle-cruisers headed for the Horn Reefs, the First and Third Light Cruiser Squadrons changed their direction also without waiting for orders, and swept to the eastward, screening the battle-cruisers. The Fifth Battle Squadron, which we must suppose originally to have been on Sir David Beatty's left, was coming up behind the battle-cruisers as fast as possible. The Second Light Cruiser Squadron, leaving the screening functions to the First and Third, made full speed to take station ahead of the battle-cruisers, where two flotillas of destroyers were already. While these movements were proceeding, a seaplane was sent up from *Engadine* which, having to fly low on account of clouds, pushed to within 3,000 yards of the four light cruisers of Von Hipper's advance force. Full and accurate reports were thus received just before the enemy was sighted in the distance.

At 2:20, when the enemy's scouting advanced craft were first seen by *Galatea*, Von Hipper was seemingly to the south of them, and according to the German account went north and east to investigate. While then Sir David Beatty was travelling southeast, east, and then northeast, we shall probably be right in supposing that Von Hipper was executing an approximately parallel series of movements out of sight to the northeast of him. Both advance forces were increasing their distance from their main forces. At any rate, neither was approaching his main force when they came into sight at 3:30, Von Hipper a few miles north of Sir David Beatty.

What was the distance at this period that separated the battle-cruisers of each side from their supporting battle-fleets? At 3:30 the German battle-cruisers headed straight for their main fleet at full speed, and met them an hour and a quarter afterward. If Von Hipper's speed was 26 knots and Admiral Scheer's 18—he had pre-Dreadnoughts with him, and it was not likely to have been greater—there would have been fifty-five sea miles separating the German forces. According to the despatch, Sir John Jellicoe at 3:30 headed his fleet toward Sir David Beatty, and came down at full speed. He came into contact with the battle-cruisers on their return from their excursion to the south at 5:45. Sir David Beatty would by this time have returned approximately to the same latitude he was on at 3:30. Had he then at 3:30 closed Sir John Jellicoe at full speed, he would have come in contact with him in, say, fifty minutes. The British fleets at 3:30, then, may have been between forty and forty-five sea miles apart, against the German fifty-five.

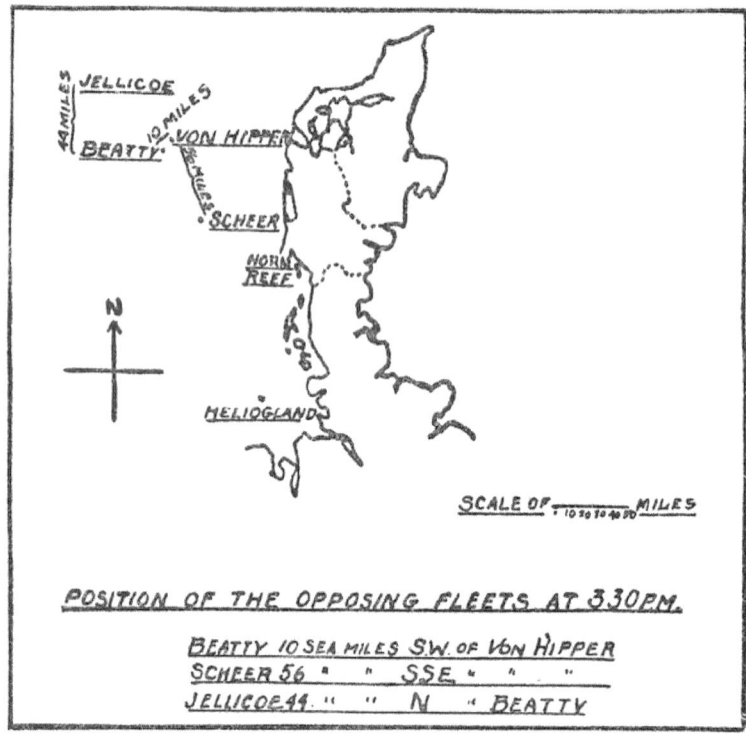

It has been said that both sides fell into a strategical error in dividing their forces. This criticism has been prominent in the neutral Press; but it arises from a confusion of thought. On neither side were the battle-cruisers considered as anything but scouting forces, which in all sea campaigns have been, because it is a necessity of the case, maintained at suitable distances from the main force. The only division of forces proper on the British side was the presence of four battleships with Sir David Beatty. But as we see from the despatch, for some reason a squadron of three of Sir David's battle-cruisers was with the main fleet, and the Fifth Battle Squadron seems to have been taking its place.

The only evidences of a strategical blunder in the disposition would be, first, a failure of the chosen plan to bring the Germans to action, next a failure to defeat them when brought to action, because of inability to concentrate the requisite strength for the purpose at the critical point. It is surely a sufficient reply to say that the German Fleet was brought to action, and that any incompleteness in the victory arose, not from there being insufficient forces present, but owing to circumstances making it impossible to employ them to the greatest advantage.

The Action: First Phase

When the enemy was sighted at 3:30, Sir David formed his ships for action in a line of bearing, so that, in the northeasterly wind, the smoke of one ship should not interfere with the fire of the rest. His course was east-southeast, and he was converging on that of the enemy, who was steering rather more directly south. By the time the line was formed the range was about 23,000 yards, and at twelve minutes to four had been closed to 18,500, when both sides opened fire simultaneously. When the range had closed to about 14,000 yards or less, parallel courses were steered and kept until the end of this phase of the engagement. The Fifth Battle Squadron, consisting of four ships of the *Queen Elizabeth* class, under the command of Admiral Evan-Thomas, at the time when Sir David formed his battle-line, was about 10,000 yards off—not straight astern of the battle-cruisers, but bearing about half a right angle to port.

The course that would bring them immediately into the line of the Battle Cruiser Fleet, then, was not parallel to that steered by Sir David Beatty, but a course converging on to it. It was this that enabled them, with their inferior speed, to come into action at eight minutes past four, though only then at the very long range of 20,000 yards.

The interval had been singularly unfortunate for the British side.

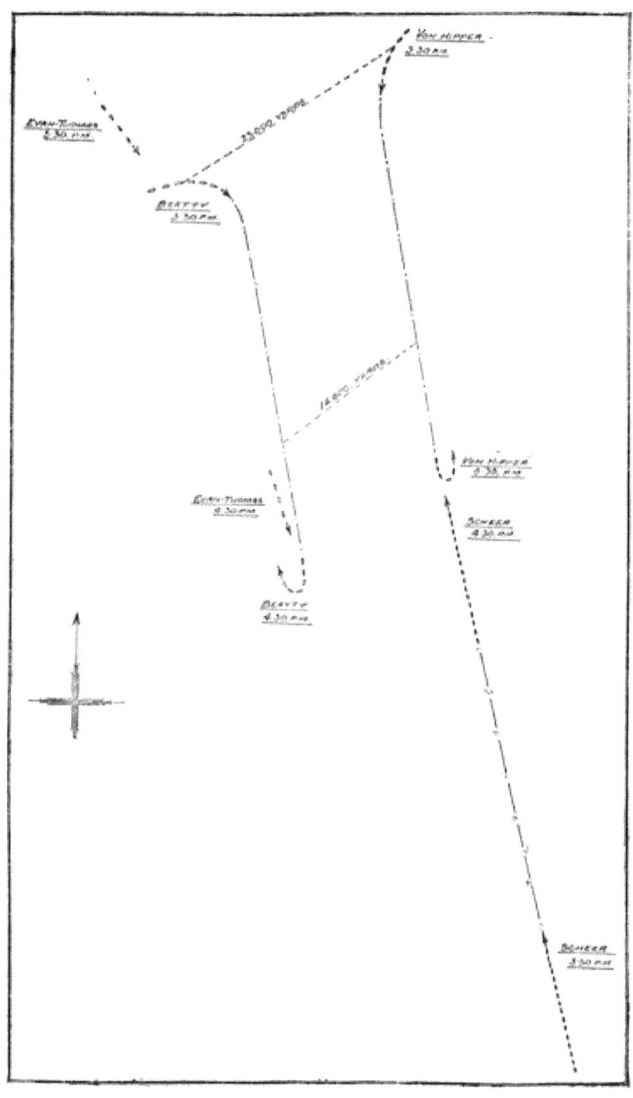

The first phase; from Von Hipper's coming into view, until his juncture with Admiral Scheer

Indefatigable (Captain Sowerby) had the misfortune to be hit by a shell in a vulnerable spot. The destruction of the ship was instantaneous, and almost the entire personnel, including the ship's very gallant Captain, was lost. An exactly similar misfortune later befell *Queen Mary*. Neither ship had, in any sense of the word, been overwhelmed by the gunfire of the enemy.

Indeed, when *Queen Mary* went down, the enemy's fire, which had been singularly accurate and intense in the first phase of the action had, as the vice-admiral says in his despatch, slackened. The superior skill, due chiefly to the wider experience of the British fire-control organisations, had already begun to tell—the enemy's fire-control being evidently unable to survive the damage, and losses of action.

Sir David Beatty's main force was thus reduced first by one-sixth, and then by one-fifth of its number, so that he was now left with four ships against the German five. But three of these ships disposed of broadsides of 13.4's, the fourth employing a gun equal to the most powerful in the German armament. In weight and power of broadside the British cruisers still had the advantage, and it is clear that their rate of fire was faster, and their aiming and range-keeping more effective.

Just as the Fifth Battle Squadron came into action at ten minutes past four, a brisk and dramatic encounter took place between the light craft of the two sides. Two flotillas of destroyers and one squadron of light cruisers, it will be remembered, were stationed well ahead of the British flagship. Eight units of the Thirteenth Flotilla, together with two of the Tenth and two of the Ninth, had been designated for making an attack on the enemy's line as soon as an opportunity offered. The opportunity came at 4:15. A destroyer attack is of course a torpedo attack, and is delivered by the flotilla engaged in steering a course converging toward that of the enemy. The destroyers must be well ahead of their targets if the attack is to be effective, so that the torpedo and the ship attacked shall be steering toward each other. These boats proceeded then, at 4:15, to initiate this manoeuvre toward the enemy.

It was almost simultaneously countered by an identical movement by the enemy, who had a considerable preponderance of force—fifteen destroyers and a cruiser against the British twelve destroyers. These two forces met before either had reached a position for effecting its main purpose, *viz.*, the torpedo attack on the capital ships. A very spirited engagement followed. It was a close-quarters affair, and was carried through by the British destroyers in the most gallant manner and with great determination. Two of the enemy's destroyers were sunk, and

British battle-crusers opening fire—opening battle action on the 31st May

what was far more important, it was made quite impossible for him to carry through a torpedo attack. None of our boats went down.

But just as the enemy's boats had been unable to get a favourable position for attacking our battle-cruisers, so, too, the English boats, delayed by this engagement, were unable to get the desired position on the enemy's bow for employing their torpedoes to the best advantage. Three of them, however, though unable to attack from ahead, pressed forward for a broadside attack on Von Hipper's ships, and naturally came under a fierce fire from the secondary armament of these vessels. One of them, *Nomad*, was badly hit, and had to stop between the lines. She was ultimately lost. *Nestor* and *Nicator* held on between the lines until the German Battle Fleet was met.

For a full half hour these two boats had been either fighting an almost hand-to-hand action with the enemy's boats, or had been under the close-range fire of Von Hipper's battle-cruisers. They now found themselves faced by the German Battle Fleet. But they were at last in the right position for an attack. Both closed, in spite of the fire, to 3,000 yards and fired their torpedoes. It is believed that one hit was made. *Nicator* escaped and rejoined the Thirteenth Flotilla, but *Nestor*, though not sunk, was stopped, and had to be numbered amongst the losses when the action was over.

While this had been going forward, the artillery action between the two squadrons of battle-cruisers continued fierce and resolute. Sir Evan-Thomas's battleships did their best with the rear of the enemy's line, but were unable to reduce the range below 20,000 yards, if, indeed, they were unable to prevent the enemy increasing it. At 4:18 a second palpable evidence that the British fire was taking effect was afforded by the third of Von Hipper's ships bursting into flames. The first evidence was, of course, the falling off in the rate of the enemy's fire, and the still more marked deterioration in its accuracy.

It will be remembered that the Second Light Cruiser Squadron, under Commodore Goodenough, had got to its action station ahead of Sir David Beatty's line a little while before the engagement opened with Von Hipper at half-past three. This squadron maintained its position well ahead, and at 4:38 reported the advent of Scheer with a German battle squadron from the south. They would then be from 20,000 to 24,000 yards off. Until *Southampton* sent in her message at 4:38, the British Admiral had no reason for knowing that the enemy Battle Fleet was out. Not that the knowledge would have affected the plan he actually carried out, for the immediate attack on Von Hipper

German battleships turn away after coming under fire

was right in either event. But it was obvious that, with only four battle-cruisers, it was out of the question continuing the action as if the forces were equal. The Fifth Battle Squadron was out of range, and the vice-admiral's first business was to concentrate his force, and then to judge how to impose his will upon the enemy in the matter of forcing him up to action with the Grand Fleet.

The junction with Admiral Evan-Thomas could obviously not be delayed; as obviously the manoeuvre was a dangerous one, for as each ship turned it would be exposed to the enemy's fire without being able to reply. Had only speed of junction to be considered, the battle-cruisers could have been turned together when the rear ship on the old course would have become the leading ship on the new. The turn could probably be accomplished in less than three minutes. But seriously as the German fire had depreciated, it was not a thing with which liberties could be taken. Sir David Beatty, therefore, turned his ships one by one, thus keeping three in action while the first was turning; two while the second was turning—the first and second coming into action on a reverse course as the third and fourth turned from the old. At no time, then, was the fire of the British squadron reduced below that of two ships.

No sooner had Sir David turned than Von Hipper followed his example, and as the vice-admiral led up on the new course, he met Evan-Thomas with his four battleships directing a fierce fire on Von Hipper. These two squadrons were on opposite courses, and the change of range was rapid. The conditions for hitting were extremely difficult. Evan-Thomas was not yet in sight of the German Battle Fleet, and the vice-admiral told him to turn, as he had done, and to form up behind him. By the time this manoeuvre was completed—that is, within a quarter of an hour of Sir David Beatty having begun his own turn—the head of Admiral Scheer's line had got within range, and a brisk action opened between the leading German ships and the rear ships on the British side.

During this quarter of an hour, Commodore Goodenough in *Southampton* pushed south to ascertain the precise numbers and composition of the German force. It was of course of great moment, not only to the vice-admiral but to the commander-in-chief that the enemy's strength should be ascertained as accurately and as soon as possible. But to do this the commodore had to take his squadron under the massed fire of the German Dreadnoughts. He held on until a range of about 13,000 yards was reached and, having got the information he wanted, returned to form up with the Cruiser Fleet on its northerly course. His squadron was hardly hit: for though the fire was intense, here, too, the change of range was rapid, and far too difficult for the German fire-control to surmount.

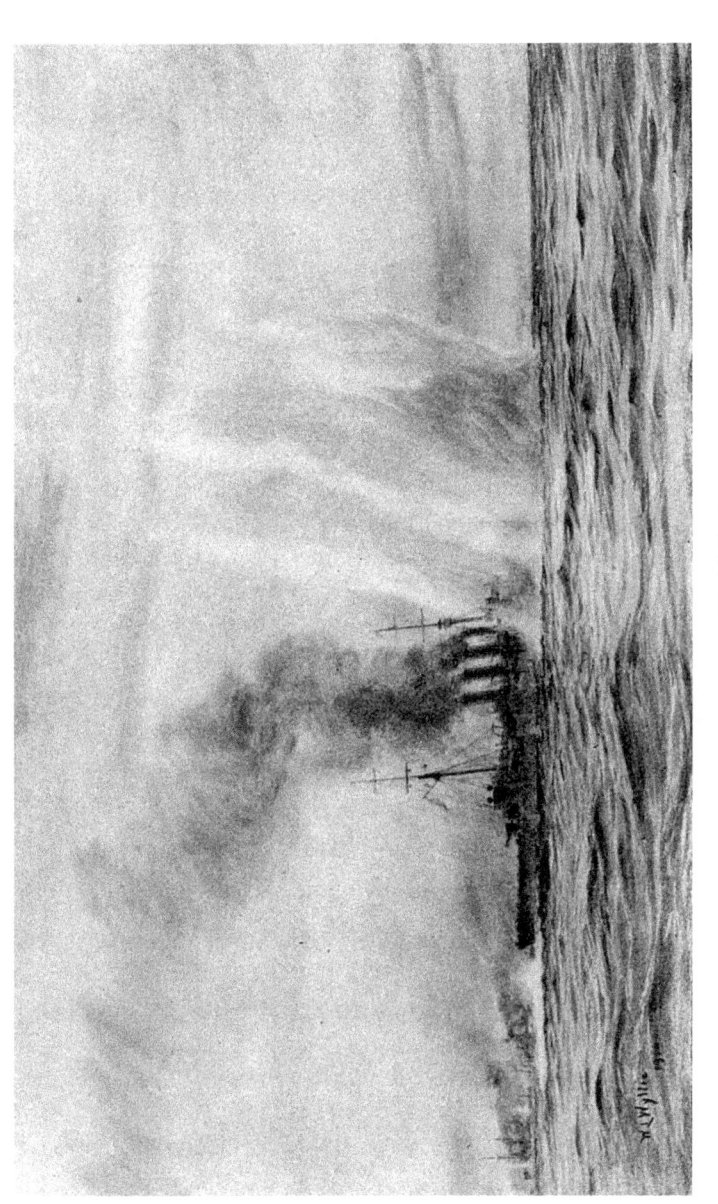

British light cruiser H.M.S. *Southampton*

CHAPTER 22

The Battle of Jutland (Continued)

4. THE SECOND PHASE

The flotillas and light cruiser squadrons were now regrouped—some ahead, some alongside of the battle-cruiser and battleship squadrons, and the whole steered to the northward, keeping approximately parallel to and well ahead of the German line. From the time when Scheer came into action at 4:57 until six o'clock, Sir David Beatty kept the range at about 14,000 yards. Both sides must have had some anxious moments during this critical hour. Sir David Beatty knew what Admiral Scheer did not—for the weather was too thick for the Zeppelins to give him the much-needed information—that he was falling back on Sir John Jellicoe, when of course overwhelming force could be brought to bear. His business was to keep Admiral Scheer in play, while exposing his ships, especially his battle-cruisers, as little as possible, consistent with their maintaining an efficient attack upon the enemy.

Sir David was criticised for exposing his ships imprudently. Is this criticism well founded? Von Hipper's battle-cruisers were at the head of the German line, but one had certainly fallen out of action by five o'clock, and one more was to leave the line in the course of this holding action. The battle-cruisers, however, did not affect the situation, for the German Fleet's speed was that of the pre-Dreadnoughts in the rear, and this could not have exceeded 18 knots and was probably less. But the slowest ship in Sir David Beatty's squadron could make at least 24.

Nothing, therefore, could have been simpler than to have taken the whole force out of reach of Scheer's guns whenever he chose. Had there at any stage been the remotest chance of the lightly armoured battle-cruisers being exposed to smothering fire from the German battleships, the danger could have been averted by the expedient of putting on more speed. Beatty's main preoccupation, however, was not this. It was undoubtedly the fear that Scheer might retreat before the Grand Fleet could get up. He had, therefore, first to act as if he were a promising target, next to be ready with a counter-stroke if the Germans showed any sign of flight. How did he meet the first necessity of the position?

By keeping the range at 14,000 yards, at which the heavier projectile guns of the British artillery would have a distinct advantage over the German batteries, and by keeping so far ahead that it was impossible for Admiral Scheer to bring the fire of concentrated broadsides to bear, not only was an absolute inequality of gunnery conditions avoided, but it is probable that, so far as tactical disposition went, Sir David Beatty, as throughout the action, had so handled his ships as to be actually superior in fighting power over the forces he was engaging. I say "so far as tactical disposition was concerned," advisedly, because a new element came into action at this point which favoured first one and then the other, and was ultimately to make long-range gunfire altogether nugatory.

Already between a quarter past four and half past, light mists had been driving down, and even before a quarter to five the outlines of Von Hipper's squadron were becoming vague and shadowy to the British gun-layers. Between half-past five and six these conditions got very much worse. It handicapped the fire-control severely, and already they were beginning to feel, what the commander-in-chief says was a characteristic of the whole period during which the Grand Fleet was intermittently in action, *viz.*, the extreme difficulty of using range-finders in the shifting and indifferent light. How local and variable the mist was may be judged from the fact that the British line was not only free from mist, but was outlined sharply against the setting sun—thus giving a great advantage to the German rangefinders.

It was this that largely neutralised the advantage which Sir David Beatty had so skilfully derived from the superior speed of his ships. No ships were lost on the British side during this part of the action. But it can hardly be doubted that had the conditions of visibility been the same for both sides, the head of the German line would have suffered more severely than it did from the Fifth Battle Squadron's 15-inch guns. But, as we have seen, one of the battle-cruisers had to haul out severely damaged, and certain others showed unmistakable evidence of having suffered severely.

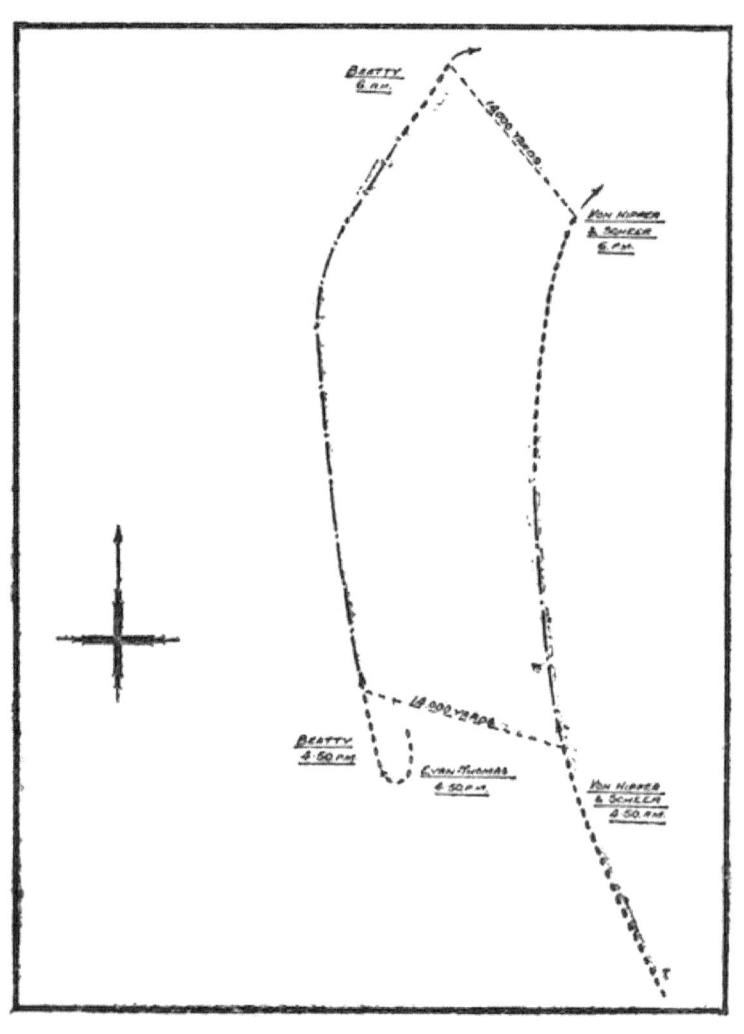

The second phase; Beatty engages the combined German Fleet, and draws it toward the Grand Fleet

In this phase of the action, as in the first, the British destroyers made attacks on the German line, and it is believed that one ship, seen to be hopelessly on fire and emitting huge clouds of smoke and steam, owed her injuries to a torpedo fired by *Moresby*.

What was Admiral Scheer's idea in following up the British squadron as he did? He knew that he had not the speed which would enable him to catch it. It was almost impossible—for he was now the pursuing squadron—to hope for any success from a destroyer attack. There was a risk that he might be caught and forced to engage by the Grand Fleet. There are, it seems, two explanations of his action. In the first place, he knew that Von Hipper had already sunk two of the British vessels. It was worth a considerable effort to try and get more, and in face of these losses Sir David Beatty's movements may have looked so extremely like flight as to make him think that he had, to this extent, the upper hand, and that the British Admiral would be unlikely to risk his force again by seeking a close action. Apart from the risk of the Grand Fleet being out, then, there seemed to be everything to gain and nothing to lose by carrying on the chase.

But is it quite certain that his action was altogether voluntary? What would Sir David Beatty's action have been had Scheer attempted to renounce the fight? There can be no hesitation in answering this question, for we only have to look at what Sir David actually did at six o'clock, when the Germans got news of the Grand Fleet's approach and had to change tactics immediately. We shall find in this the clue to what would have happened had Scheer attempted to change course and withdraw earlier in the action.

The governing factors of the situation were, first, Beatty's superior speed; secondly, his superior concentration of gun power, and, lastly, the greater efficacy of his guns at long range. The difference between the speed of the slowest ships in the British fast division, say 24½ knots, and that of the slowest in the German main squadron, say 18, was 6½ knots at least.

If Scheer had attempted simply to withdraw, he must have reversed the course of his fleet, either by turning his ships together or in succession. In the first case, the simplest of manoeuvres would have brought the British Fleet into the **T** position across the German rear. And with a six-knot advantage in speed, Sir David could even have attempted the final tactics of Admiral Sturdee at the Falkland Islands, and pursued the flying force with his four battle-cruisers, engaging them from one side, and the Fifth Battle Squadron attacking them

British destroyer of the 13th Flotilla

from the other. So disastrous, indeed, must this manoeuvre have been to the Germans that it need not be considered as thinkable. The alternative was to lead round from the head of the line, when the choice would have arisen between a gradual change of course and a reverse of course, *viz.*, a sixteen-point turn.

The objections to the sixteen-point turn were precisely similar to those to turning the fleet together, with, perhaps, the added objection that the British would have had two lines of ships to fire into instead of only one—an advantage which would not have been counterbalanced by the enemy keeping one or two broadsides bearing, for they would be the broadsides of ships under full helm, and it is highly improbable that their fire would have been effective. When Scheer actually did break off battle, we shall find that he turned his fleet in succession through an angle of 135°. There were special reasons that made it obligatory he should do this, and special conditions which made it possible. Until he met the Grand Fleet, there was nothing to force him to turn, and the counter-stroke on which he relied to rob the turn of its chief dangers would not have been operative against the two squadrons of fast ships under Sir David Beatty's command.

Had Scheer attempted such a turn as he actually made at 6:45, or had he initiated and continued such a manoeuvre as he began at six o'clock, Beatty's speed advantage would have enabled him to maintain his dominating position ahead of the German line. He could either have manoeuvred to get round between Scheer and his bases, with a view to heading him north again, or, if he judged it hopeless to expect the Grand Fleet to reach the scene in daylight, could himself have reversed course and pounded the weak ships at the end of the German line unmercifully.

In any event, while it would be an exaggeration to say that he had the whip-hand of the enemy, it is no exaggeration to say that his force was so formidable and so fast as to make escape from it anything but a safe or a simple problem. The utmost Scheer could have hoped for would have been a long defensive action until darkness made attack impossible, or winning the mine-fields made pursuit too dangerous.

These considerations cannot be ignored in asking why it was that Scheer followed the British admiral so obediently in the hour and a quarter between 4:57 and 6 p.m. But still less must we forget that had Scheer known earlier that the Grand Fleet was out, he would certainly have preferred the risk of a pursuit by Beatty to the chance of having to take on the whole of Sir John Jellicoe's battle fleet.

British battleships led by the H.M.S. *Iron Duke* flagship

At twenty-five minutes to six Admiral Scheer began hauling round to the east, changing his course, that is to say, gradually away from the British line. Sir David supposes that he had by this time received information of the approach of the Grand Fleet. This information might have come from Zeppelins, though in the weather conditions this would seem to have been improbable; or it might have come from some of his cruisers, which were well ahead, and had made contact with Hood's scouts. But is this quite consistent with what Admiral Jellicoe says of Hood's movements?

> At 5:30 this squadron observed flashes of gun-fire and heard the sound of guns to the southwestward. Rear-Admiral Hood sent *Chester* to investigate, and this ship engaged three or four enemy light cruisers at about 5:45.

It is not stated that Rear-Admiral Hood saw the German light cruisers, and it seems improbable, then, that they saw him. Admiral Scheer could not have changed course at 5:35, because of the action of his scouts with *Chester* at 5:45. But her presence may have been signalled to him as soon as she was seen, and he may have concluded that the news could have but one significance, *viz.*, that the Grand Fleet was coming down from the north. But is it altogether impossible that Scheer began his gradual easterly turn before suspecting that the Grand Fleet was out? Was he not, perhaps, already aware of the dangers of getting too far afield, and beginning that gradual turn which might keep Sir David Beatty's ships in play as long as daylight lasted, without giving the openings which a direct attempt at flight would offer?

Whatever the explanation of the movements, the enemy began this gradual turn and Sir David turned with him, increasing speed, so as to maintain his general relation to the head of the German line. At ten minutes to six some of the Grand Fleet's cruisers were observed ahead, and six minutes later the leading battleships came into view. The moment for which every movement since 2:20 had been a preparation had now arrived—the Grand Fleet and the German Fleet were to meet.

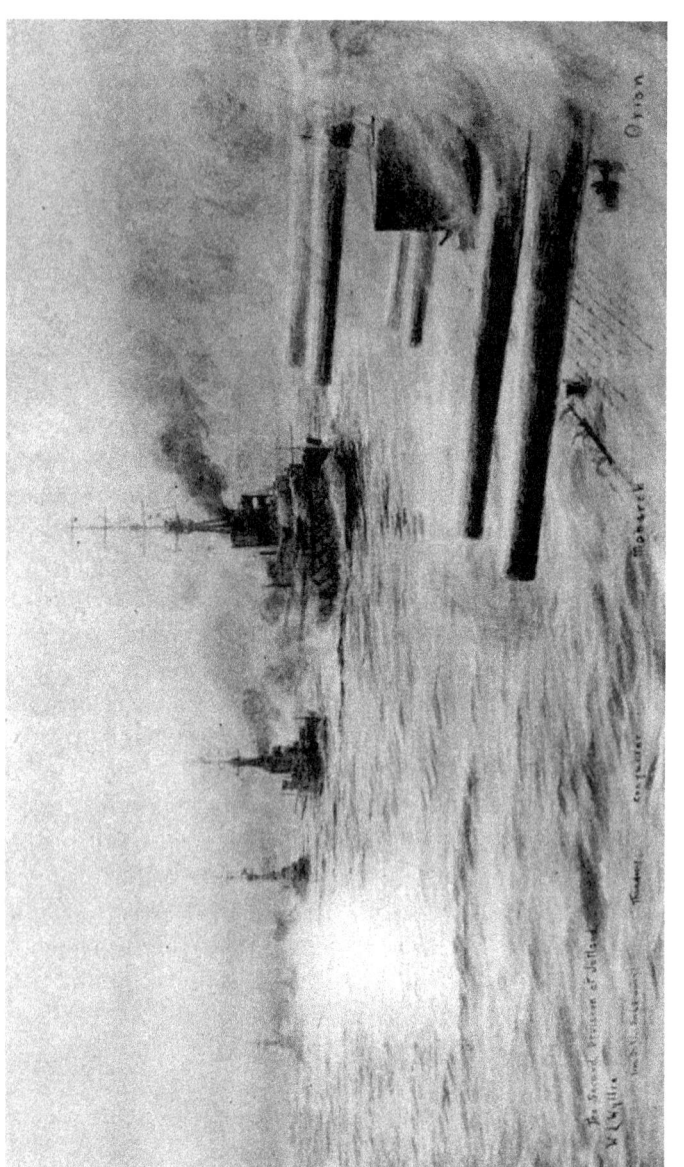

British 2nd Division of Battleships

CHAPTER 23

The Battle of Jutland (Continued)

5. The Three Objectives

The issue of the day would now depend upon how the commanders of the three separate forces appreciated the tasks set to them; the principles that governed the plans for their execution; the efficiency of their command in getting those principles applied; the resolution and skill with which the several units executed each its share in the operations. It was easy enough to define the task of each leader. Sir David Beatty had so far completely justified what seemed the general strategic plan of the British forces. He had driven the German fast divisions back to their main fleet, he had held that fleet for an hour and a half, and had brought it within striking distance of the overwhelmingly superior main forces of his own side. He had lost two capital ships and three destroyers to achieve his end to this point. He had the sacrifice of some thousands of his gallant companions to justify. Neither a parade nor a "gladiatorial display," only the utter rout and destruction of the enemy's fleet, could pay that debt. His task was not, therefore, complete. He had to help the Grand Fleet to deliver its blow with the concentration and rapidity that would render it decisive.

It was already obvious that rapidity would be vital. The weather conditions had been growing more and more unfavourable to the gunnery on which the British Fleet would rely for victory. Everything pointed to the conditions growing steadily worse. It was a case of seizing victory quickly or missing it altogether. Had there been no shifting mists there would have been two and a half or three hours of daylight on which to count. But with lowering clouds and heavy vapours, clear seeing at 10,000 or even 5,000 yards might be as impossible two hours before as two hours after sunset. Everything pointed, therefore, to this: the British attack would have to be instant—or it might not materialize at all. The vice-admiral commanding the Battle-Cruiser Fleet saw his duty clearly and simply. But to decide exactly what action he should take was a different thing altogether.

No less clear was the task of the British commander-in-chief. Twelve miles away from him was the whole naval strength of the enemy, 150 miles from his mine-fields, more than 200 from his fleet bases. Against sixteen modern battleships, he himself commanded twenty-four—a superiority of three to two. His gun-power, measured by the weight and striking energy of his broadsides, must have been nearly twice that of the enemy; measured by the striking energy and the destructive power of its heavier shells, it was greater still. Opposed to the enemy's five battle-cruisers, there were four under the command of Sir David Beatty and three led by Rear-Admiral Hood. Against the six 18-knot pre-Dreadnoughts that formed the rear of the German Fleet, with their twenty-four 11-inch guns firing a 700-pound shell, there were Rear-Admiral Evan-Thomas's four 25-knot ships of the Fifth Battle Squadron, carrying thirty-two 15-inch guns, whose shells were three times as heavy and must have been nine times as destructive. This force, vastly superior if it could be concentrated for its purpose, had to be deployed for a blow which, if simultaneously delivered at a range at which the guns would hit, must be final in a very brief period.

The German admiral could never have had the least doubt as to his task. His business was to save his fleet from the annihilation with which it was manifestly menaced. So far fortune had been kind. The British Battle-Cruiser Fleet had done what the Germans had expected it to do. It had engaged promptly and determinedly and its losses, surprisingly enough, had been suffered, not while it was holding a force greatly superior to itself, but while engaging Von Hipper, whose ships were less numerous and more lightly armed. Though Scheer did not expect an encounter with the Grand Fleet, he was very far from being unprepared, should it come. Accordingly, when at six o'clock he realised that the supreme moment had arrived, he was probably as little in doubt as to his method of executing his task, as to the character of the task itself.

The Tactical Plans
Admiral Scheer's tactics

The tactics of Admiral Scheer were a development and an extension of those of Von Hipper on January 24 of the previous year. If his task was to break off action as soon as possible and to keep out of action until darkness made fleet fighting impossible, means must be found of thwarting or neutralizing the attack of the British Fleet while it lasted, of evading that attack at the earliest moment, and of preventing its resumption. He could only neutralize the attack in so far as he could thwart the fire-control and aiming of the enemy by the constant or intermittent concealment of his ships by smoke. He could only evade attack by preventing the overwhelming force against him being brought within striking distance. Recall for a moment the lessons of the Dogger Bank. In his retreat Von Hipper had put his flotillas to a double task.

For the first two hours of that engagement he had checked the speed of his battle cruisers to cover *Bluecher*. When the British Fleet had so gained on him that its artillery became effective, he realised that the case of *Bluecher* was hopeless and that, unless prompt measures were taken, the case of the battle cruiser would be little better. *Bluecher* was, therefore, abandoned to her fate and *Derfflinger*, *Seydlitz*, and *Moltke* concealed by smoke. Simultaneously, or almost simultaneously, a veritable shoal of torpedoes was launched across the path on which *Lion* and her consorts were advancing. The smoke baffled the gun-layers, the changed course forced on the battle-cruisers baffled the fire-control. The Germans gained immunity from gunfire and, in the pause, changed course and got a new start in the race for home.

Then the first of a succession of rendezvous for submarines placed on the pre-arranged line of the German retreat, repeated this tactic of diversion just before *Lion* was disabled. The intervention—an hour later—of a second protecting picket of submarines was decisive, for, on realising their presence, the officer who had succeeded Sir David in command broke off pursuit. It was on these tactics on a greatly extended scale and developed no doubt by assiduous study and repeated rehearsal, that Scheer now had to rely.

The circumstances of the moment were exceptionally favourable for their employment. The conditions of atmosphere that made long-range gunnery difficult, made the establishment of smoke screens to render it more difficult still, exceptionally easy. The wind had dropped, the air was heavy and vaporous, the ships were running from one bank of light fog into another. It was a day on which smoke would stay where it was made, clinging to the surface of the sea, mingling with and permeating the water-laden atmosphere. Further, these were just the conditions in which, were a torpedo attack delivered at a fleet by the fast destroyer flotillas, the threat would have an element of surprise that would be lacking in clear vision. Such menaces, then, should they have any deterrent effect on the enemy's closing, would be likely to have a maximum effect. The respite from gunfire, the delay in the reformation of the fleet for pursuit, each could be the longest possible.

Two considerations must have caused Scheer the gravest possible anxiety. In the first place, smoke screens would not protect the van of his fleet. What if the British used their speed to concentrate ships there and crush it? Secondly, as destroyer attacks could only be delivered from a point in advance of the course of the squadrons it was hoped to injure or divert, the method on which he relied, first for breaking off from, and then evading, action could not be used until he had the British Fleet on his quarter or astern.

Now at six o'clock the British Fleet was dead ahead of him. Its fleet's speed must have been three, and may have been four, knots greater than his own. He had four powerful ships, six or seven knots faster still, on his port bow at a range of only 14,000 yards, supported by a 25-knot squadron only three knots slower and of enormous gun power. How was he to turn a line of twenty-one ships to get the whole of this force behind him, without some portion of it being overwhelmed in the process? For to turn in succession would be to leave first the centre and the rear, and then the rear entirely unsupported as the leading ships escaped.

As we have seen in a previous chapter, until the enemy's artillery was neutralised, it was out of the question to do anything but to turn on a flat arc, so that so long as it was necessary or possible, all the ships should act in mutual support. The crux of the situation was this: The Grand Fleet was but twelve miles off, a distance that could be shortened to easy gun range in ten or twelve minutes. What if the whole of this force were in a quarter of an hour brought parallel to, and well ahead of, his own? To engage it defensively by gun power would be useless for the odds were hopeless. To turn the head of the line sharply would be to purchase a precarious safety for the van by the certain immolation of the centre and the rear. Scheer must have seen that, were things to develop along this line, he would have no choice but to turn his whole fleet together, a dangerous and desperate manoeuvre, but permissible because the time would have come for a *sauve qui peut*.

But while these considerations may have caused him some anxiety, there were other elements to reassure him. Years before the war, the Germans had discovered and grasped what seemed the fundamental strategic idea that had shaped British naval strategy. It was that the *rôle* of our main sea forces in war was to be primarily defensive. Our fleet was to consist of units individually more powerful than those of competing navies. As to numbers, we were aiming at possessing these on an equality with the two next largest powers combined. It was a policy that permitted of an overwhelming concentration against the most powerful of our competitors, the Germans, while still maintaining substantial forces the world over. It was a presumption of this policy that the use of the sea would in war be ceded to us by our enemies, and would remain virtually undisturbed until our main forces were not only attacked but defeated. Numbers and individual power made an attack by inferior forces seem the most remote of all contingencies, and defeat impossible.

From this theory the Germans derived a corollary. It was that, as the British ideal was concerned not primarily with victory, but in avoiding defeat, we should probably not face great risks to destroy an enemy—and obviously no enemy could be destroyed without great risks—but rather would be chiefly preoccupied with averting the destruction, not only of our whole fleet, but even of such a proportion of it as would deprive us of that pre-eminence in numbers on which we seemed chiefly to rely. Hence, in the preamble of the last Navy Bill which the government got the *Reichstag* to accept before the war, it was plainly stated that the naval policy of the German Higher Command did not aim at possessing a fleet capable of defeating the strongest fleet in the world, but would be satisfied with a force that the strongest fleet could not defeat, except at a cost that would bring it so low that its world supremacy would be gone.

The underlying military conception was that the group then controlling the British Navy would not fight, and the underlying political conception that, should this group be replaced by leaders of a more aggressive complexion, the price we should pay for a sea victory would be a combination of the world's other sea forces against us, they being prompted to this by their long-felt jealousy of Great Britain's navalism.

In May, 1916, the bottom had fallen out of the political argument. There was no naval power that was the least jealous of Great Britain. The submarine campaign had disgusted all with Germany's sea ethics, and the whole world would have rejoiced had sea victory, which was necessary before the submarine could be finally defeated, been won. But on the military argument the Germans were on surer ground.

They had certain substantial reasons for believing that they had not misread the psychology of our Higher Naval Command. Indeed, if Jutland left them or the world in any doubt about the matter, their interpretation was to receive the most striking of all confirmations by a statesman who had not only been First Lord of the Admiralty, but had personally selected the commander-in-chief on this eventful day, and had no doubt been a party to, if he had not inspired, the strategy which the Grand Fleet was to observe.

Mr. Churchill left the world in no uncertainty at all that, in his opinion—which, presumably, was that not only of the Boards over which he had presided, but of those from whom it had been inherited—the British Fleet, without a victorious battle, enjoyed all the advantages that the most crushing of victories could give us, and that it was for the Germans and not for us to attempt any alteration in the position at sea. Beyond this, however, Scheer not only had it in his favour that the British commander-in-chief might, under such inspiration, hesitate about the risks inseparable from seeking a rapid decision at short range; he seemed to have a definite and official confirmation of a further theory, *viz.*, that to avoid a certain form of risk was almost an axiom of official British doctrine.

Von Hipper's escape at the Dogger Bank, unexplained it is true in Sir David Beatty's despatch, had been complacently attributed by the British Admiralty to the unexpected presence of enemy submarines. The immediate abandonment of the field in the presence of this form of attack, so far from being made the subject of Admiralty disapproval, seems to have been endorsed by the continuous employment of the officer responsible. Scheer could then look forward to his torpedo attack not only as holding a menace over the British Fleet that might endanger its numerical superiority. It seemed to be a menace specifically accepted as one not in any circumstances to be encountered.

Still, for all that, there was uncertainty in the matter. The sport of bull-fighting owes its continuance solely to the fact that the instincts of each brute playmate in that cruel game are exactly identical with those of every other. However busy any bull may be with a tossed and disembowelled horse, it is a matter of mathematical certainty that a red cloak dangled before his eyes will divert him from goring the rider. The animal's reactions to each well-known pin-prick or provocation are inevitable. The safety of every *toreador*, *picador*, and *matador* depends not on their power of meeting the unexpected, but upon the rapidity, deftness, and agility with which they can first time the movements which long experience has taught them to expect, and then execute the counter-stroke or evasion which an old-established art has prescribed. Scheer, it seems to me, showed something more than rashness in relying on a German analysis of our naval mentality, and upon a single instance—and endorsement—of that mentality in action, as if it established a rule of conduct as irrevocable as instinct. But, then, it must be understood, he had no choice.

Sir David Beatty's Tactics

At six the Grand Fleet was five miles to the north, approximately twelve miles from the enemy. It could not come into action in less than a quarter of an hour. The speed of *Lion, Tiger, Princess Royal*, and *New Zealand* was twenty-seven knots, at least eight, possibly nine or even ten knots faster than that of the enemy. The head of the enemy's line bore southeast from the flagship. Scheer, already aware of Sir John Jellicoe's approach, was beginning his eastward turn. Beatty realised that at full speed he could head the German Fleet, so that by the time the Grand Fleet's deployment was complete, he would be in a commanding position on the bow of the enemy's van. It would probably not be possible for Evan-Thomas to gain this position, too.

But there was no reason why he should. Assuming Sir David's purpose to be the realisation of the most elementary of tactical axioms, *viz.* to strike as nearly as possible simultaneously with all the forces in the field, Evan-Thomas would be just as useful at one end of the line as the other. The twenty-four ships of the Grand Fleet, led by the battle cruisers and with the four *Queen Elizabeths* as a rear squadron, would outflank the enemy at both ends of his line.

The realisation of the plan would depend entirely upon the pace of the Grand Fleet in getting into action. Had all the divisions of the Grand Fleet kept their course at full speed until reaching the track of Sir David Beatty's squadron, the starboard division would have cut that line in about ten minutes and the port division in about twelve and a half to thirteen. There would have been an interval of five miles between the leading ships. Even at twenty-seven knots the four battle-cruisers led by *Lion* could hardly have got clear of the port division and, to avoid collision, all would have had to ease their speed slightly. But undoubtedly at 6:15 or, at least, 6:20, a line might have been formed exactly in Sir David Beatty's track.

Had this line followed him as he closed down after Hood at 6:25 the enemy would have been completely outflanked at both ends of his

H.M.S. *Tiger* and other battle-cruisers

line and even surrounded at its head. There would have been half an hour between the Grand Fleet getting into action and the failure of the light. It is difficult to suppose that, at ranges of from 11,000 yards to 8,000, the guns of the Grand Fleet could not have beaten the High Seas Fleet decisively. Scheer could not have turned. His choice would have been between annihilation and a flight *pêle-mêle*.

Not only does it seem that some such deployment as this was manifestly possible; it looks as if it was exactly this deployment that Admiral Beatty had expected. On any other supposition his manoeuvre in throwing first his own and then Hood's battle cruisers into a short-range fight with the Germans was to run the gravest risks of disaster, without any high probability of justifying it by a final defeat of the enemy. If he expected the Grand Fleet to deploy on to his course and so come into action with its entire strength, possibly within fifteen, certainly within twenty minutes of the enemy being sighted, then to have incurred the loss, not of one but of half of his and Hood's ships would have been amply justified.

The manoeuvre he executed—judged not as a self-contained evolution but as part of a large plan—was, of course, one of the most brilliant and original in the history of the naval war. For the first time for more than two thousand years two fleets met of which a section of one had nearly a 50 *per cent.* superiority in speed over the other. This fast squadron was sent at top speed to hold and envelop the enemy's van. It was calculated to, and it did, arrest that van by sinking the leading ship and throwing the remainder into confusion. It was not a movement that interfered with the deployment of the Grand Fleet in the least degree. It was one, on the contrary, that would have covered it most effectively, and to a great extent must have concealed its character from the enemy.

But, further, being carried through at a speed which probably exceeded that which any enemy flotilla could maintain in the open sea, the manoeuvre must have made it impossible for Scheer to get his destroyers into the right position for a torpedo attack, either upon the deploying ships or upon the Grand Fleet once deployed. For to attack to advantage, the flotillas must have been brought up ahead of the British battle-cruisers, a manifest impossibility.

Had the Grand Fleet as a whole, then, been in action in Sir David Beatty's wake from 6:20 on, it is almost certain that, with all his fleet in action at short range, against guns almost twice as numerous as his own and more than three times as powerful Scheer could not have ventured upon changing the course of his fleet at all. He could not have done so, that is to say, while attempting to keep his ships in line. He might, as we have seen, have turned all his ships together in undisguised flight, he could not have kept them in fighting formation while withdrawing from a fight in these circumstances.

Sir John Jellicoe's Tactics

Before speculating as to the plans or discussing the tactics of the British commander-in-chief, two factors which influenced the situation must be kept in mind. The first is, that the positions of the two fleets and of the enemy had been the subject of a forecast by dead reckoning in both flagships. It is to be supposed that Sir David Beatty kept Admiral Jellicoe informed from time to time of the position, speed, and course of his fleet and of the enemy, and that from these data the lines of approach had been calculated. Each flagship made its own calculations and, being made by dead reckoning, there was a discrepancy between the two, which the commander-in-chief describes as inevitable. It resulted from this that both were equally surprised when, at four minutes to six, *Lion* and *Marlborough* came within sight of each other. Whatever plan of action was adopted could not, if it was intended to meet the situation of the moment, have been the subject of long forethought or preparation.

The second factor was the difficulty of seeing anything at long range. This, in the first place, had prevented any rectification of the misunderstanding as to positions, such as might easily have been done had the scouting cruisers of the two fleets come into sight earlier. It followed, next, that the Commander-in-Chief of the Grand Fleet did not probably see a single ship in the enemy's line until ten or twelve minutes *after* seeing the leading ship of the British Battle-Cruiser Fleet. His plan of deployment, then, orders for which must have been given some minutes before the deployment was complete, *could not have been based upon his own judgment of the situation after seeing the enemy, but must have been dictated, either by some general principle of tactics applied to the information as to the enemy's position, speed, and course, as given by the vice-admiral, or it must have been part of a plan suggested by the vice-admiral.*

There is nothing in the despatch to say whether Sir David Beatty communicated anything more to the commander-in-chief than the bearing and distance, first, of the enemy's battle cruisers, then of his battleships. But it seems irrational to suppose that Sir David did not announce what he intended to do or failed to suggest how best he

H.M.S. *Iron Duke*, Admiral Jellicoe's Flagship, opening fire at approximately 6.15pm 31st May

could be supported.

If the despatches are silent as to the nature of Sir David Beatty's plan, they are equally silent about the commander-in-chief's. We are told simply that he formed his six divisions into a line of battle and are left to infer the character and the direction of the deployment from internal evidence. The facts, so far as they can be gathered from the despatch seem to be as follows:

The Grand Fleet came upon the scene in six divisions on a S.E.-by-S. course. This means that the six divisions were parallel with the leading ships in line-abreast, with an interval of approximately a mile between each division. A line drawn through the leading ships and continued to the west would have cut the line of Sir David Beatty's course after six o'clock, if that also had been similarly continued, making an angle of about 33 degrees. The division on the extreme right, led by *Marlborough*, flagship of Vice-Admiral Sir Cecil Burney, sighted Sir David Beatty's squadron at six o'clock. At the same time Sir David reported the position of the enemy's battle-cruisers, three of which were still at the head of the German line. The speed of the Grand Fleet was probably at least twenty knots, if not twenty-one.

The six divisions seem to have continued their former course for ten or twelve minutes, when all the leading ships turned eight points—or a right angle—together to port, the second, third, and fourth ships in each division following their leaders in succession, so that, very few minutes after the leading ship had turned, the fleet would be on a line at right angles to its former course, and steering N.E. by E. If the leading ship continued on the new course, the fleet would then be heading at an angle of 56 degrees *away* from the enemy. A fleet so deployed would now be brought into action by the leading ship turning again, either to a course parallel with the enemy or converging towards it.

It seems probable that it was some such manoeuvre as this that took place, from the fact that the starboard (or right hand) division, which became the rear division after deployment, got into action so early as 6:17, at a range of 11,000 yards, that is, a thousand yards nearer to the enemy than Sir David Beatty's track, while the port division, now the leading, did not open fire till sometime after 6:30, when, as we learn from the despatch, the British fleet was on the bow of the enemy. This means that the courses were parallel, but that the leading British divisions were well ahead of the enemy.

Both fleets, in other words, were still steering to the east. The track of the Grand Fleet was, therefore, parallel, not only to that of the enemy, but to that of Sir David Beatty up to 6:25, but by some considerable amount, probably 2,000 yards farther from the High Seas Fleet. At 6:50 the leading battle squadron was 6,000 yards N.N.W. from *Lion*. The Grand Fleet had not formed up astern of the Battle-Cruiser Fleet. It had not come into action as a unit simultaneously. It had not deployed either on the enemy or on the British fast division.

(*Vide The Fighting at Jutland* edited by H. W. Fawcett & G. W. W. Hooper—The personal experiences of 45 Sailors of the Royal Navy at the Great Battle at Sea, 1916, and *Kiel and Jutland* by Georg von Hase, the famous Naval Battle of the First World War from the German perspective; Leonaur 2011.)

CHAPTER 24

The Battle of Jutland (Continued)
(*For diagrams illustrating this chapter, see end of book.*)

6. THE COURSE OF THE ACTION

What in fact happened was this. Beatty, as we have seen, had led due east at six o'clock, closing the enemy from 14,000 yards to 12,000 yards, and was overhauling the head of his line rapidly. At 6:20 Hood, in *Invincible*, with *Inflexible* and *Indomitable*, was seen ahead returning from a fruitless search for the Germans, which he had made to the southwest an hour before. Hood was one of Beatty's admirals with the Battle-Cruiser Fleet temporarily attached to the Grand Fleet. When, therefore, his old commander-in-chief ordered him to take station ahead, he had not the slightest difficulty in divining his leader's intentions. It was characteristic of this force that the rear-admirals and commodores in command of the unit squadrons acted without orders throughout the day.

Hood formed before the *Lion* and led down straight on the German line. By 6:25 he had closed the range to 8,000 yards and had *Lützow*, Von Hipper's flagship, under so hot a fire that she was disabled and abandoned almost immediately. By an unfortunate chance his own flagship, *Invincible*, was destroyed by the first and almost the only shell that hit her, the rear-admiral and nearly all his gallant companions being sent to instant death. But their work was done and the van of the German fleet was crumpled up.

Scheer by this time had had his fleet on an easterly course for five and thirty minutes, waiting for the opportunity to turn a right angle or more, so as to retreat under the cover of his torpedo attacks. Up to this time the main body of his fleet had only been under fire for a brief interval, during which the rear division of the Grand Fleet had

Destruction of the British Armoured Cruiser H.M.S. *Black Prince*

been in action. Scheer had, no doubt, watched the deployment of the Grand Fleet and had realised that the method chosen had not only given him already a quarter-of-an-hour's respite, but had supplied him with that opportunity for counter-attack and the evasion it might make possible, which he had been looking for. The battle cruisers were well away to the east. The van and centre of the Grand Fleet, though well on his bows, were only just beginning to open fire.

It is probable that the van was now converging towards him and shortening the range. Scheer was trying to make the gunnery as difficult as possible by his smoke screens, but probably soon realised that, if the range was closed much more, his fleet would soon be in a hopeless situation. At about a quarter to seven, therefore, he launched the first of his torpedo attacks. This had the desired effect. The commander-in-chief, says:

> The enemy constantly turned away and *opened the range* under the cover of destroyer attacks and smoke screens as the effect of British fire was felt.

"Opening the range" means that the object of the torpedo attacks had been attained. For a quarter of an hour or more the closing movement of the Grand Fleet was converted into an opening movement. Scheer had prevented the close action that he dreaded. He had gained the time needed to turn his whole force from an easterly to a south-westerly course.

Sir David Beatty's account of his movements up to now is singularly brief:

> At six o'clock, I altered course to east and proceeded at utmost speed. . . . At 6:20 the Third Battle Squadron bore ahead steaming south towards the enemy's van. I ordered them to take station ahead. . . . At 6:25 I altered course to E.S.E. in support of the Third Battle-Cruiser Squadron, who were at this time only 8,000 yards from the enemy's leading ship.

Nothing is said of his movements in the next twenty minutes, he continues:

> By 6:50, the battle-cruisers were clear of our leading Battle Squadron, then bearing N.N.W. three miles from *Lion*. (*Lion* was now third ship in the line). I ordered the Third Battle Cruiser Squadron to prolong the line astern and *reduced to eighteen knots*.

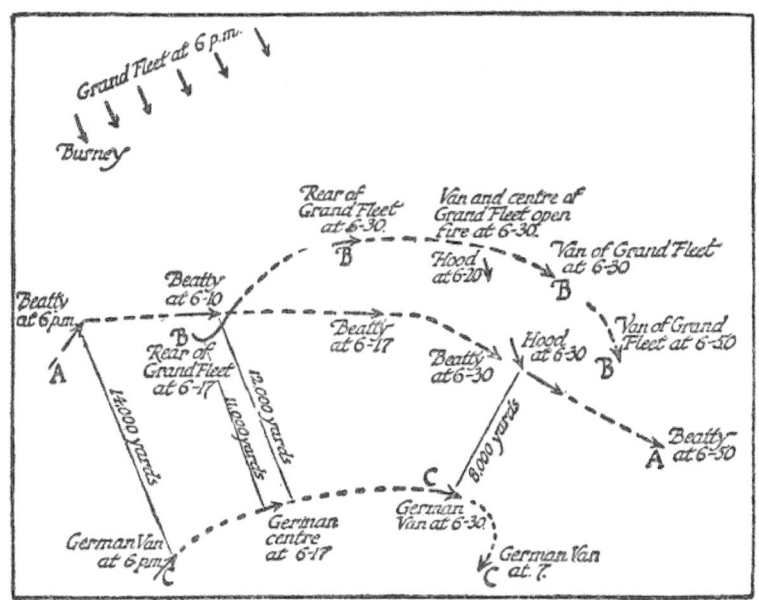

A. Battle-Cruiser Fleet; B. Grand Fleet; C. German Fleet
Sketch plan of the action from 6 p.m. when the Grand Fleet prepared to deploy, till 6:50 when Admiral Scheer delivered his first massed torpedo attack.

There was nothing now to hurry for. The daylight action was, in fact, over. For that matter good visibility was at an end. From 6:0 to 6:50, though never perfect, it had been more favourable to us than to the enemy. Could the British forces have been concentrated for united effort during this period, what might not have resulted? But from 6:0 to 6:17 Scheer had been engaged by Sir David Beatty's four battle-cruisers only. For a short period after 6:17 it was engaged by some ships of the rear division as well. From 6:30 till the torpedo attacks broke up the Grand Fleet's gunnery, it was engaged intermittently and at longer range by all three of the main squadrons. But by this time Sir David Beatty had passed ahead, and the survivors of the enemy's van had begun their turn.

The German Retreat

The next phase of the action was a fruitless chase of the enemy from seven o'clock until 8:20. Sir David Beatty says:

At 7:6, I received a signal that the course of the fleet was south.

. . . We hauled round gradually to S.W. by S. to regain touch with the enemy (who were lost to sight at about 6:50), and at 7:14 again sighted them at a range of about 15,000 yards. . . . We re-engaged at 7:17 and increased speed to twenty-two knots. At 7:32 my course was S.W. speed eighteen knots, the leading enemy battleship bearing N.W. by West. . . . At 7:45 p.m. we lost sight of them.

The two quotations I have made from Sir David Beatty's despatch divide themselves naturally in this way. The first deals with the plan he had attempted to make possible and to share, the second describes his course after that plan had proved abortive. Between them they make it clear that Sir David kept an easterly course at full speed from six o'clock till 6:25. He then turned a quarter of a right angle to the south, that is, to his right, and held this course for twenty-five minutes when, having lost sight of the enemy and, the Grand Fleet being still three miles from him, he dropped his speed from say twenty-seven or twenty-eight knots and awaited developments.

As soon as he heard that the Grand Fleet, after recovering from the first torpedo attack, had turned south in pursuit of the Germans, he increased his speed by four knots, hauled round to the southwest, found and re-engaged the enemy at 7:14. By this time, as we have seen, the enemy's whole line would be following the leading ships on a southwesterly course, so that Sir David Beatty's movements between 6:0 and 7:14 were approximately parallel to those of the enemy. He had been able to keep parallel by availing himself of his ten or eleven knots' superiority between 6:0 and 6:50 and by his four or five knots' superiority between 7:0 and 7:14.

On hearing that at last he was to be supported, Sir David Beatty raised his battle-cruiser speed to twenty-two knots and made a last effort to get in touch with the retiring enemy. He soon found and engaged him at a range of 15,000 yards and contact coincided with a sudden improvement in the seeing conditions. Four ships only, two battle-cruisers and two battleships, evidently the van of the enemy's line, were visible, and these were at once brought under a hot fire, which caused the enemy to resort to smoke-screen protection, and, under cover of this he turned away to the west. At 7:45 the mist came down again and the enemy was lost to sight.

The First and Third Light Cruiser Squadrons were then spread out. They swept to the westward and located the head of the enemy's line again, and at 8:20 the battle-cruisers—whose course had been southwest up to now—changed course to west and got into action apparently with the same four ships as before, at the short range of 10,000 yards. The leading ship soon turned away emitting high flames and with a heavy list to port. She had been brought under the fire of *Lion*. *Princess Royal* set fire to one of the two battleships. *Indomitable* and *New Zealand* engaged a third and sent her out of the line, heeling over and burning also. Then the mist came down once more and the enemy was last seen by *Falmouth* at twenty-two minutes to nine.

The commander-in-chief is far less explicit as to the occasions on which his ships got into action. The action between the battle fleets, he said, lasted intermittently from 6:17 to 8:20. At 6:17 we know that Burney's division got into action, and at 6:30 until sometime up to 7:20 the other divisions also. But no details of any kind of encounters later than that are mentioned. It is clear that after 6:50 the weather made any continuous engaging quite impossible. There was a second torpedo attack during the stern chase—and once more the enemy "opened the range."

THE NIGHT ACTIONS AND THE EVENTS OF JUNE 1

The form that the deployment actually took, and the fifteen minutes' respite from attack won by the torpedo attack at 7:40 which enabled Scheer to get his whole fleet on to a southeasterly from an easterly course were, tactically speaking, the explanation of the German escape on the 31st. It is more difficult to understand exactly why they were not brought to action on the following day. Very little is actually known of what happened in the course of the night, and the despatches throw little light on it because, though many incidents are mentioned, very few have any definite hour assigned to them. The facts, so far as they can be gathered, are as follows:

The Grand Fleet seems to have lost sight of the Germans altogether after 8:20 and Sir David Beatty's scouts saw the last of their enemy at 8:38. The vice-admiral continued searching for forty minutes longer and then fell back east and to the line which was the course of the Grand Fleet when he was last in touch with it by wireless. Both fleets seem to have proceeded some distance south and to have waited for the night in the proximity of a point about equi-distant—eighty miles—from the Horn Reef and Heligoland. One destroyer flotilla, the Thirteenth, and one light cruiser squadron were retained with the capital ships for their protection. The rest were disposed, as the commander-in-chief says:

> In a position in which they could afford protection to the fleet and at the same time be favourably situated for attacking the enemy's heavy ships.

They must have been placed north of the British forces. No British battle or battle-cruiser squadron was attacked during the night, but the Second Light Cruiser Squadron, which was disposed in the rear of the battle line, got into action at 10:20 with five enemy cruisers, and at 11:30 *Birmingham* sighted several heavy ships steering south or west-southwest. The Thirteenth Flotilla, which seems to have been associated with the Second Light Cruiser Squadron astern of the battle fleet, reported a large vessel half an hour after midnight, which opened fire on three of the flotilla, disabling *Turbulent*. At 2:35 another, *Moresby*, sighted four pre-Dreadnoughts and had a shot at them with a torpedo. We are not told the course they were steering.

The destroyers sent out to attack the enemy got several opportunities for using their torpedoes, three of which were probably successful, and a fourth attack resulted in the blowing up of a ship. The despatch does not say, however, whether the destroyers were able to keep in wireless communication with the main fleet, whether any were instructed to keep contact with the enemy and just hang on to him till daylight; whether, in fact, either the commander-in-chief or Sir David Beatty had any authentic information at daylight as to the enemy's formation or movements. *Champion's* encounter with four destroyers at 3:30 is the only occurrence we hear of after daybreak, until the engagement of a Zeppelin at 4:0 a.m. All we are told is to be gathered from these words of Lord Jellicoe's:

> At daylight, June 1, the Battle Fleet, being then to the southward and westward of the Horn Reef, turned to the northward in search of enemy vessels and for the purpose of collecting our own cruisers and torpedo-boat destroyers.... The visibility early on June 1 (three to four miles) was less than on May 31, and the torpedo-boat destroyers, being out of visual touch, did not rejoin until 9 a.m. The British Fleet remained in the proximity of the battlefield and near the line of approach to German ports until 11 a.m. on June 1, in spite of the disadvantage of long distances from fleet bases and the danger incurred in waters adjacent to enemy coasts from submarines and torpedo craft. *The enemy, however, made no sign*, and I was reluctantly compelled to

the conclusion that the High Sea Fleet had returned into port. Subsequent events proved this assumption to have been correct. *Our position must have been known to the enemy*, as at 4 a.m. the fleet engaged a Zeppelin for about five minutes, during which time she had ample time to note and subsequently report the position and course of the British Fleet. The waters from the latitude of the Horn Reef to the scene of the action were thoroughly searched.... A large amount of wreckage was seen, but no enemy ships, and at 1:15 p.m., it being evident that the German Fleet had succeeded in returning to port, course was shaped for our bases, which were reached without further incident on Friday, June 2.

At this time of year and in this latitude, it will be daylight some time before 3:30. The fleet, therefore, made for the scene of the action at this hour—principally, it would seem, to pick up the cruisers and destroyers—and remained in its proximity until 11 a.m., when the waters between the Battle Fleet and the Horn Reef were searched. The commander-in-chief does not tell us of any search made for the enemy at all. But from the fact that he had gone northward to look for his own destroyers and cruisers, it is evident that, whatever information he had got during the night, pointed to the probability of the enemy having retreated from the battlefield not south or west, but east and northwards. At 8:40 on the previous evening he was last reported at a point 120 miles from the Horn Reef lightship, bearing almost exactly northwest from it. It is highly probable that at least ten of the German ships had been struck by torpedoes, in addition to the one sunk.

And though *Lützow* was the only ship sunk by gunfire, many others had suffered very severely. If the fleet's maximum speed before the action was eighteen knots, it is highly improbable that after the action it exceeded fifteen. At fifteen knots it would have taken the Germans eight hours to reach the Horn Reef lightship, had they started for that point directly after contact with the British main squadrons was lost. Having suffered so severely and escaped so miraculously, it was not only obvious that Scheer's one idea on June 1 would be to make the most of his luck and get safely home, it was also to the last degree probable that he would shape a course for home which would bring him soonest under the protection of whatever defences the German coast could offer. He would not, that is to say, attempt to regain Heligoland by trying to get round the British Fleet to the south and west, and then turn sharply east to Heligoland; he would probably try to creep down the Danish and Schleswig coasts, where wounded ships might, if necessary, be beached, and the islands might supply some form of refuge if the situation became desperate.

It was on this route also that the submarines sent out to cover the retreat could be stationed. The best chance of bringing the Germans once more to action on the morning of June 1 would then appear to have been a sweeping movement towards the Horn Reef. The German fleet could not possibly have reached this point before half-past four, and probably not before half-past six. The fast, light forces and the battle-cruisers could have got across to the Schleswig coast in two and a half hours and the battleships before seven o'clock.

If the despatch tells us all that was done, one is rather driven to the conclusion that the commander-in-chief assumed that it was not our business, but the Germans' business, to resume the action. Why else should he say that "the enemy made no sign"? or exult in the fact that he knew from his Zeppelin at four o'clock where the British fleet was if he liked to look for it? Why should the enemy make a sign? Was it not obvious after the events of the preceding day that he could have but one idea and that was safety? Scheer and Von Hipper had certainly done enough for honour. They had inflicted heavier losses than they had suffered. If they could get home, they had anything but a discreditable story to tell.

If the commander-in-chief really thought it was not his first duty to find and bring the enemy to action again; if the risk of approaching the Jutland coast seemed too great; if the frustration of any ulterior object the enemy might have contemplated the day before seemed cheaply purchased by the losses the Battle Cruiser Fleet had suffered, so long as our main strength at sea was not impaired, then the proceedings on June 1, as communicated to us, are perfectly intelligible.

Yet there must have been many among his officers and under his command who took a diametrically different view. After engaging for the last time at 8:40 on the previous evening, Sir David Beatty says:

> In view of the gathering darkness, *and of the fact that our strategical position was such as to make it appear certain that we should locate the enemy at daylight under most favourable circumstances*, I did not consider it desirable or proper to close the enemy battle fleet during the dark hours. I therefore concluded that I should be carrying out your wishes by turning to the course of the fleet,

reporting to you that I had done so.

On the events of June 1 Sir David Beatty's despatch is silent, but it is obvious that it was not his opinion overnight that the morrow should be spent in waiting for the enemy to give a sign, but that, on the contrary, it was certain that he could and should be found and brought to action.

CHAPTER 25
Zeebrügge and Ostend

In the course of the night April 22–23, an attack was made on the two Flemish bases, Ostend and Zeebrügge, with a view to blocking the entrances of both by the familiar method of sinking old cement-filled ships in the narrow fairway. At Ostend the block-ships were grounded slightly off their course, and a few days later a second attempt was made. The Zeebrügge block-ships got into their chosen billets and are safely grounded there. The latter port, in spite of official denials, was for many months made almost useless to the enemy, and it is probably safe to assume that the value of Ostend, where *Vindictive* lies across the fairway, is considerably diminished. Material results, therefore, of high importance were achieved by this enterprise.

The operations are worth examining on three quite independent grounds. First, what is the strategical value of their objective? How, that is to say, would the naval activities of Great Britain and her Allies gain by Zeebrügge and Ostend being, for some months at least out of action? And, conversely, what would the enemy lose? Unless we are satisfied that the gain must be substantial—apart altogether from the moral effect—we should obviously have a difficulty in justifying, not the losses in ships incurred, which were trivial and easily replaced, but the losses in picked men, which were irreparable. Secondly, the incident is clearly worth examining for its tactical interest. What were the difficulties the vice-admiral in command had to overcome? By what weapons, devices, and manoeuvres did he attempt to effect his purpose? Third, what was the morale effect?

Strategical Object

There is now only one theatre of the war, and in this the issue of civilization or barbarism must be decided by military action. The event depends upon the capacity of the sea power of the Allies to deliver in France all the fighting men and all the war material that Allied ships can draw from Asia, from Australia, from South America, from the United States, and from Canada, and then deliver either directly into France, or first into British ports, and then from Britain into France. To beat the German Army is ultimately a problem in sea communications. The whole of these have to pass through the bottle-neck of the Western end of the Atlantic lanes. Into an area south of Ireland and north of Ushant, a hundred miles square, every ship that comes from the Mediterranean, from the Cape, from Buenos Ayres, Rio, the West Indies, or the Gulf of Mexico, from the Atlantic seaboard of America, must come.

Secondary only to this are the areas that feed ships into it, or into which the ships that pass through it are dissipated on their way to the several ports—the Mediterranean, the Bay of Biscay, the English Channel, St. George's Channel, the Irish Sea. It is in these, when it is driven from the main funnel point of traffic, that the submarine must do its work. The defeat of the submarine, when at large, turns upon three factors: (1) the under-water offensive—that is, mine-fields, that will tend to keep it within certain areas; (2) the efficiency with which ships liable to attack are protected by convoy; and (3) the skill and persistence with which submarines, once on their hunting grounds, are in turn hunted. To maintain a cross-Channel barrage, the enemy surface craft must be handicapped in every possible way. The second and third factors of anti-submarine war make heavy demands on material, on personnel, and on skill, judgment, and organisation.

Here the decisive material factor is the number of destroyers available for both forms of work. When it comes to a close-quarters fight, no craft that has a speed of less than thirty knots, that cannot maintain itself in any weather, that does not possess a large cruising radius, can be of the first efficiency. The larger petrol-driven submarine-chasers and the many special craft which are built for various purposes in connection with the defensive campaign, all have their field of utility. But for the final power to rush swiftly on to a submarine if it is momentarily seen afloat, and for covering the area into which it can submerge itself, while the destroyer approaches with depth bombs, the destroyer, if only from its superior speed, stands supreme as the enemy of the U-boat. From the very earliest days of the submarine work it has, then, been axiomatic that every measure which will put a larger number of destroyers at our disposal should be taken at almost any cost. How does the work at Zeebrügge and Ostend help us, both in this respect and in a mining policy?

At these two ports our enemy was able to maintain a very considerable destroyer force. Its activities were necessarily mainly confined to work in darkness or in thick weather. But in such conditions its efficiency was of a very high order. The public only heard of its activities when it shelled some point of the coast of Kent, or raided our trawlers or other patrols, and, in all conscience, it heard of these activities often enough. Yet we were inclined to suppose them unimportant because their material results were insignificant. The news that a cross-Channel barrage was in course of establishment gave them a new value. But their value to the enemy should not be measured by the casualties they inflicted on our light craft, nor by their occasional excursions into the murder of civilians on shore. It lay in the fact that the enemy's force permanently withdrew from the anti-submarine campaign numerous destroyer leaders and destroyers which had to be maintained at Dover to cope with it.

From Zeebrügge to Emden—the nearest German port—is, roughly, three hundred miles by sea, and it does not need elaborate argument to show that if Zeebrügge and Ostend are permanently out of action the problem of dealing with enemy craft in the narrow seas is totally and entirely changed. With these gone, the East Coast ports became the natural centres from which to command the waters between Great Britain and Holland. They are fifty miles nearer Emden than is Dunkirk. If any German destroyers got west and south of Dunkirk, and the news of their presence were cabled to an East Coast base, destroyers could get between the enemy and his ports without difficulty. Thus, enemy surface craft, based upon German ports, would practically be denied access to Flemish waters altogether, and this by the East Coast and not by the Dover forces. In other words, the Dover patrol forces would, by the closing of Ostend and Zeebrügge, be set free for the highly important work of aiding in the anti-submarine campaign—and there is certainly no naval need that is greater.

The strategical objective, therefore, which Admiral Keyes put before himself in his expedition was, so far as he could, to set back the enemy's naval bases by no less than three hundred miles. Its importance as setting free new forces, both for the direct attack on submarines, and for saving the mine-layers from attack, cannot be exaggerated, for it was a step—and a great step—forward in making sure of the sea communications on which all depends. It must be conceded, then that the results Admiral Keyes had in view amply justify a very considerable expenditure both of material and men. Let us next ask ourselves what kind of material he chose, and how he proposed to use his forces with utmost economy and maximum tactical effect.

Sir Roger Keyes's Tactics

The purposes of the expedition, as we have seen, were to block the exit of the canal at Zeebrügge and the entrance of the small, narrow harbour at Ostend with old cruisers filled with cement, the removal of which would be an operation of a lengthy and tedious kind. Incidentally, the plan was to effect the maximum destruction of war stores and equipment at Zeebrügge and to sink as many as possible of the enemy vessels found in either port, and finally, to inflict on the enemy the maximum possible losses of personnel. By blocking the canal, the value of Zeebrügge was reduced from being an equipped base to being a mere refuge. As there were two points of attack, the expedition naturally resolved itself into two distinct, but simultaneous, undertakings.

The simpler, the less dangerous, the less ambitious, but, as the event showed, the more difficult operation of the two, was the attempt to block Ostend. The larger, more complex, and infinitely more perilous undertaking, but because of its very complications, ultimately easier, was the attempt at Zeebrügge. In its broad outlines, the scheme was to get the ships as near as possible without detection, and then to trust to a final rush to gain the desired position. Concealment up to the last moment was to be secured by smoke screens. At Ostend the problem was simply to run two or three ships into the entrance—that is, to get them into position before the enemy's artillery made it impossible to manoeuvre. If the Ostend attempt failed, it was largely because a sudden change in the weather conditions robbed the smoke screens, which were to hide the ships, of their value, so that the operation of placing the block-ships accurately was made almost impossible.

The operation of blocking such entrances has, of course, long been familiar. The exploit of Lieutenant Hobson in the Spanish-American War, is fresh in the memories of all sailors. This failed through the steering gear of the blocking-ship being destroyed by gunfire at the critical moment. The Japanese attempted the same thing on a large scale at Port Arthur but with anything but complete success. If the first Ostend effort, then, fell short of finality, we have the experience of these earlier precedents to explain and account for it.

I have dealt with Ostend first because, after the preliminary bombardment, nothing more could have been attempted than to force the ships into the harbour entrance and sink them there. But at Zeebrügge a far more intricate operation was possible. Zeebrügge is not a town. It is just the sea exit of the Bruges Canal, with its railway connections, round which a few streets of houses have clustered. The actual entrance to the canal is flanked by two short sea walls, at the end of each of which are guide lights. From these lights up the canal to the lock gates is about half a mile. A large mole protects the sea channel to the canal from being blocked by silted sand. The mole is connected to the mainland by five hundred yards of pile viaduct. The mole is nearly a mile long, built in a curve, a segment amounting to, perhaps, one-sixth of a circle, the centre of which would be a quarter of a mile east of the canal entrance, while its radius would be three-quarters of a mile. It is a large and substantial stone structure, on which are railway lines and a railway station, and has been turned to capital military account by the enemy, who erected on it aircraft sheds and military establishments of many kinds.

The general plan was to bombard the place for an hour by monitors and, under cover of this fire, for the attacking squadron to advance to the harbour mouth. Then, when the bombardment ceased, *Vindictive* was to run alongside the mole, disembark her own landing party and those from *Iris* and *Daffodil*, who were to overpower the enemy protecting the guns and stores while the old submarines were run into the pile viaduct to cut the mole off from the mainland, thus isolating it. Meanwhile, other forces were to engage any enemy destroyers or submarines that might be in the port. Finally, the block-ships were to be pushed right up into the canal mouth and there sunk. The success of the latter part of these operations turned upon the extent to which the enemy could be made to believe that the attack on the mole was the chief objective.

To ensure success against the mole, several very ingenious devices were brought into play. The main landing parties were placed in *Vindictive*. This cruiser—which displaced about 5,600 tons, and had a broadside of six 6-inch guns—was fitted, on the port side, with "brows," or landing gangways, that could be lowered on the mole the moment she came alongside. All the vessels of the squadron were equipped with fog- or smoke-making material, which would veil the force from the enemy until he sent up his star shells and, in the artificial light, would conceal the character, numbers, and composition of the force as completely as possible. It seems that a shift of wind at the

The Zeebrugge raid

critical moment—here, as at Ostend—robbed this plan of some of its anticipated efficiency.

At some point of the approach, then, apparently just before *Vindictive* rounded and got abreast of the lighthouse, the presence of the invaders was detected, and they were saluted first by salvoes of star shells and next by as hot a gunfire as can be conceived. *Vindictive* lost no time in replying. Her six 6-inch guns—and no doubt her 12-pounders as well—swept the mole as long as they could be fired, and, once alongside, the "brows"—only two out of eighteen seem to have survived the heavy gunfire—were lowered, and officers and men "boarded" the mole.

The earlier accounts stated that this landing was effected in spite of the stoutest sort of hand-to-hand fighting, that the enemy was overcome and driven back, and that the landing party then proceeded to the destruction of the sheds and stores. The plans had included the blowing-up of the pile viaduct, which connects the stone mole with the mainland—by means of one or two old submarines charged with explosives, and so virtually converted into giant torpedoes. These did their work most effectively, and had the enemy been in occupation of the mole, his force would have been isolated. But, as a fact, the mole was not occupied, and the enemy relied upon machine- and gun-fire organised from the shore end of the mole for making the landing impossible. In spite of a withering fusillade, a considerable landing party of marines and bluejackets got ashore, though Colonel Elliott and Commander Halahan and great numbers of their men were killed in the attempt. Those that got on the mole proceeded to destroy, as far as possible, the sheds, stores, and guns, and then turned their attention to the destroyers moored against its inner side.

Meantime, the only enemy destroyer that seems to have had steam up tried to escape from harbour, and was either rammed or torpedoed and instantly sunk. Others, less well prepared, were either boarded, after the resistance of their crews had been overcome, and, it must be presumed, sunk also. Others, again, were attacked by motor launches, which preceded and helped clear a way for the block-ships. Whether an attempt on the lock gates was made or even contemplated, we have not been told; but the main purpose of the expedition, the sinking of at least two out of the three old *Apollos* in the right place, was achieved with precision.

The moment the block-ships were in place, the purpose for which the mole was occupied was gained, and the order was rightly given for an immediate retreat. The work had been done, and there was no knowing what new resources the enemy could have brought to bear had time been wasted. Many of the vessels, including *Vindictive*, had been holed by 11-inch shells. But *Vindictive's* damages were not of a serious kind, and the whole force was able to withdraw in safety, with the exception of one destroyer and two motor launches. The destroyer is known to have been sunk by gunfire. The successful withdrawal of the expedition is conclusive evidence that the enemy was demoralised.

For such close-quarters work Admiral Keyes, naturally enough, armed his forces as for trench fighting. *Vindictive* carried howitzers on her forward and after decks, and her boarding parties were liberally armed with grenades and flame-throwers as well as with rifles, bayonets, and truncheons. Machine-guns also seem to have been landed, so that hand-to-hand fighting was prepared for in the full light of the most recent war experience. The plan, it should be noted, was to have included aeroplane co-operation to supplement, if not to assist, the work of the monitors; but the change in the weather appears to have interfered with this part of the programme, and may quite easily have made any accurate work by the monitors impossible also.

It is, first of all, patent that the expedition was thoroughly thought out in all its details, and therefore closely planned. An accurate study of the enemy's defences had been made, and suitable means of avoiding his attack or overcoming his defences had been elaborately worked out. It is equally clear that almost to the moment when the attack was made, the weather conditions were those which the plan contemplated as necessary to success, and that it was only the sudden, unexpected change in the wind that threatened the Ostend part of the operations with partial failure and made the Zeebrügge operations more costly in life than they should otherwise have been.

When it is remembered that the approaches to Ostend and Zeebrügge are commanded by very formidable batteries, armed with no less than 120 guns of the largest calibre, and that the mole and the sides of the canal bristled with quick-firing 12-pounders and larger pieces, it will be realised that, to the enemy, any attempt actually to bring an unarmoured vessel, with her cement-laden consorts, right up either to the mole or to the actual mouth of the canal must have appeared an undertaking too absurdly hare-brained for anyone but a lunatic to have attempted. It was just because Sir Roger Keyes had evaluated the enemy's defences with exactitude and had thought out and adopted, first, methods of evading his vigilance and, next, manoeuvres that would *for the necessary period* make his weapons useless, that it was possible not only to make the attempt, but to realise the very high degree of success that has apparently been won.

The essence of the matter, of course, was to take the enemy by surprise. At first sight, it may appear a curious way of putting him off his guard, that he should for an hour be bombarded by monitors and aeroplanes. But the vice-admiral probably reasoned that this would lead, as it often does, to the crews of the big guns taking shelter underground until the attack is over. If the monitors were placed at their usual great distance from ports, and were concealed by smoke or fog screens, the enemy gunners would know that it was merely idle to attempt to reply to their fire. If nothing was to be possible in the way of response until daylight, the gun-layers were just as well in their shell-proofs as anywhere.

Under cover, then, of this long-range bombardment, and concealing his squadron by the ingenious fog methods invented by the late Commander Brock, Sir Roger Keyes made his way within a very short distance of the veiled lights at the end of the mole. It was at this point that the wind shifted and the presence of the squadron was revealed to the enemy. There was a brief interval before the big guns could be manned, and it was doubtless owing to this that *Vindictive* got alongside before more than one 11-inch shell had struck her. Once under the shelter of the mole, she was safe from the larger pieces, and only her upper works could be raked by the smaller natures.

Attack on the Mole

The policy of attacking the mole and making that appear to the enemy the central affair, was a fine piece of tactics. The engagement which developed there was in fact, a containing action, which left the execution of the main objective to the other forces, and its purpose was to prevent the enemy from interfering too much with them. Nelson, it will be remembered, cut out a block of ships in the centre of the enemy's line at Trafalgar, occupying them so that their hands were full, and preventing both them and the van from coming to the succour of the rear. The main operation was the destruction of the rear by Collingwood. Here it was *Vindictive*, her landing party, that played the Nelson *rôle* while the vice-admiral, in *Warwick*, himself directed the crucial operation, namely, the navigation of the block-ships to their billets.

The moment they were blown up and sunk the purpose of the

expedition was fulfilled, and *Vindictive's* siren recalled all those from the mole who could get back to the ship. The actual fortunes of the fight on the mole itself, while of thrilling human interest owing to the extraordinary circumstances in which it was undertaken, were of quite subsidiary importance. The primary object, it must be borne in mind, was not the destruction of the mole forts, or of the aeroplane shed, or of whatever military equipment was there, or even of killing or capturing its garrison. These were only important in so far as their partial realisation was necessary to relieving the block-ships from the danger of premature sinking.

This is a matter of real capital importance and of very great interest, for it is, I think, not difficult to realise that, had similar circumstances existed at Ostend—had it been possible, that is to say, to occupy the defenders and distract their attention on some perfectly irrelevant engagement—the requisite time would have been given to those in command of the block-ships to make sure of getting them into the right position. As things were, they were threatened by the fate which made Hobson's attempt at Santiago a failure. With the whole gun-power of Ostend concentrated upon the blocking-ships, there was not a minute to be wasted. But with the enemy's fire drawn there would have been the leisure which alone could make precision possible. (*Vide The Raids on Zeebrugge & Ostend 1918: The Royal Navy Attacks on the German Occupied Belgian Coast During the First World War—Ostend and Zeebrugge* by C. Sanford Terry & *Zeebrugge Affair* by Keble Howard C. Sanford Terry & Keble Howard; Leonaur 2016.)

Morale Effect

The attack on Zeebrügge and the two successive attacks on Ostend, carefully planned and boldly and resolutely carried out, achieved a very high measure of success. It was natural enough, on the first receipt of the news, that we should all have been carried away by our wonder and admiration at the astonishing heroism that made it possible to carry through so intricate a series of operations, when every soul engaged was seemingly aware of the desperate character of the enterprise, when no one could have expected to return alive, when the enemy's means seemed ample, not only for the killing of everyone engaged, but for the immediate frustration of every object that they had in view, and so made most of the astounding gallantry and daring of all concerned.

For over four years now we have had a constant recurrence of such feats of courage, and repetition does not lessen their power to intoxicate us with an overwhelming admiration of those who are the heroes of these great adventures. But we should be misconceiving the significance of these events if we were to measure their importance either by the ordered daring of those engaged, or by their successful execution, or by their immediate military results, great and far-reaching as these were.

The thing was more important as affording conclusive evidence that the British Navy, as inspired and directed from headquarters, had now abandoned the purely defensive *rôle* assigned to it by ten years of pre-war, and three and a half years of war, administration. It meant that the fleet had escaped from those counsels of timorous—because unimaginative and ignorant—caution, which had checked its ardour and limited its activities since August, 1914. The effect may be incalculable. The doctrine that every operation which involved the risk of losing men or ships must necessarily be too hazardous to undertake, was thus shown to be no longer the loadstone of Whitehall's policy. The navy was at last set free to act on an older and a better tradition.

It is indeed on this tradition that on almost every occasion the navy has, in fact, acted when it got a chance. When *Swift* and *Broke* tackled three times their number of enemy last year, and *Botha* and *Morris* six times their number this year, the gallant captains of these gallant vessels did not wait to ask if the position of their ships was "critical" or otherwise; but, with an insight into the true defensive value of attack—which, seemingly, it is the privilege only of the most valorous to possess—went straight for their enemies, fought overwhelming odds at close quarters, and came out as victorious as a rightly reasoned calculation would have shown to be probable.

Similarly, on May 31, 1916, Sir David Beatty, when his force of battle-cruisers, by the loss of *Indefatigable* and *Queen Mary*, had been reduced below that of the enemy, persisted in his attack upon Von Hipper and, by demoralising the enemy's fire, provided most effectively for the safety of his own ships. Losses did not make him retreat then, nor, when Scheer came upon the scene with the whole High Seas Fleet, did he withdraw from the action—his speed would have made this easy—though the odds were heavy against him. He kept, on the contrary, the whole German Fleet in play, drawing them dexterously to the north, where contact with the Grand Fleet would be inevitable.

And, when the contact was made, his last effort to break up the German line was to close from the 14,000 yards, a range he had prudently maintained during the previous two hours, to 8,000, where his guns would be more certainly effective, realising perfectly that no loss of ships in his own squadron would signify, if only the entire destruction of the German Fleet were made possible by such a sacrifice. It would not be difficult to give scores of incidents in which individual admirals and captains have shown the old spirit under new conditions.

But, save only for the crazy attack on the Dardanelles forts—and this is hardly a precedent we should rejoice to see followed—we have looked in vain for any sign of naval initiative from Whitehall. The explanation lies in the fact that we had no staff for planning operations, nor the right men in power for judging whether any proposed undertaking was based on a right calculation of the value of the available means of offence and defence. The events, therefore of the night of the 22nd and the early hours of the 23rd were of quite extraordinary importance, for they marked an undertaking needing long and elaborate preparation, and one which could not have been brought to a successful issue had it not enjoyed from its first inception the enthusiastic support of the Admiralty. But this is not all. Not only was this an Admiralty-supported undertaking, it was one that, unlike the Gallipoli adventure, was carried through on right staff principles. There was a definite, well-thought-out plan—careful preparation for every step in the right selection of men and means for its execution.

I think it is right to put this forward as the most important aspect of a significant, stirring, and successful enterprise. It is the most important because the news meant so very much more than that Zeebrügge was blocked, that Ostend was crippled, and that an expedition—at first sight perilous beyond conception—had been carried through with losses altogether disproportionate, either to its dangers or to the results achieved. The news meant that a new direction either had been, or certainly can, and therefore must, now be given to our naval policy. In the spring of 1917, sceptics were asking if the army could win the war before the navy lost it.

Why, they said, if our land forces can force a way through what we were told were impregnable fortifications, should the greatest sea force in the world be impotent against an enemy who slinks behind his forts with his surface craft, while devastating our sea communications with his submarines? Is naval ingenuity, they asked, so crippled that we can neither protect our trade against the submarine at sea, nor block the enemy's ports so that the submarine can never get to sea? The critics replied that all was well with the navy, but that all was sadly wrong with its official chiefs. The reorganisation of the Admiralty was immediately followed by the adoption of the convoy principle—and submarine losses were reduced to half. This long-advocated measure, the recently inaugurated barrage at Dover, and now the events of the morning of April 23, have justified the critics and the changes in method and men which they urged. Zeebrügge had been in the enemy's hands since September, 1914, and it took us three and a half years, not to discover a man capable of attacking it, but in developing an Admiralty capable of picking the man and giving him the right support before the attack could be made. If a similar spirit had actuated a properly constituted Admiralty all these years, what might not the navy have accomplished?

In the previous year the emancipation of the navy had gone forward apace. And not the least significant of the stages in the process were first the appointment of Admiral Sir Roger Keyes to be head of the Planning Division at the Admiralty, next his removal from the Admiralty to Dover, next the inauguration of the Channel barrage, and finally his surprising and masterly stroke at the Flemish ports. The enumeration of these stages is worth making, for they mark the genesis of the plan we have seen achieved. It was, if I am correctly informed, quite understood when Admiral Keyes went to Dover that his mission was temporary.

If he was sent to do the things which he has done, and now that he has done them is taken back to Whitehall, then it might seem as if we might look forward to an aggressive policy at sea more worthy of the superb force which we possess, and more consonant with its glorious heritage than anything which we have witnessed in the past. And if Sir Roger cannot be spared from his new command, so auspiciously inaugurated, then we must trust that some other of equal brains and spirit has already taken or will take his place. Zeebrügge and Ostend, then, will figure in naval history, not only as the names of achievements unique and splendid in themselves, but more famous as the harbingers of still greater things to come.

Third Phase Sketches

In these sketches "A" represents the Grand Fleet, "B" Beatty's Battle Cruisers, "C" the German Fleet. A, B, C are the positions at 6; A^1, B^1, C^1, at 6:20; A^2, etc. 6:30; A^3, etc. 6:50; A^4, etc. at 7:6.

Diagrams 1 to 4 suggest movements by the three fleets consistent with the account of the third phase of the action given in Admiral Jellicoe's and Vice-Admiral Beatty's despatches.

Diagram 1 shows the Grand Fleet continuing on its course from 6:0 till about 6:15, when the leading ships of the six divisions turn together to port, forming a line on a course at right angles to their original course. This movement carries the starboard divisions nearer to the enemy's line than the track of Sir David Beatty's squadron. Admiral Sir Cecil Burney was the leader of these divisions, and so got into action at 11,000 yards at 6:17.

Diagram 2 shows the continuation of these movements from 6:20 to 6:30. Vice-Admiral Jerram's divisions, leading the line, turn east parallel to Sir David Beatty's course, the centre and rear following him. At 6:30 Sir David Beatty who had meantime been joined by Hood, makes a further turn to the S.E., to attack the head of the German line.

Diagram 3. Between 6:30 and 6:50 Scheer sends out his destroyers to attack the Grand Fleet and under cover of his attack begins to turn from east to south and then southwest.

Diagram 4. 6:50 to 7:6. The German turn has been completed; Sir David Beatty has dropped speed at 6:50 and continues at 18 knots until, at 7:6, he hears that the Grand Fleet has turned south. The movements of the Grand Fleet between 6:30 and 7:6 are, of course, purely conjectural.

At 6:30 some of the ships opened fire on the Germans, and at about five minutes to seven *Marlborough* was hit by a torpedo. The torpedo attack delivered between 6:30 and 6:50 was the first of the two "under cover of which the enemy increased the range," as Admiral Jellicoe describes.

Diagram 5 shows the form of deployment by the Grand Fleet, which it is suggested Sir David Beatty must have expected, for it would have brought the whole of the battleship squadrons into action astern of *Lion* by 6:20 or 6:25. With Hood's force falling in ahead of the battle-cruisers, the Germans would have been overlapped at either end of their line which, for twenty-five or thirty minutes, would thus have been under the massed fire of one hundred and fifty 12-inch, one hundred and forty 13.5-inch, and sixty 15-inch guns, and the difficulty of organising a torpedo attack would have been greatly enhanced.

It is to be remembered that, while at no time good, the light between 6 and 6:50 was more favourable to the British Fleet than to the enemy. After 6:50 the intervals of good vision were few and short.

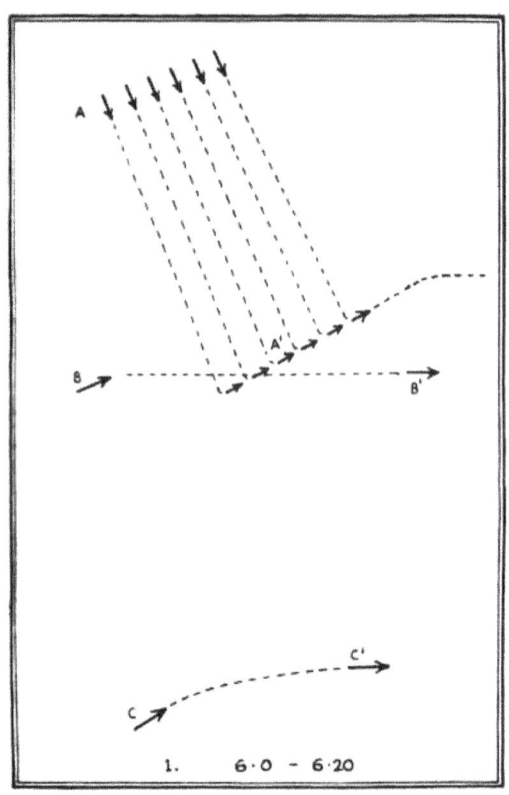

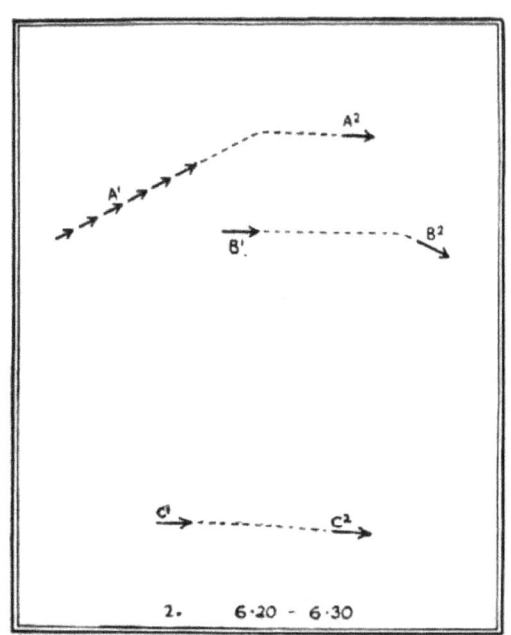

2.   6·20 - 6·30

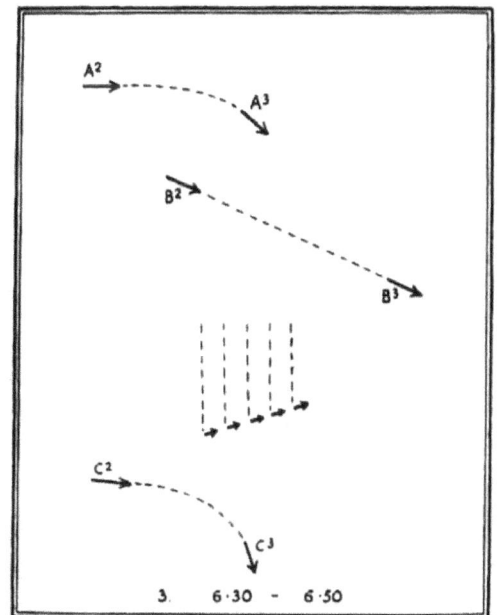

3.   6·30 - 6·50

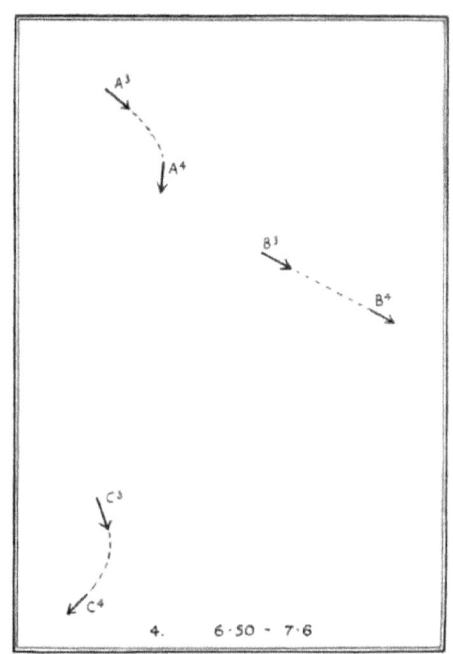

4.   6·50 - 7·6

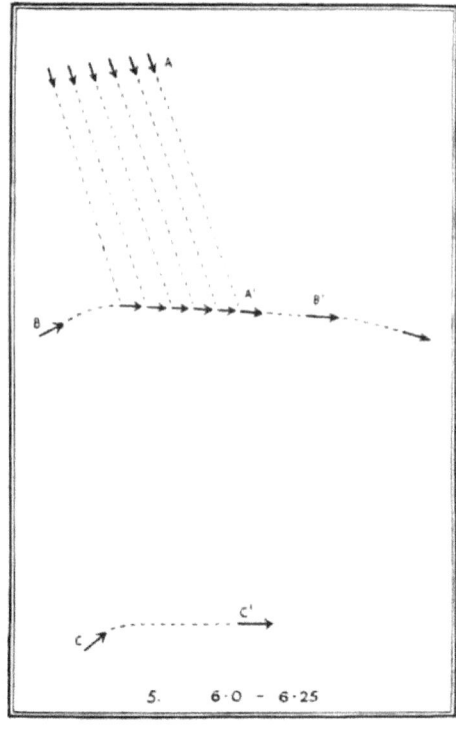

5.   6·0 - 6·25

www.ingramcontent.com/pod-product-compliance
Lightning Source LLC
Chambersburg PA
CBHW031620160426
43196CB00006B/206